LIONHEARTED LEADERSHIP

Surround Yourself with Lions,
No More Chicken Scratch

Empowering Teams to Embrace Courage,
Strength, and Unity in the Workplace

IBRAHIM M. ALARIFI

Copyright © 2024 By Ibrahim M. Alarifi

All Rights Reserved

Paperback ISBN = 978-2-293-10742-0

Table Contents

Preface 4

Acknowledgments 6

Chapter 1: The Lion's Den 8

Chapter 2: Identifying Your Pride 42

Chapter 3: Roar with Purpose 85

Chapter 4: Courageous Conversations 124

Chapter 5: Leading by Example 168

Chapter 6: Adopting Resilience 209

Chapter 7: The Heart of Collaboration 251

Chapter 8: Empowering the Pack Delegation and Trust 278

Chapter 9: Celebrating Wins 309

Chapter 10: Continuous Growth 342

Chapter 11: Adapt and Overcome 382

Chapter 12: Legacy of Lions 417

Preface

In today's rapidly changing, often turbulent world, excellent leadership is needed more than ever. The struggles of organizations in implementing change, building teamwork, or driving innovation involve competent and brave leaders. Lionhearted Leadership: Surround Yourself with Lions, No More Chicken Scratch aims to equip leaders with the mindset and tools to create resilient, high-performing teams that thrive during adversity.

The metaphor of lions versus chickens is a striking reminder of the sharp contrasts in behavior and mindset that may define teams. As symbols of strength, courage, and unity, lions personify those qualities that every great leader attempts to instill within his or her organization. By direct contrast, the timid nature of chickens reflects the pitfalls of complacency, fear, and lack of direction. The book calls upon leaders to give their teams the environment they need to let the potential roar with confidence and relevance away from the dining cacophony of mediocrity toward the path of greatness.

Throughout the chapters, we will cover the core concepts of lionhearted leadership, from building a fearless team culture to empowering through effective delegation and recognition. Each chapter is designed to inspire and provide practical strategies that leaders can implement immediately. We'll look into real examples and case studies that illustrate in the application how these concepts have been embraced by organizations, in reality, to overcome challenges and achieve remarkable results.

As you read this book, I invite you to reflect on your leadership style and team dynamics. Are you creating an environment in which courage and collaboration thrive? Are you inspiring your pride to rise above fear and into their strengths? By filling your organization with lions and leading a culture of bravery and accountability, you can transform your organization into a force to be reckoned with that can accomplish anything.

In a world of high stakes and constant change, it's time to leave the chicken scratch of indecision and doubt behind. Let us take this journey together to unleash the lionhearted leaders within us all. Whether you're a seasoned executive or an emerging leader, this book will help you build a legacy of strength, resilience, and relentless commitment to excellence.

Welcome to Lionhearted Leadership. May the roar of your pride be heard!

Acknowledgments

Writing Lionhearted Leadership: Surround Yourself with Lions, No More Chicken Scratch has been an inspirational and collaborative journey. I am very grateful to all who have contributed to this effort. First and foremost, I would like to thank my family for their love and support. Your belief in my vision has been a constant source of motivation. To my partner, thank you for your patience and understanding during the countless hours spent writing, researching, and refining ideas. Your insights and feedback have shaped this book in ways I cannot fully express.

I would like to extend my heartfelt appreciation to all my mentors and colleagues who shared their wisdom and experiences. Your insight has been instrumental in forming my ideas about what good leadership and teamwork look and feel like. Special thanks to Ehtisham Altaf for your early encouragement and for challenging me to think critically about leadership dynamics. Your influence has been pivotal in my growth as a leader and writer. To the numerous leaders and teams that shared their stories and insights, thank you for your openness toward meaningful discussion. Your real-world examples have enriched this book by providing a practical foundation for the concepts discussed herein. Your experiences will inspire others to engage in lionhearted leadership within their organizations.

I would also like to acknowledge the dedicated professionals in the publishing industry who have helped bring this book to life. Your expertise and commitment to quality have ensured that this work reaches its fullest potential. A special thanks to my editor, Alyssa Matesic, for your meticulous attention to detail and insightful suggestions that have greatly enhanced the clarity and impact of the writing.

Finally, to the readers of this book, thank you for your interest in developing your leadership skills and fostering a culture of courage and collaboration. I hope the principles and strategies within these pages resonate with you and empower you to lead with heart and conviction. Let us create an environment where the teams thrive and roar like lions, leaving behind the shackles of doubt and fear. So, on this lionhearted leadership journey, let us surround ourselves with lions and have our organizations be beacons for the strong and resilient.

CHAPTER 1

The Lion's Den: Creating a Fearless Team Environment

Introduction

The core of any effective company is an enduring group setting where individuals feel secure sharing concepts, taking risks, and being open. Right here, I will research the idea of a "lion's den," an encouraging yet difficult area that enables participants to flourish. Like lions in the wild, who draw stamina plus defense from each other, groups must create trust funds and mental security for advancement and maximum efficiency. An endured group setting begins with acknowledging that anxiety hinders imagination and impairs better efficiency [1,2]. Disengagement happens when staff members fear sharing concepts or making blunders, bringing about mediocrity in society. The opposite of that is a fearless environment, where openness can enable sharing opinions without the looming knife of criticism or retribution over a team member's head. This chapter will explore the essential elements contributing to such an environment, providing practical strategies for leaders to implement [3].

I will emphasize the role of psychological safety as something that, first and foremost, should be the bedrock of any high-functioning team: how leaders can instill trust, encourage vulnerability, and guarantee respectful communication, at which innovation and collaboration thrive. Further, I discuss the role of constructive feedback and how one can use it to strengthen relationships and group dynamics [4].

I will explore, using real examples and case studies, a variety of organizations that have led cultural transformations in making fearless environments a priority. In tangible terms, these stories illustrate the business dividends from investment in team morale and well-being- extraordinary results that organizations can achieve when their members feel empowered and valued [5]. Remember your team dynamics as I enter the lions' den in this chapter. Do you lead an environment that lets your members roar with pride, or is fear and uncertainty holding them back? This chapter will equip you with the knowledge and the tools to empower you to make your team a cohesive pride of lions ready to take on any challenge together and realize true greatness [6, 7].

Let me take the first step necessary in the team environment for lionhearted leadership: be fearless. Let's create that den where every voice can be heard, every contribution valued, and every team member empowered to unleash their inner lion.

1.1 Establishing Psychological Safety

Psychological safety is a key characteristic of high-performing teams. It provides an atmosphere in which individuals feel secure taking risks, sharing ideas, and voicing concerns without the threat of negative consequences. On job teams where psychological safety thrives, team members are more likely to engage in open dialogue, challenge each other constructively, and collaborate effectively. This gives birth to a secure feeling that lets the teams be innovative and creative and explore new opportunities without the feeling of restraint caused by the fear of making mistakes.

The leader must first identify the importance of psychological safety in a team. When employees feel that there is no punishment or ridicule for being candid over their thoughts and feelings, they are bound to feel more open about their mistakes and ways of seeking help. This leads to a continuous improvement culture where learning from failures is embraced. Leaders are hugely important in modeling that behavior: being vulnerable, sharing their struggles, and showing it is okay not to be perfect. They will create an environment where the team members do not hesitate to share their experiences.

Figure 1.1 Establishing psychological safety.

Communication is another critical element in the development of psychological safety. Leaders should establish transparent and open channels for dialogue, whether through regular team meetings or confidential feedback systems. Actively seeking input from all team members ensures everyone feels valued and heard. When individuals know their contributions are acknowledged, they are more likely to participate in discussions and share their insights. The leader should show receptivity towards feedback so that all voices are recognized and valued irrespective of the rank in a team.

It's beyond communication; it's creating that culture to support experimentation and risk. Leaders must get people out of their comfort zone and inform them that mistakes are part of the learning curve. And leaders set norms that minimize the fear of failure by emphasizing effort and innovation. Recognizing and celebrating contributions furthers that safety culture and shows team members that their input is welcomed and vital to the team's success. Establishing psychological safety requires an ongoing commitment, thus requiring consistent effort. These benefits are worth investing in a resilient, engaged, high-performing team.

1.2 Encouraging Open Dialogue

Open dialogue involves a sense and use of understanding and cooperation within any given community. It opens up an environment where people feel safe enough to express their views and experiences and allows them to share ideas richly. Persons holding open conversations within themselves can challenge the assumptions and expand their thinking. This exchange strengthens the relationship and builds respect for a culture of empathy. By inviting diverse voices into the discussion, I can better take on complicated issues, innovate solutions, and meet the needs of everyone.

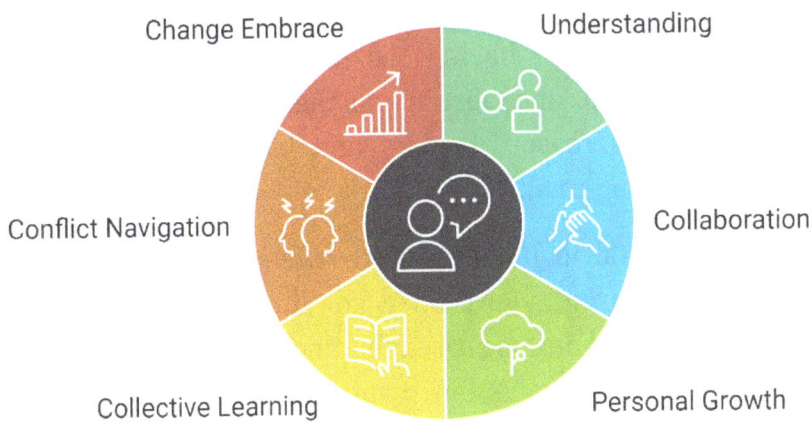

Figure 1.2 Open dialogue is essential for adopting understanding and collaboration.

Also, encouraging open dialogue nurtures personal development and learning in the group. I encourage critical thinking and emotional intelligence by sharing opinions and listening to others. Participants may feel a deeper connection and sense of belonging when they realize their shared humanity from different views. Organizations and communities that value open communication are better prepared to deal with conflicts and change. Encouraging an open dialogue is an added advantage and necessary to make the atmosphere genuinely inclusive and alive for all.

1.2.1 Creating a Culture of Trust

A culture of trust provides the basis for any organization or community to achieve success and sustainability. Trust lies at the base of relationships, collaboration, communication, morale, etc. This makes people show more initiative by sharing innovative ideas and being involved in their work or community. On the other hand, not having trust results in apathy, miscommunication, and hostility in the atmosphere of such a society. For this reason, leaders and team members should prioritize building trust.

It is instrumental in building trust, wherein the organization must be transparent. Here, open communication in flow and decision-making should be cared for. The same can be facilitated through periodic updates, an open-door policy, and feedback forums. When people understand why certain decisions have been made and are informed about organizational objectives, they are more likely to buy into and follow through with those goals. Furthermore, leaders should model trust in their actions and promise through consistency in follow-through. That means delivering on commitments, owning up to mistakes, and not misrepresenting challenges. Where leaders are vulnerable and authentic, others follow suit in a safe space to converse openly.

Other key components that help build trust include encouraging a sense of belonging and becoming inclusive. In such a situation, team members are better positioned to trust one another. This may be achieved by recognizing individual contributions, celebrating diversity, and having a say in decision-making. Opportunities for team bonding through team-building activities or less formally can strengthen relationships and build trust. Ultimately, a trust-based culture lets people cooperate unafraid, take risks, and innovate. Such a culture drives the company or community toward great success.

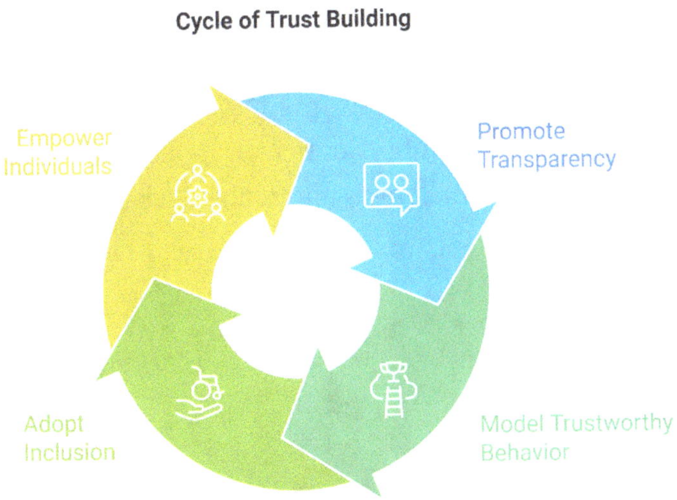

Cycle of Trust Building

Figure 1.3 Trust building cycle.

Trust is gained in an atmosphere that promotes transparency and good examples of trustworthy behavior, and inclusivity leads the way. Hence, an organization should consider these things more for better performance and a healthy atmosphere where people can contribute freely. Trust cannot be built in one day; it grows with time through continuous actions and a shared commitment toward mutual respect and understanding. Where there is trust, the potential to grow and achieve becomes unlimited.

1.2.2 Defining Team Values and Norms

Defining team values and norms is crucial for establishing a cohesive and effective work environment. Team values represent the core principles that guide behavior and decision-making within the group. These values often reflect the organization's broader mission and vision, aligning individual motivations with collective goals. By articulating values such as integrity, collaboration, and innovation, teams articulate a shared notion of what matters, influencing their sense of purpose and direction. When staff members are clear about these values, they more easily navigate challenges and make decisions in tune with the group's spirit.

Figure 1.4 Building a cohesive team environment.

Other than values, norms are the unspoken guidelines on interaction and expectations within the team. The norms will involve the communication styles, ways the team deals with conflict, accountability, and work ethics. Established norms ensure a predictable environment in which the team members know what to expect from others, advancing teamwork with fewer misunderstandings. These refer to such norms as giving constructive feedback, listening to each other, or observing deadlines. By agreeing on those norms and revisiting them regularly, teams ensure commonality in their actions, which leads to better performance and closer relationships among the team members.

1.3 Addressing Conflict Constructively

Conflict is inevitable in any team dynamic; however, how that conflict is dealt with makes a world of difference in relationships and team effectiveness. Constructive conflict resolution means viewing disagreements as opportunities for growth rather than barriers. The first step in this process is to create a safe space where team members can freely express their opinions and concerns. Encouraging open communication and active listening advances a culture where differences can be openly discussed. This approach helps avoid suppressing or ignoring any conflict that may lead to resentment and further complications.

Table 1.1 Simple example of how it can be structured in Markdown format.

Team Values	Description
Integrity	Upholding honesty and strong moral principles.
Collaboration	Working together effectively to achieve common goals.
Innovation	Encouraging creativity and new ideas in problem-solving.
Respect	Valuing each team member's contributions and perspectives.
Accountability	Taking responsibility for actions and commitments.

When conflict occurs, it should be approached with resolution in mind and not blame. This might be achieved using tactics such as "I" statements to express feelings without blame and, in turn, elicit a better reception of the message. Once all parties' underlying interests and motivations are known, what was a contested situation turns into a collaborative effort to solve a problem. Shared objectives and values are a good starting point for finding commonalities among team members. Instead of focusing on the issue, focusing on the solutions can turn conflicts into opportunities that ignite creativity, improve relationships, and ultimately enhance cohesion and performance within the team.

1.3.1 Recognizing and Mitigating Fear Factors

Fear can seriously impair performance, creativity, and collaboration in an organization or team. "But when these fear factors are identified and mitigated, a healthy work environment results in feelings being free to be expressed, risks are taken, and dialogue open without trepidation. Some of the more notable dimensions are fear of failure, criticism, and change. Knowing these elements is where developing a culture that allows growth and innovation can start.

The most prevalent fear factors involve the fear of failure. Employees would be more unwilling to initiate any new proposals or even take leadership, as it is seen that once there is a mistake, the result in most cases is condemnation and possibly punitive action. To reduce this fear, organizations should have a growth mindset where mistakes are seen as learning rather than failure. As such, the leadership should model it by being candid with their setbacks and lessons learned. Moreover, an enabling feedback culture may further make people feel secure.

Constructive feedback, therefore, should be developmental and not critical. This would enable the person to comprehend that their contribution to any endeavor was unsuccessful; they are still valued.

Another high level of fear pertains to the fear of peer criticism or judgment. This will stifle creativity and openness in communication because such team members may need clarification about how their ideas will be received. To that effect, teams should set norms for psychological safety: an environment where team members feel safe taking interpersonal risks. This would include frequent team-building exercises and/ or open forums for sharing ideas. Besides this, leaders need to allow for diverse opinion expression and actively celebrate participation by all team members so that every single member of the team will feel their voice heard.

Change may also cause paralyzing fear in organizations driven by transitions or uncertainties, such that new processes, technologies, or changes in leadership are anxieties of uncertainty. Breaking down such fears requires leaders to communicate candidly about the 'why' of change and how that would benefit the organization and its staff. It can be a means of support through training or resources. It may also enable the team members to own the change and minimize potential resistance.

In other words, seeing plus reducing concern is vital to constructing depend on a favorable and also reliable workplace. Establishing a society that approves failure as a possibility to find, encourages free speech, and successfully takes care of adjustment will certainly assist any company in conquering those anxieties standing in the means of development. When staff members feel secure and sustained, they connect much better, team up with others, and add to your company's success. Eventually, resolving these worry elements will enhance individual health and improve group efficiency with technology.

1.3.2 Building Inclusivity in Team Dynamics

Structure incorporation in group characteristics involves developing a collective plus cutting-edge atmosphere where each staff member feels valued and encouraged. Incorporation indicates surpassing having varied employees to identify and commemorate all people's distinctions in point of view, histories, and experiences. A group that focuses on incorporation develops its analytic capacities plus safeguards high worker fulfillment plus retention. For this, a company has to use calculated techniques that take on interaction, understanding, and connectedness among its labor force.

Primarily, addition can be constructed by unlocking precise lines of interaction and urging candid conversations. Leaders are accountable for making their staff members not hesitate to reveal their sights and experiences without anxiety or judgment honestly. This will certainly be dramatically assisted by normal check-ins, devices for confidential responses, and comprehensive conferences that everybody can add. Look for the input of all participants, specifically underrepresented ones, and make certain their voices, points of view, and understandings are listened to and considered in decision-making. Reliable interaction and energetic listening training would help staff members identify the significance of valuing numerous viewpoints and embrace a more inclusive environment.

The organization may also provide training programs that enable team members to recognize their biases and understand how they impact their behaviors and decisions. This allows a team to work toward equitable practices that ensure equal access to opportunities and resources. Moreover, a relationship of mentorship programs with diversified personnel amidst experienced team members could help bridge gaps in the development process. In developing all team members, an organization commits itself to inclusiveness and empowers them to reach their full potential.

Inclusive culture also concerns celebration and a sense of belonging. Teams must always appreciate and celebrate the unique backgrounds, cultures, and perspectives brought in by their members. It might be through cultural awareness events, team-builders highlighting diverse traditions or celebrating cultural holidays. By cultivating a sense of belonging, team members will feel more connected and attached to the group, developing collaboration and creativity. Furthermore, leaders should model behaviors inclusively through respect and appreciation for diversity in practice. The management's instructions in its inclusivity establish the structure, at which point they can bring the remainder with each other.

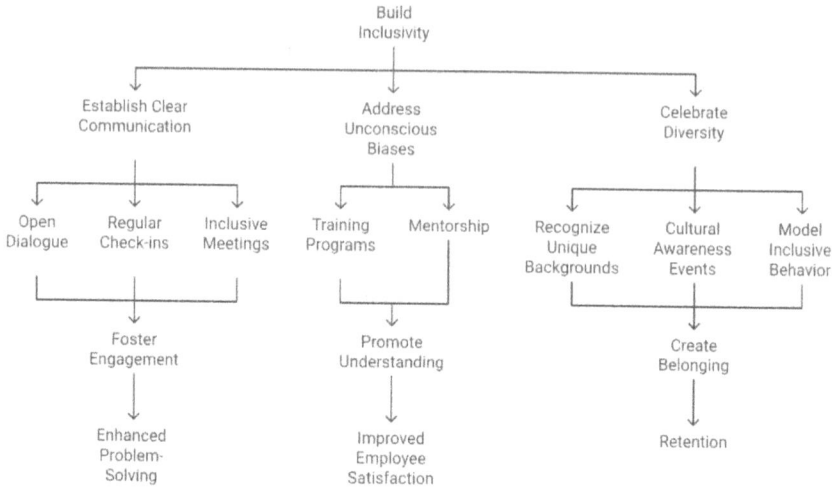

Figure 1.5 Building inclusivity in team dynamics.

Inclusivity within group characteristics develops the foundation of an effective office society where every person can add plus succeed. Organizations can contribute to an atmosphere that values everybody's payments by working on open interaction networks, caring for subconscious predispositions, and proactively commemorating variety. As groups become extra comprehensive, they drive total efficiency and take on a feeling of coming from that gas interaction together with imagination. Inevitably, inclusiveness is not a purpose; it's a procedure that takes dedication, recognition, and activity in all events.

1.4 Encouraging Risk-Taking and Innovation

The basis of motivating risk-taking and advancement exists with companies that aim to be ever-relevant in today's fast-moving and altering setting. In several ways, development occurs when one takes danger to try out originalities and assumptions.

Nevertheless, too many groups might be afraid of attempting brand-new points because they could fall short, gain objection, or anticipate effects from the company. The motivation of imagination in a dangerous society needs to encourage the staff members to introduce unique suggestions without worrying about revenge.

One of the key elements to encourage risk-taking is an enabling environment for experimentation. The leadership can provide this environment by clearly communicating that failure is necessary for innovation. If the team members know that any mistakes are tolerated and, even further, represent valuable learning opportunities, they are more likely to make bold moves. In this regard, innovative efforts, which might have failed, should be celebrated. For instance, highlighting case studies of those projects that did not succeed but came out with valuable insights will encourage others to think out of the box. Also, give them time and resources for brainstorming and experimentation that eliminate the employees' hounding pressure for immediate results using performance metrics.

Apart from creating a safe space to try new things, an organization should develop a collaborative and communicative mindset. Diversity in teams brings many different perspectives that lead to the generation of new ideas. Collaboration between departments and disciplines would facilitate tapping into the combined creative potential of human capital. The different brainstorming sessions, cross-functional workshops, and innovation challenges would lead to motivation in sharing and evolving ideas. Moreover, feedback loops should be established where team members' views can be put forward and received with constructive responses from their colleagues. In this way, the value of the ideas will be increased, and a sense of ownership and commitment will be developed.

Besides, leaders have a very important role in modeling risk-taking behavior. When leaders take calculated risks and share those experiences, successes, and failures, they set a powerful example for the team. Innovation can be demystified by transparency like this, inviting employees out of their comfort zones. Leaders must, therefore, emphasize and recognize people and teams showing creativity and initiative; they need to reinforce that taking calculated risks is recognized and encouraged within the company. Celebrating achievements, whether big or small, can motivate others to pursue their innovative ideas fearlessly.

Therefore, risk-taking and innovation are important for organizations that seek to remain competitive and responsive. By allowing a safe environment to take a chance on trying something new, developing collaboration, or modeling risk-taking behavior, leaders can create a culture of valuing creativity and encouraging employees to explore new possibilities. Innovation drives risk and empowers people to contribute meaningfully to an organization's success. When the teams are supported in their endeavor, it will make them push boundaries, challenge the norms, and develop breakthrough solutions that will always move the organization forward.

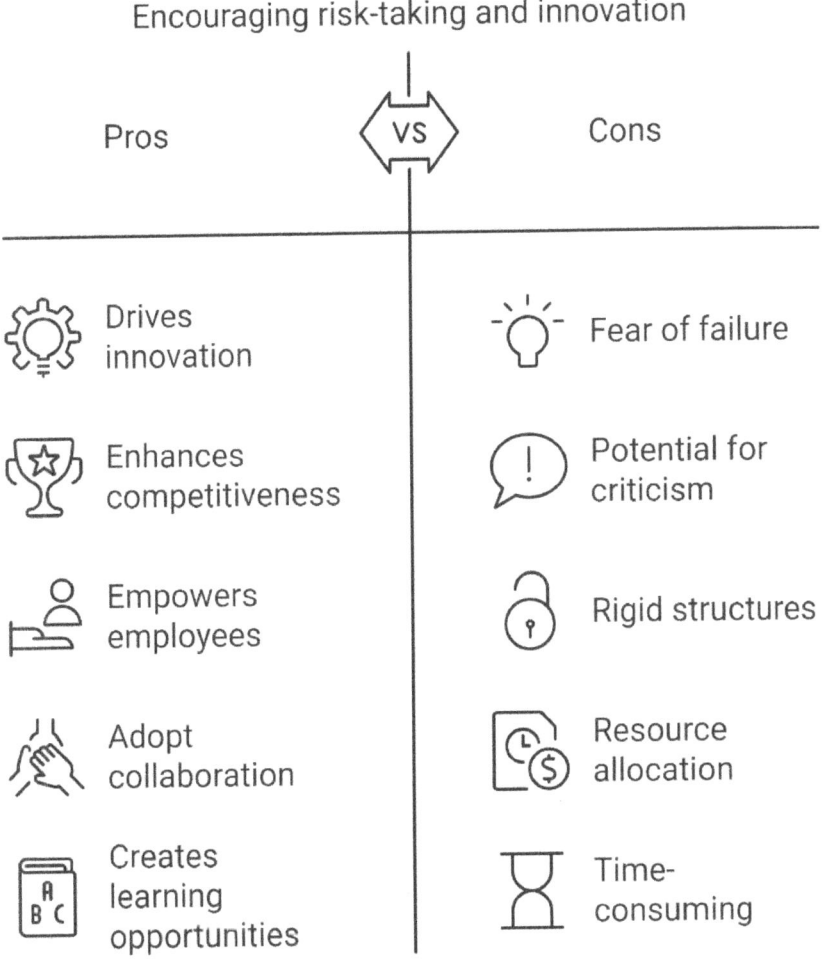

Figure 1.6 Compression of encouraging risk-taking and innovation

1.4.1 Setting Boundaries for Healthy Discourse

The boundaries around healthy discourse are important for any environment dealing with collaboration, whether a workplace, community groups, or online platforms. Healthy discourse allows everyone to freely share their thoughts and ideas while maintaining constructive and respectful discussions. Without predetermined limits, conversations spiral into fruitless debates or poisonous communications, choking imagination and collaboration. Standards established an atmosphere of interaction in which various points of view can be shared and contemplated.

Among the first steps in boundary-setting regarding healthy and balanced talks is specifying the values that would result in such communications. Organizations must express concepts like regard, energetic listening, and open-mindedness. All individuals will recognize what they get from the interaction via clear interaction.

For example, the grounds for considerate exchange are currently established by urging staff members to pay attention without disturbing others, not to mention striking others directly. In addition, establishing ground rules for conversation, like concurring not to make individual assaults or disparaging language, will certainly make the environment enjoyable. Assisting conferences with an organized strategy can additionally sustain healthy and balanced speech. This could consist of utilizing a mediator or facilitator to direct discussions and ensure that all could talk, handling the moment to avoid prominence by solitary voices over others.

Round-robin sharing, where each adds, in turn, is one strategy of stabilizing involvement to ensure all voices are listened to. This helps lessen the chances of conversations going astray and creating conflicts or hurtful disputes. Establishing a program in conversations can likewise minimize the chance of tangential conversations that result in conflicts. The other essential attribute of establishing limits is developing room for sharing different points of view. Healthy and balanced discussion requires that individuals feel comfortable sharing varied viewpoints without retaliation. Inquisitiveness, including concerns and difficulties, helps normalize the expression of various views. A "no-shaming " strategy recognizes that individuals will not be shamed for their views but urged to clarify themselves, sustain a position, and discover in the discussion.

Lastly, it is essential to assess plus reassess these limits routinely. Equally, as groups alter with the addition of brand-new participants, so does a dedication to healthy and balanced conversation. Via normal check-ins or interaction technique workshops, the relevance of established borders can be reiterated and means might be discussed as to which those limits might be challenging to keep. This continuous discussion ensures that the rhetoric standards stay pertinent and valued. Establishing the restrictions for healthy and balanced unsupported claims is important to produce an enabling atmosphere where individuals feel free to share their concepts and have useful conversations.

A company would certainly show regard and impartiality by assisting with structured conversations, ensuring security in sharing arguments, and reviewing the borders. Healthy and balanced unsupported claims settle regarding group characteristics, technology, and analytic abilities, leading to much better partnerships and, for that reason, higher outcomes for all concerned.

1.4.2 Implementing Regular Team Check-Ins

Group check-ins are a crucial advancement in interaction and using partnerships to guarantee placement in a group. These conferences allow staff members to share updates concerning their jobs, difficulties, and successes, each causing an extra joint with an effective office. Check-ins can take numerous types plus rhythms from day-to-day to regular or bi-weekly; they supply a location for employees to get in touch with and involve each other meaningfully. Among one of the most crucial benefits normal group check-ins give is far better interaction.

When individuals become hectic at the office, they typically become siloed and might be required to comprehend or recognize partnership chances. Check-ins allow everybody to share progression, review the method's challenges, and request their associates' assistance. With this open line of interaction, assumptions are crystal clear, driving openness and responsibility within the group. When staff members understand what others are doing and encountering it, it brings assistance along with sources, developing friendships or common objectives. Besides enhancing interaction, constant check-ins likewise pay for a method of official comments and representation.

They can be made useful: colleagues can review what jobs are available and what are not. These continual comment cycles will assist in the early discovery of prospective concerns to ensure that the group might change before issues intensify. Furthermore, check-ins can add to people's individual plus specialist advancement by urging individuals to establish objectives on their plus and, later on, assess those objectives. Employees who feel sustained in individual development are more likely to remain involved.

An additional essential advantage of normal group check-ins is that they urge a favorable society. They enable time to commemorate successes, whether large or small. Commemorating specific coupled with group accomplishments constructs a feeling of coming from amongst staff members and encourages them to succeed. Check-ins might additionally consist of team-building tasks coupled with icebreakers that assist in boosting partnerships together with partnership within the team. By giving center stage to connectivity and engagement, teams can adopt a more inclusive and supportive environment, ultimately elevating overall morale and productivity.

With a well-defined structure and purpose, one would establish routines for effective team check-ins. These should be set regularly, daily, weekly, or biweekly so that check-ins become part of the team's rhythm. Every meeting should have a defined agenda that might include any updated issues, discussing challenges, and providing feedback. This will help keep the meetings focused and time-efficient, which will keep them engaging without being a burden. Second, understanding the preferred format and topics of the check-ins from team members can help tailor the meetings to their liking and fulfill their needs.

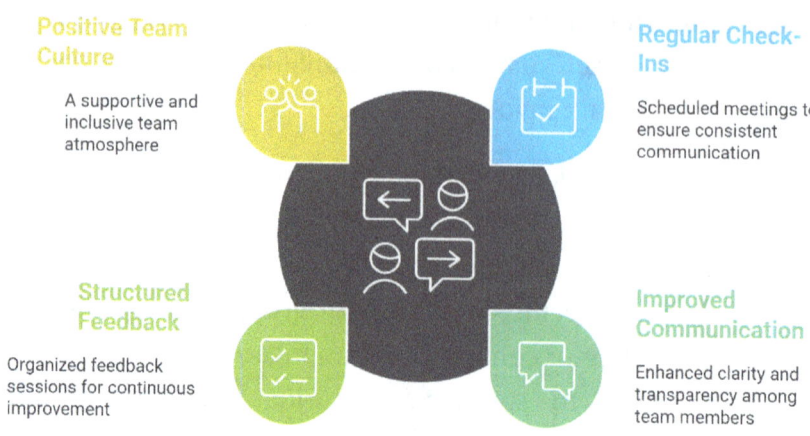

Figure 1.7 Implementing regular team check-ins.

In this respect, regular team check-ins can be a powerful means for effective communication, adopting the spirit of teamwork, and furthering individual and team growth. Indeed, with a more systematic approach toward such sessions, teams can develop better collaboration, proactively address complicated issues, and celebrate their successes. Regular check-ins will allow all team members to feel connected, supported, and motivated to put in their best efforts for the organization's higher performance and overall success.

1.5 Celebrating Vulnerability and Authenticity

Celebrating vulnerability and authenticity must be a core constituent in nurturing a culture of trust, collaboration, and innovation at work. By creating an environment where team members can be themselves, including their fears, challenges, and unique perspectives, creativity is nurtured, and relationships are strengthened. By embracing vulnerability and authenticity at work, one encourages the well-being of the team's individuals, positively reinforcing team dynamics for better performance and higher job satisfaction.

The concept of vulnerability is usually labeled as a weakness, but it is one of the strong points that helps team members bond with each other firmly. When leaders model it through sharing experiences, fears, and mistakes, they tell others that vulnerability is okay. Openness like this welcomes members to share thoughts and feelings; thus, an inclusive environment wherein all are heard is adopted. For instance, leaders can share personal experiences about the challenges they had to go through, pointing out what was learned and the growth resulting from such experiences. That way, leaders de-sanitize their persona, encouraging others to accept their vulnerabilities and creating an empathetic, supportive culture.

Authenticity, on the other hand, is about being true to oneself and a free expression of oneself, thoughts, feelings, and values. When team members' authenticity is encouraged at work, teamwork engagement and productivity will increase. The employees will be more creative since they are not confined to behaving in a specific corporate persona, meaning they can freely express their identity. It helps an organization be more genuine because the employees can express their diversity and experiences through numerous activities, such as storytelling, team building, or projects celebrating diversity. Such activities improve one's knowledge base and build better relationships in your team since members learn to respect and appreciate each other's differences.

These values need to be taught in the habit formation of organizations so that vulnerability and authenticity can be celebrated. Regular check-ins, feedback sessions, and open forums can provide a safe space for sharing thoughts and feelings. Besides, training programs concerning emotional intelligence and effective communication will help team members have the necessary tool kit to be authentic yet sensitive to the feelings of others. It means creating an environment where vulnerability is welcome: setting the norms to prioritize respect and understanding and feeling supported by all team members when experiences are shared.

This will also mean innovation; team members will feel free to propose bold ideas. The chances are more open toward taking risks and thinking creatively, thus driving the organization forward to breakthrough solutions and higher competitiveness. Also, teams that allow vulnerability are resilient because they can face challenges together by drawing on each member's strengths and perspectives.

Figure 1.8 Celebrating vulnerability and authenticity in the workplace.

Vulnerability and authenticity should be celebrated to instill trust, collaboration, and innovation in the workplace. When organizations allow team members to be themselves and create sharing opportunities, they can build better relationships and generate more engagement. As leaders model the concepts of vulnerability and authenticity, the pathway is designed for a more inclusive and supportive environment that propels the team into tremendous success and fulfillment. Embracing these qualities benefits individuals and strengthens the organization by creating a thriving culture where all can contribute their best.

1.5.1 Measuring Team Engagement and Morale

The engagement and morale of a team provide a good insight into the organization's health from the employees' point of view. High levels of engagement translate into better performance, reduced turnover rates, and higher overall job satisfaction. A no-low morale projects an individual who becomes disengaged, less productive, and has high attrition. It is, therefore, essential to note here that organizational team engagement and morale need to be judged and improved regularly for specific practical reasons.

The typical form of measurement of team engagement is employee surveys. Such a survey can include questions referring to job satisfaction, perceived support from management, opportunities for professional development, and general workplace culture. Quantitative and qualitative questions enable staff to state opinions in the most orderly manner and allow space for open feedback. For example, the questions on the Likert scale can establish the magnitude of the feelings towards certain aspects of their work. On the other hand, with open-ended questions, root problems may spring to light, which quantitative measures cannot indicate. Performing such studies is a lengthy method of developing the moment patterns and aids the administration in determining locations to address.

Besides, a company might examine worker interaction with normal individual check-ins and efficiency analyses. These discussions can give a fantastic understanding of the individual experiences of private team participants. Supervisors can review job desires and obstacles coupled with comments in a nonjudgmental setting, developing depending on open interaction.

This assists the supervisor in raising spirits while providing the staff members with an opportunity to vent their views, be listened to, and be valued. In addition, urging peer comments might enhance this procedure, as staff members can gain insight into each other's degrees of interaction that supervisors might not see. Various other efficient methods to determine group spirit include observing characteristics and habits in the work environment. A very involved group generally shows high cooperation, excitement, and dedication.

On the other hand, disengagement might be identified by enhanced lack, minimized involvement in group tasks, or absence of effort amongst participants. Through normal focus on these, leaders can rapidly develop where morale is moving and take the required actions very early to avoid points from getting worse. Additionally, exit interviews with the employees leaving can provide significant insights into the culture and morale of the organization, thus indicating where to make improvements.

Organizations then must interpret the results of data collected thoughtfully and communicate findings back to the team. Transparency of engagement metrics builds ownership and accountability among employees. It is important to communicate areas of metrics where improvements are being shown and to recognize weaknesses. In doing so, organizations can collaborate to generate action plans on concerns that will lead to better employee buy-in and commitment to the change initiative.

Lastly, measuring engagement and morale should be continuous rather than a one-time activity. A constant feedback culture at work may allow employees to express views regularly and thus keep the organization abreast of their team's needs. It can be implemented as informal check-ins, suggestion boxes, or routine team discussions on morale and engagement.

In other words, team engagement and morale are essential to measure because they contribute to developing a good and functioning team environment. It would be rather valuable if the organization could obtain a notion about the employee experience through questionnaires, one-on-one questionnaires, observation techniques, and open dialogues. This is how continuous measurement and adjustment ensure morale and drive engagement to enhance overall work performance, making work more satisfying for all involved.

1.6 Case Study: Creating a Fearless Team Environment

The fear-less team environment spurs innovation and resiliency in today's fast-moving and competitive business world. The case study explores how the mid-sized technology company Innovatech created a workplace cultural shift focusing on psychological safety, creativity, better collaboration, and higher employee satisfaction.

Innovatech is the epitome of software solutions, and teams need more cohesion. Employees at Innovatech rarely shared ideas or complaints because they were afraid of being reprimanded or snubbed. Such an environment clipped the creative wings of the employees and lessened their morale. Soon, the management decided to implement some strategies to help build a fearless workplace where employees could express themselves freely.

The first step in this transformation was a hard look at what it is. Innovatech conducted anonymous surveys to learn more about what employees thought was happening with safety and openness amongst the team members. Results showed that what leadership thought was happening and what employees experienced were far apart. To address this, the leadership team planned workshops on psychological safety led by a third-party consultant specializing in organizational behavior.

These workshops were the basis on which the team members discussed vulnerability, embracing failure to rise as an opportunity for learning. These elements of success were. These elements of success were encouraging open dialogue, modeling vulnerability, and holding regular check-ins to help build a climate where employees felt empowered and free to share ideas and take risks. The cascading positive results increased innovation to boost collaboration and employee satisfaction-indicating that cultivating a fearless culture can be one of the primary drivers of organizational success. This case can serve as a multi-dimensional example for any organization that wants to enhance teamwork and build an innovative and engaging workplace.

1.7 Key Point Donald Trump's potential re-election in 2024

> **Strong Base Support:** Trump maintains a loyal and energized base that is committed to his policies and leadership style.

Former President Donald Trump has built a formidable cadre of dedicated supporters who stick by his policies and kind of leadership. This steadfast nature of loyalty does not simply reflect partisan loyalty but reflects deep emotional attachment and shared values with millions of Americans. It becomes important to explain such support dynamics, as the explanation provides insights into Trump's political influence and, more generally, the landscape of American politics.

This is attached to an identity and a feeling of belonging, constituting the heart of Trump's base [8]. Many feel he represents their interests and values, especially concerning economic policy, immigration, and national security. Trump's "America First" agenda has been well-received among the working-class Americans who have been left out by shifting economic trends and globalization. His pledges to strengthen American manufacturing, protect American jobs, and advance national interests strike a strong chord, particularly in areas that have suffered from economic downturns. The result is a brand of allegiance that can largely transcend party ranks due to the perception by many of his followers that he represents their grievances and hopes [9].

> **Emphasize Direct Communication**
> Use social media to bypass traditional media and connect directly with supporters.
>
> **Branding is Key**
> Create a strong, recognizable brand that resonates with your audience.

Besides, Trump's leadership style-brashness, forthrightness, frankness-has drawn his base to him. He challenges traditional ways of doing political business, and many supporters appreciate that he will speak bluntly about issues others avoid. It puts him in a different category from the mainstream politician and builds a sense of authenticity with his base. During his presidency, Trump's heavy use of social media, especially Twitter, led him to go directly into the supporter base and route around traditional media filters. This line of communication has galvanized his base; they feel their voices are finally being heard, and they have a personal stake in the political process.

These rallies and events orchestrated by Trump amplify this sense of community and energize support. These gatherings are more than political events; they serve as social spectacles where supporters unite to express their enthusiasm and solidarity. The rallies are usually electric, full of chants, slogans, and a sense of shared purpose. This reinforces loyalty, embeds a grievance culture, and frames the resistance from what is commonly seen as the threat to their cause from political elites and the media. So, in effect, it's the policy for which Trump's supporters rally and build a collective identity that fortifies their commitment to his leadership.

More significantly, Trump's framing of issues has resonated with his base and galvanized their support. His rhetoric often taps into the feelings of the dispossessed and cultural anxiety; positioning against rapid social change, he depicts himself as a defender of traditional American values. By addressing concerns about immigration, crime, and economic security, Trump effectively rallies his base around the idea of a shared America that is under threat. This energizes his supporters and galvanizes his army into action through grassroots organizing, voting, or advocacy [10]. Donald Trump enjoys base support with a loyal, energized following that is deeply committed to his policies and leadership style. This support is an identity, appreciation for his frankness, and the rallies—the shared communal experience. By speaking to the frustrations and wants of his base, Trump has ignited a strong, long-lasting political movement. As politics in America continue to shift, understanding this base will prove increasingly important for addressing the intricacies of today's political world.

Reference

1. Brown, B. (2018). Dare to lead: Brave work. Tough conversations. Whole hearts. Random House.

2. Duhigg, C. (2016). Smarter faster better: The secrets of being productive in life and business. Crown Business.

3. Edmondson, A. C. (2019). The fearless organization: Creating psychological safety in the workplace for learning, innovation, and growth. Wiley.

4. Google. (2016). Project Aristotle: Understanding team effectiveness. Retrieved from https://rework.withgoogle.com/print/guides/5721312655835136/

5. Grant, A. (2013). Give and take: A revolutionary approach to success. Viking.

6. Kahn, W. A. (1990). Psychological conditions of personal engagement and disengagement at work. Academy of Management Journal, 33(4), 692-724. https://doi.org/10.2307/256287

7. Lencioni, P. (2002). The five dysfunctions of a team: A leadership fable. Jossey-Bass.

8. Schein, E. H. (2010). Organizational culture and leadership (4th ed.). Jossey-Bass.

9. Desjardins, L. (2016). 24 things Donald Trump is promising to do. *PBS News*.

10. Fair Observer. (2019). It's simplistic to assume Trump's devoted voters are irrational. *Fair Observer*.

CHAPTER 2

Identifying Your Pride: Recognizing Strengths and Talents

Introduction

Recognizing and accepting one's strengths and talents is a changing process in a world created on the frontiers of competition and achievement [1, 2]. This chapter, "Identifying Your Pride: Recognizing Strengths and Talents," is a foundational exploration into the essence of self-awareness and personal growth. Understanding our unique abilities empowers us to navigate challenges more effectively and allows us to appreciate our individuality and contributions to the broader community [3, 4].

Identifying our strengths and talents is not self-promotion but essential in developing natural self-esteem and self-confidence [5, 6]. Often, people are plagued with self-doubt and the tendency to belittle their abilities, considering the norms dictated by society or society's comparisons one's making toward peers [7]. This chapter must eliminate some of these barriers by prompting readers to think profoundly about their experiences, values, and skills [8, 9]. Using such a process of reflection, one would henceforth develop pride in what has been achieved and realize the intrinsic value of one's talents.

The chapter shall also explain the identification of strengths by introducing practical resources and methodologies, such as self-assessments, peer feedback, and mindfulness practices. This approach will show how personal strengths may be expressed in creative problem-solving, effective communication, or leadership capabilities [10]. It is through recognizing and celebrating our unique talents that we build self-awareness, positioning ourselves for the pursuit of opportunities to which we are passionate about and value [11, 12].

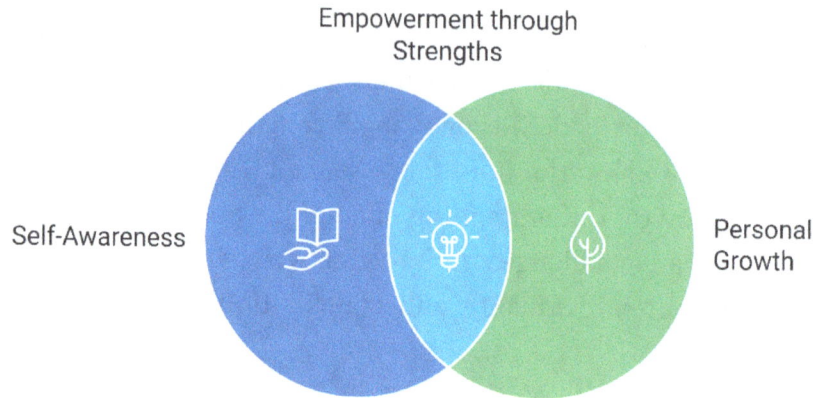

Figure 2.1 Recognizing and embracing one's strengths and talents.

Ultimately, "Identifying Your Pride" calls for readers to accept strengths as a power source. In so doing, we nurture a culture of valuing uniqueness and allow others to start the journey into self. The following steps within this chapter will enable us to identify and celebrate unique strengths individually; in that sense, we create pathways into individual and collective growth [13].

2.1 Conducting Skills Assessments

Conducting skills assessments is a vital process for individuals and organizations aiming to understand and leverage their strengths and capabilities effectively. These assessments provide valuable insights into existing skills, highlight areas for development, and inform strategic decision-making regarding career paths, team dynamics, and training initiatives. By systematically evaluating abilities, individuals and organizations can adopt growth, enhance performance, and align efforts with overarching goals.

Clearly defining the objectives is the first step in conducting a skills assessment. The goal could be to explore personal strengths, prepare for a career transition, or determine team competencies. In such cases, individuals must practice introspection. This will include the ability to engage in personal questions related to past experiences, achievements, and challenges. Situations, where one feels particularly effective or engaged, may indicate core competencies and interests that might not otherwise be obvious.

On the other hand, organizations apply more formalized methods of assessing skills, most using surveys, self-assessments, and competency frameworks. The survey may be designed to assess technical and soft skills, giving an overall perspective of the employees' capabilities. Through self-assessments, personnel are prompted to be honest about assessing their skills for their strengths and avenues of development to be recognized. Besides this, organizations can use 360-degree feedback mechanisms, whereby peers, supervisors, and subordinates can give input about an individual's skills and behaviors. A holistic approach like this provides a well-rounded perspective and may uncover blind spots that individuals cannot see for themselves.

After the information has been acquired, it should be analyzed and interpreted to yield meaningful results. The individual analyses will show trends that may give an idea of an individual's skills and the opportunities available. Aggregating and analyzing data may also inform an organization's talent management strategies, training programs, and succession planning. Understanding the skills, including the emergence of new roles and competencies, allows leaders to make informed decisions about resource allocation and development initiatives.

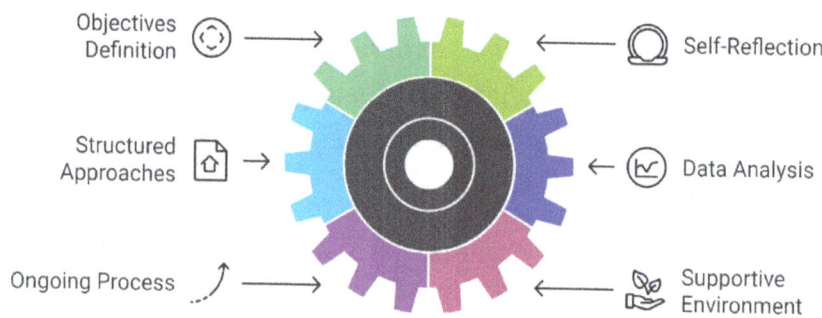

Figure 2.2 The Dynamics of Skills Assessment.

Some might consider abilities analyses an occasion, yet they must be dealt with as a procedure. The normal analysis will permit both organizations and individuals to be fast in this ever-before-transforming setting. As sectors constantly progress and adjust to brand-new innovations, the expertise for success likewise adjusts. This routine evaluation allows prompt recognition of ability voids and training requirements, therefore making staff members and companies affordable.

Lastly, a making-it-possible setting needs to be produced where comments are offered and renovations are constantly made.

This, for people, indicates that development attitude abilities are vibrant and can be created via initiative coupled with knowledge. A discovery and development-supportive business society improves the value of abilities evaluation by motivating workers to take an energetic passion in their development. Ability analysis is a powerful method that is useful for people and companies.

In terrific information, abilities evaluation reveals people's strengths and growth areas, while companies tactically align skills to organizational purposes through organized evaluation. Accepting analysis as a continual procedure produces a society of development and versatility that inevitably results in much better efficiency and satisfaction for all concerned.

2.2 Utilizing Strengths-Based Frameworks

Some might occasionally consider abilities evaluations; however, they must be dealt with as a procedure. The routine analysis will permit individuals and companies to be fast on their feet in this ever-before, ever-transforming setting. As sectors constantly advance and adjust to brand-new innovations, the expertise for success likewise adjusts. This routine evaluation allows prompt recognition of ability voids plus training requirements, making staff members and companies affordable.

Ultimately, an encouraging atmosphere ought to be developed where comments are provided and enhancements are continually made. This suggests that developing the way of thinking abilities is vibrant and can be established via initiative and knowing. A knowledge- and development-supportive business society improves the significance of abilities analysis by motivating staff members to take an energetic passion in their development.

Essentially, abilities evaluation is a powerful technique that settles for people and companies. In excellent information, abilities evaluation reveals people's stamina and advancement locations, while companies tactically align ability with company purposes via organized analysis.

Embracing analysis as a constant procedure develops a society of development and versatility that inevitably leads to much better efficiency and fulfillment for all concerned. This approach empowers them to discover and utilize their natural communication, solving problems, creating, or leading rather than focusing on what is lacking. Focusing on such strengths could raise motivation, engagement, and overall well-being.

The most well-known strengths-based framework is the Gallup StrengthsFinder, which identifies individual talents across various domains. This tool allows the person to understand their topmost strengths and equips them with insight on applying them in their personal and professional lives. It is found that organizations working on identifying strengths elicit the worth of employees and that they are better prepared to deliver value toward the team's objectives. This helps improve productivity and higher satisfaction from employees by aligning their roles and responsibilities with their strengths, building a culture of collaboration and appreciation.

Adopting strength-based approaches in teams fuels collaboration and communication. Knowing other team members' strengths dramatically affects how one works with them effectively. In such a case, a team would develop far more complicated projects since individuals would contribute different dimensions or skills. This boosts morale within the team and creates an incentive toward innovation because of the diversity of ideas and talents used in creating a more dynamic solution.

Moreover, the use of strengths-based frameworks may heighten leadership effectiveness. This is when leaders identify and build strengths among their members, creating a climate of trust and empowerment. When leaders focus on what is done right, they can develop plans for growth instead of remediation development plans. This improves individual performance and builds a resilient and capable team.

Figure 2.3 Strengths-Based Framework Impact

An enabling culture that allows open communication and feedback should be adopted within the organization to successfully implement a strengths-based framework. This would be further reinforced by regular check-ins, coaching sessions, and team-building activities involving strengths. Training programs would incorporate The strength-based philosophy within the organization's culture.

In other words, the strengths-based framework unleashes a transformational personal and organizational development approach wherein people have a new paradigm of engagement, collaboration, and innovation. That paradigm shifts the focus from individual weaknesses to strengths. Recognizing and leveraging unique talents might create greater job satisfaction and fulfillment for individuals. Putting employees in the right roles and responsibilities based on their relative strengths would bolster productivity and a positive workplace culture. Embracing a strengths-based approach empowers individuals and perpetuates collective success, creating a thriving environment where all can bring in their best.

2.2.1 Identifying Key Roles and Responsibilities

Recognizing significant roles and responsibilities within a team or organization is vital in ensuring maximum performance, effective teamwork, and realizing strategic goals. Well-defined roles make the team member aware of their contributions and how these fit within the organization's broader goals. With well-set responsibilities, an organization will enhance efficiency, reduce confusion, and increase accountability among team members.

Identifying key roles begins with a critical look into organizational objectives and determining the resultant objectives. In this regard, consultations with stakeholders are conducted to help us understand the broader vision and what specific deliverables are expected from different teams. By aligning roles with organizational goals, teams can ensure that the efforts of every member meaningfully contribute to the overarching mission, infusing a sense of purpose and direction.

Once the objectives are well-defined, the subsequent step will detail the activities and work involved in meeting those objectives. This may often be a role or responsibility assignment matrix, such as the RACI-Responsible, Accountable, Consulted, Informed matrix. This tool will help clarify who is responsible for each task, who has decision-making authority, and who needs to be kept informed through the process. By visualizing roles and responsibilities in this way, teams can prevent overlap and ensure that all necessary tasks are covered without redundancy.

At this stage, communication is the key. Discussing the roles with the team members instills a feeling of ownership and responsibility. When people contribute to developing their role, they are most likely to show interest in it and believe in their team's success. That is how discussion can be made in regular team meetings and one-on-one conversations. Some adjustments and improvements can be made.

Recognizing the essential duties at the workplace likewise calls for recognizing every participant's toughness and abilities. A duty meaning from a strengths-based strategy ensures complete work satisfaction and maximizes efficiency. By aligning duties with personal toughness, companies can utilize their labor force's varied abilities, enhancing effectiveness and technology. For example, the one with exceptional interaction abilities will certainly manage customers better, while the one with durable evaluation abilities will perform far better on jobs including information.

When duties are developed, reviewing and reassessing them frequently is crucial. As business requirements progress and jobs alter, adaptability is crucial. Normal check-ins and efficiency analyses provide opportunities to review any required duty changes, permitting groups to stay nimble and receptive to brand-new difficulties or possibilities.

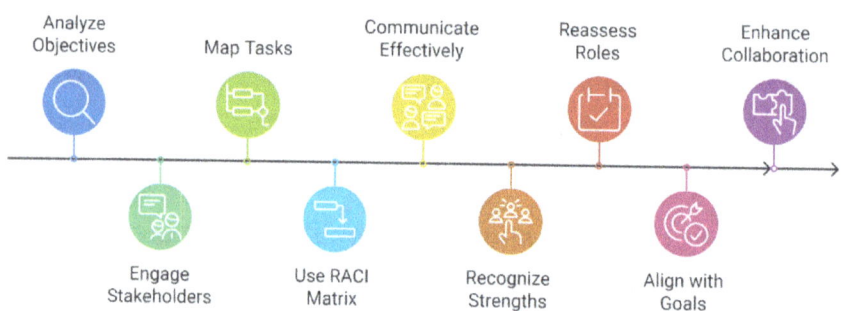

Figure 2.4 Identifying Key Roles and Responsibilities.

Secret duties and duties are the structure of reliable group characteristics in addition to business success. Well-defined duties straightened with business objectives, high degrees of interaction amongst staff members, and a focus on leveraging each individual's bits of stamina in a collective atmosphere all advantage companies by creating much-needed responsibility together with general far better efficiency. Clearness makes it possible for group performance plus affects a favorable office society where staff members feel valued plus encouraged to add their finest initiatives. As daily passes, the company continually discovers plus develops; well-defined functions and duties will certainly be essential for proceeded success along with long-lasting objectives.

2.2.2 Development of a Culture of Recognition

Establishing a company's appreciation of society favorably affects worker involvement, inspiration, and work environment fulfillment. A setting abundant in appreciation boosts people's spirits and adds favorably to business society by raising performance and boosting retention. Arranging methodical consent and the event of staff member payments produces an establishment where individuals feel valued and encouraged to stand out. Acknowledgment society would certainly be fired up by recognizing that staff members should recognize their initiatives.

Acknowledgment can take several forms, from casual appreciation to thank-you notes to official honors and public acknowledgments. In developing this sort of society, acknowledgment must become a vital top priority of the company. It begins with the top: the tone is established when leaders proactively attempt to acknowledge and commemorate their groups' success. It states quantities regarding top priorities connected to admiration in the work environment.

One way to establish a society of acknowledgment is to carry out normal acknowledgment programs. These can be points such as worker of the month, peer-to-peer acknowledgment systems, or turning point events. Establishing formal mechanisms for recognition can help organizations make acknowledgments routine, expected, and average in the workplace. Such programs should be inclusive and accessible to all employees so that contributions from all levels and departments are valued. This helps provide a feeling of being present and promotes the spirit of comradeship among team members.

Besides formal programs, organizations can improve their culture through informal practices. Encouraging managers and peers to show real-time appreciation for specific actions greatly influences employee morale. Small things, like verbal praise during team meetings or handwritten notes, will make them feel valued. Again, training in effective recognition techniques will allow leaders to provide meaningful feedback and celebrate successes authentically.

Table 2.1 The key components and strategies for developing a culture of recognition within an organization

Component	Description	Strategies
Leadership Commitment	Leaders model recognition behaviors and prioritize appreciation as a core value.	• Set clear expectations for recognition practices. • Share success stories in meetings.
Formal Recognition Programs	Structured initiatives to acknowledge employee contributions and achievements.	• Employee of the Month awards. • Annual recognition ceremonies. • Milestone celebrations.
Informal Recognition	Casual and spontaneous ways to acknowledge employees in daily	• Verbal praise in team meetings.

Practices	interactions.	• Handwritten thank-you notes.
		• Celebratory emails.
Peer-to-Peer Recognition	Encouraging employees to recognize each other's contributions adopts camaraderie and support.	• Implement a digital recognition platform.
		• Create a "kudos" board for public acknowledgments.
Training for Managers	Equip leaders with the skills to provide meaningful recognition and feedback.	• Conduct workshops on effective recognition techniques.
		• Role-playing scenarios for practice.
Use of Technology	Leverage digital tools to facilitate and document recognition efforts.	• Utilize recognition software for tracking and celebrating contributions.
		• Create a dedicated channel for recognition on communication platforms.
Feedback Mechanisms	Regularly gather input from employees to assess the effectiveness of recognition initiatives.	• Conduct surveys to measure employee satisfaction with recognition.
		• Hold focus groups for deeper insights.
Sustaining the Culture	Continuous efforts to maintain and improve recognition practices over time.	• Review and revise recognition programs based on feedback.
		• Celebrate recognition successes to reinforce the behavior.

Second, leveraging technology is very significant in furthering the culture of recognition. Many organizations today use digital platforms on which employees can globally recognize the contributions of their fellow employees. These platforms can create instant feedback, creating a repository of shared successes that allows the recognition to be visible and reinforces the sense of community. Making recognition more accessible through the incorporation of technology will ensure that recognition becomes part of the daily rhythm of work.

Measurement and collection of feedback from employees are paramount in maintaining a culture of recognition. Surveys and focus groups help indicate the trend of recognition in an organization and where improvement is needed. Asking for input shows that an organization is committed to creating a culture of appreciation and helps it make strategic adjustments to meet employee needs better.

A positive, recognition-based culture is thus a powerful means of ensuring maximum employee engagement and satisfaction. By prioritizing recognition at all levels of the organization, implementing both formal and informal acknowledgment practices, and leveraging technology, organizations can adopt an enabling environment for employees to aspire and contribute positively in pursuit of organizational goals. Such a culture enhances morale, leading to more team collaboration, innovation, and loyalty, ultimately benefiting organizational performance. The strong culture of recognition will be a point of differentiation in the race to attract and retain top talent as businesses grapple with complexity in the modern workplace.

2.3 Building Diverse Teams for Holistic Strength

As companies today pursue a worldwide allied globe, alternative toughness plus continual success are related to the structure of varied groups. Variety comes about in several measurements, varying from race and sex to age, sexual preference, and social history, moving even more to varied experiences together with different points of view. Organizations stand to get suggestions along with techniques that drive development, creative thinking, and analytic when embracing an inclusive atmosphere where varied voices are listened to and valued.

Amongst the numerous crucial values of varied groups is the richness of points of view they bring right into conversations. When individuals from various histories interact, they make certain to add to others with distinct understandings from their experiences. Such a variety of ideas might cause detailed services to intricate concerns where participants test each other's presumptions to prompt the reasoning of others. For instance, a task group of people with various social histories might use various methods regarding the point of view of an advertising and marketing project. This permits the messaging to reverberate with a bigger target market. The capability to introduce and adjust comes to be essential in a market that is transforming rapidly.

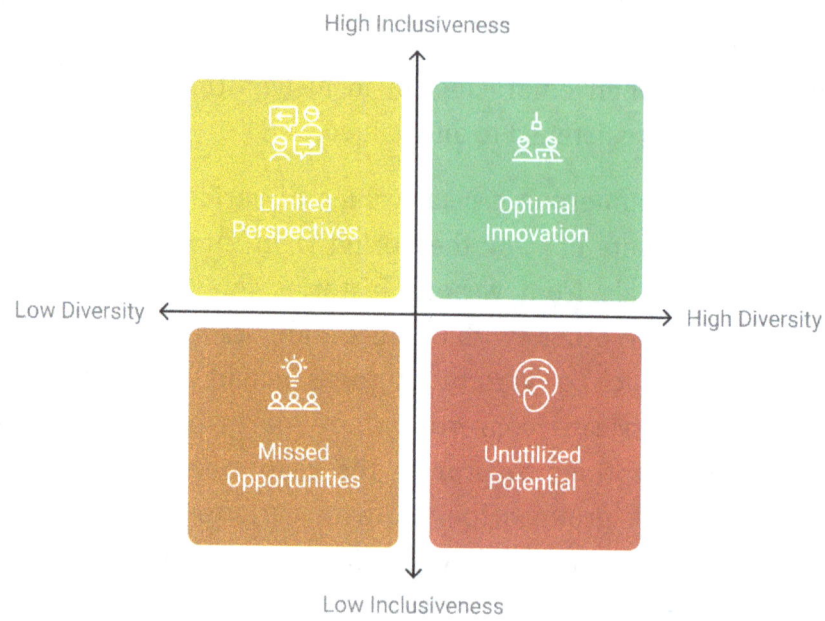

Figure 2.5 Diversity and Inclusiveness in Organizations.

Apart from this, diverse teams are more creative and innovative. Organizations with diverse teams are more likely to develop innovative products and services. This is partly because diverse teams do a much better job of recognizing market gaps and understanding different customer segments' needs. When the teams represent the diversity of the customer base, they can come up with more relevant and practical solutions. This results in higher customer satisfaction and strengthens brand loyalty and market position.

Another major business benefit of building diverse teams is that such teams contribute to an inclusive workplace culture. Indeed, a culture of diversity offers psychological safety; that is, individuals feel free to express themselves without judgment.

Such openness furthers collaboration and trust, team cohesion, and morale. Those employees who are made to feel included and valued will be more engaged and motivated, leading to better performance and reduced turnover.

But that requires intention and commitment from the top. In short, an organization intentionally seeks to recruit and retain diverse talent by making its hiring practices equitable and inclusive. This may be as basic as assessing work summaries to remove prejudiced language, blind employment techniques, and varied neighborhood involvements to bring in a broader range of candidates. Furthermore, companies require normal training in variety, equity, and addition to elevate understanding, give workers means to function, and value distinctions. Composited varied groups coming from various professions will certainly be considerably invited. This society can be advertised with organized team-building tasks, allowing connections and understanding amongst the staff members to be built.

This likewise covers normal check-ins and comment sessions to make everyone feel valued and that their suggestions are included in the decision-making procedure. By producing an atmosphere of sought-after and appreciated varied points of view, companies can completely optimize their groups' capacity. Essentially, varied team building is not around conference allocations or releasing company social duty tasks, yet it is an important critical factor that drives all-natural stamina within companies.

Without a doubt, companies can improve their imagination, technology, and analytic capacities by leveraging varied employees' one-of-a-kind toughness points of view. Producing a comprehensive work environment adds to staff member interaction plus contentment, causing far better total efficiency. Variety, therefore, becomes a crucial accelerator for browsing efficiently with the puzzle of the contemporary company setting, attaining durability and offering strength.

2.3.1 Encouraging Peer Feedback and Mentorship

Feedback and mentorship among peers are effective devices for developing workers and their groups, which results in much-needed assistance within any kind of company. When workers feel encouraged to provide constructive objections and participate in mentorship with others, companies can recognize their employees' maximum potential. Consequently, this enhances personal and professional growth and solidifies team and organizational performance.

Meanwhile, peer feedback forms are the cornerstones of continuous learning and improvement. While the traditional top-down evaluation models are imbalanced, a peer feedback system provides employees with insights from colleagues who understand the work and context. This feedback form can be invaluable since the peers are often better positioned to understand day-to-day challenges and successes in detail. The encouragement of open dialogue and frequent feedback sessions leads organizations to a position of transparency whereby employees can share their thoughts and suggestions.

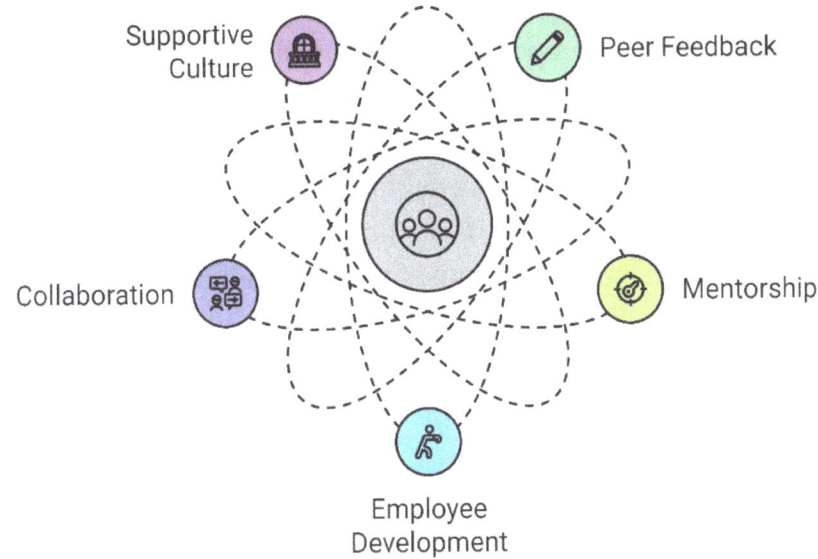

Figure 2.6 Enhancing Workplace Culture through Feedback and Mentorship.

With an articulated policy of giving and receiving feedback, along with training programs, an organization will ensure that feedback is constructive and bearable. This can also involve giving and receiving feedback workshops, focusing on specificity and positivity. Approaching this with a growth mindset, feedback is treated not as criticism but as a means of development to support this approach further. For example, a structured feedback process following the close of a project can allow employees to reflect on experiences and learn from one another within a nonjudgmental framework.

In addition to training, mentorship is critical to personal and professional development. An organization arranges less experienced workers with more experienced professionals. "The coaching connections will certainly give the mentees advice, assistance, and also understanding of just how to perform their occupations while permitting the advisors to share their know-how and develop their management abilities. This ends up being a two-way connection that benefits individuals and also provides a feeling of community. It requires accumulating a coaching society that calls for companies to develop official mentorship programs that describe purposes, assumptions, and training for coaches and mentees. Such a structure can ensure that the partnerships are effective and also contribute to the business goals.

Sources such as coaching training sessions, conversation overviews, and regular check-ins add value to such partnerships. Organizations can likewise allow casual coaching, enabling staff members to obtain support from coworkers throughout various other divisions or degrees. Furthermore, identifying and commemorating effective peer comments and coaching connections can enhance their value within the company.

Highlighting tales of impactful mentorship throughout group conferences or company-wide interactions can influence others to get involved and also participate in these methods. By showcasing the advantages of peer responses and mentoring, companies can produce a society that values continual discovery and partnership.

In other words, urging peer comments plus mentoring can produce an environment of development combined with the company's teamwork. Urging open interaction and formalized mentoring programs can aid in creating better-informed staff members, more powerful groups, and a much more encouraging workplace. This dedication to peer comments and mentoring will certainly enhance private efficiency and assist the company in its mission for success as well as survival. With firms altering constantly, it remains in these techniques that ability will certainly be established coupled with a society of continual renovation growth.

2.3.2 Creating Personal Development Plans

Creating individual growth strategies is important in establishing ability amongst people through attaining job objectives and long-lasting understanding. A well-formulated PDP provides a plan of action toward personal and professional growth. It offers the opportunity to identify strengths and weaknesses and what steps one needs to take to realize aspirations. Thus, individuals can take responsibility for their development, be better motivated, and focus their energies on satisfying personal ambitions and the organization's objectives.

Writing a personal development plan requires first carrying out some personal assessment. This requires reflecting on his skills, values, interests, and goals. SWOT analysis tools can be handy; they help an individual to get a full understanding of his standing at the moment. One can use the strengths in the development efforts, while weaknesses, on the other hand, give clear-cut direction for improvement. Besides, analysis of opportunities and threats allows one to estimate those external factors that may influence on growth.

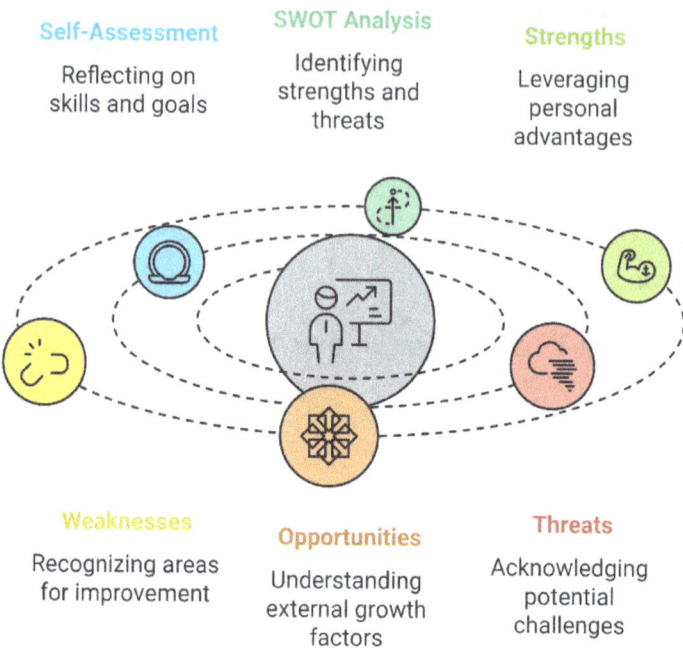

Figure 2.7 Achieving Personal Growth through PDPs.

Following self-assessment, SMART-specific, measurable, achievable, relevant, and time-bound goals should be set. The goals should reflect both the short-run and long-run aspirations, clearly focusing on the development process. For example, the short-term goal could be to finish a specific training course in three months, whereas the long-term goal could be to reach a managerial position in five years. Precise articulation of goals creates direction and a sense of purpose in the development journey.

After setting goals, a person has to specify the actions needed to realize them: on-the-job training or complementary relevant programs, searching out a mentor, and networking. Breaking large goals into small tasks will not make them overwhelming and will give a sense of direction. Example: The aim was to enhance public speaking, meaning the actions were enrolling in a workshop on Public Speaking, practicing in front of peers, and then seeking feedback regarding performance.

Also, creating a timeline for achieving each goal and action step is vital. The timeline will keep the individual accountable and allow them to assess progress made regularly. Setting deadlines for specific times can encourage commitment and create a sense of urgency, which can be motivating. Checking progress against the timeline on regular occasions will afford the chance to adjust the plan if necessary so that the individual stays on track regarding moving toward their goals.

In addition, support and feedback comprise other key components of the best personal development plans. Frankly, people must seek support and useful responses from supervisors, peers, or advisors concerning their development. Discussing development goals leads to interesting insights and resources that an individual might not have considered. Equally, sharing one's PDP with a trusted colleague will enhance accountability and mutual support.

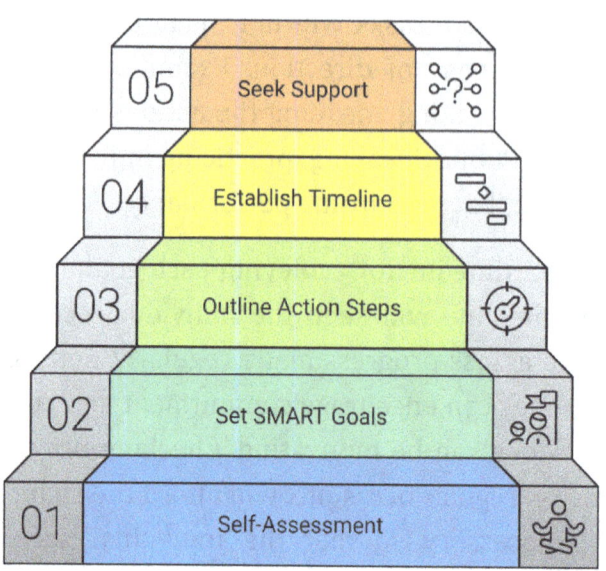

Figure 2.8 Achieving Personal Development Goals.

Finally, individual growth preparation is a solid method people use to achieve better individual and expert objectives. People can take charge of their advancement by self-assessing themselves with SMART objectives, explaining activity actions that can be taken, and developing timelines. Additionally, looking for comments and assistance creates the society for constant enhancement in the PDP. As they purchase themselves, they expand their proficiencies and capacities and add a lot more to the total success of the company to which they belong. Success in today's vibrant office relies on how well one accepts the procedure of individual advancement preparation.

2.4 Aligning Strengths with Team Goals

Aligning individual strengths with team goals is a strategic approach to enhancing team performance and collaboration for collective success. When team members support shared objectives by utilizing their unique abilities, a synergistic effect will maximize productivity and innovation. Such alignment boosts morale and develops a sense of purpose and belonging for team members through a higher drive toward involvement and commitment.

First, the team's goals must be clearly defined, aligning strengths with them. This would involve understanding the team's objectives, whether completing a project, launching a product, or improving processes. This clarity gives members an overview of where their effort fits into the overall contribution. Regular team meetings to discuss goals and progress can maintain focus and ensure open communication.

After the team objectives are defined, then the capacity of each single participant can be determined. It can then be done with the help of self-concept, peer review, or some strengths-finder instruments, such as Gallup StrengthsFinder. By then, each member's different skills, talents, and experiences are accounted for. Hence, a team can identify how to exploit the attributes to achieve stated objectives. For example, a person skilled at data analysis would be extremely important. In contrast, a colleague with excellent verbal and written communication should logically fit with customers.

Figure 2.9 Aligning Individual Strengths with Team Goals.

Effective communication should allow discussions and let the members express their strengths and how they contribute to or would like to contribute to the team's goals. This is how people own their jobs, which is the beginning of a good collaborative culture. When team members understand each other's strengths, they can start delegating better tasks, ensuring that every person works on areas where he or she can excel. This avoids frustration and maximizes efficiency.

Secondly, aligning strengths with team goals requires creating an enabling environment that advances the spirit of continuous development. Teams should regularly review their objectives and assess whether the current allocation of tasks aligns with individual strengths. This continuous analysis allows changes to be made to keep staff members focused and utilize their abilities efficiently. Offering possibilities for specialist advancement, such as training or mentoring, further improves employees' capabilities and straightens them with developing group requirements.

Acknowledging and commemorating success is necessary in maintaining the balance between toughness and objectives. Recognizing where staff members stand out enhances the significance of using their stamina. Whether it's a huge or tiny turning point, commemorating develops a favorable ambiance and motivates staff members to add their finest. The acknowledgment will also enhance the link between specific payments combined with group success, improving spirits and dedication.

This positioning will certainly entail matching individual stamina with the group's objectives and goals to enhance efficiency and create a functioning society. As necessary, groups ought to create an atmosphere where everybody feels valued and also complimentary to contribute by establishing clear objectives, examining toughness, promoting open interaction, and urging continual growth. Such placement improves efficiency and ingenuity and creates an effective feeling of group neighborhood. As companies navigate the intricacies of today's workplace, leveraging each employee's unique stamina is crucial to effectively and sustainably achieve business objectives.

2.4.1 Facilitating Team-Building Activities

Team-building workouts also assist in advertising participation, interaction, and unity in the working atmosphere. Such campaigns boost social partnerships, enabling reliance on a sensation of coming from established within a group. Efficient team-building workouts raise efficiency, analytic abilities, and a favorable job society. Specifying the purposes promotes team-building tasks.

Understanding what the group intends to accomplish in interaction, count on, or partnership assists in handpicking ideal tasks. For example, activities that involve open dialogue and active listening would be perfect for improving communication. In contrast, if the goal is to achieve trust, it would be better when it involves vulnerability and relying on each other.

Once objectives have been identified, appropriate activity selection becomes key. There can be a range of activities that different goals and teams may hold interest in. A variety of activities for team building in this area include icebreakers, like two truths and a lie or team trivia, that would help tear down barriers to get people interacting; longer activities might include problem-solving challenges or an outdoor adventure task, promoting teamwork and collaboration within a dynamic environment. Selecting activities that align with the team's interests and comfort levels increases participation and engagement.

Table 2.2 The key components and strategies for facilitating practical team-building activities.

Component	Description	Strategies/Examples
Objective Definition	Clearly define the goals of the team-building activities to align with team needs.	• Improve communication • Build trust • Enhance collaboration

Activity Selection	Choose activities that align with the defined objectives and team dynamics.	• Icebreakers (e.g., Two Truths and a Lie) • Problem-solving challenges • Outdoor adventures
Facilitator Role	Ensure the facilitator creates an inclusive environment and guides the activities effectively.	• Set clear expectations • Encourage participation • Remain neutral
Open Communication	Adopt an environment where team members feel comfortable sharing their thoughts and feelings.	• Prompt discussions during activities • Use reflective questions post-activity
Debrief and Reflection	Lead discussions after activities to reinforce learning and solidify relationships.	• Ask participants to share insights • Discuss how to apply lessons learned
Integration into Routine	Make team-building efforts a regular part of team routines to maintain engagement.	• Incorporate regular check-ins • Schedule collaborative projects
Feedback Loop	Gather participant feedback to evaluate the activities' effectiveness and improve future efforts.	• Conduct surveys or informal discussions • Adjust activities based on feedback

These team-building activities will require facilitators who can play an important role in their success. They should offer an environment that is not intimidating to any team member but comfortable enough for them to participate in. That includes setting clear expectations for behaviors and participation and inviting everyone to contribute while understanding and respecting different personalities and comfort zones. Effective facilitators maintain neutrality and provide guided discussions or activities without offering opinions so the team explores and learns from experiences.

Open communication is necessary for activities. This allows deeper relationships and better comprehension of one another's communication. The facilitators may open the discussion with reflective questions concerning the experiences, like challenges faced and how the members felt during the activities. Such reflections solidify learning and allow individuals to understand their team roles better.

It would also be important to have some debriefing and evaluation after the team has finished all the activities. The leaders of the discussions need to facilitate talks that enable team members to reflect on what they learned, how they may apply these insights in their work, and, importantly, the effects these may have on their relationships. This feedback loop reinforces lessons learned and ensures that the benefit of these activities extends beyond the event itself.

Secondly, team building could be made even more effective by incorporating it into the daily routine of the teams. Rather than taking teamwork-building as a single event, companies must use regular check-ins, projects that require collaboration, and other steady processes to keep the ball rolling. This frequent interaction will solidify relationships and open communications, finally leading to team cohesiveness.

Essentially, team building helps to a great extent in building strong and effective teams. By specifying clear goals, picking suitable tasks, plus producing a comprehensive atmosphere, assistants can improve partnership, count on, plus interaction among staff members. The understanding acquired from these tasks will certainly lead to increased efficiency and a favorable office society. As companies undergo the intricacies of a team effort, purchasing initiatives in the direction of a group structure will certainly be a core component in attaining long-lasting success and durability.

2.4.2 Using Personality Assessments Effectively

Character examinations have ended up being progressively prominent devices made use of within companies. They give beneficial understandings of how people act, such as how they function and associate with others. Using suitably can boost team effort and interaction plus individual development. Nevertheless, utilizing individuality examinations is a massive factor to consider, as well as awareness for a company that prefers an optimal advantage.

The trick to using character analysis effectively hinges on picking an ideal tool. Many different assessments are available, including the MBTI, the DiSC assessment, and the Big Five Personality Traits model. Each one provides different insight and focuses on various aspects of personality. Organizations should choose assessments that best suit their needs and may wish to consider certain aspects, including team-building exercises, leadership development, and employee engagement. Understanding the organization's strengths and limitations helps ensure that the right tool fits the organization's needs.

Figure 2.10 Effective Use of Personality Assessments.

Once the tool has been chosen, one has to consider how best to establish conditions that will make participants feel comfortable. This is evident in explaining to them the purpose of the assessment and how the results will be applied. If individuals know that the intention is to affect personal and team development and not to label or pigeonhole them, they are more likely to respond openly to the process. Giving background information about the tool can ease tension and ensure honest participation.

After the administration is complete, organizations must recognize the value of interpretation and discussion. The goal is to organize group discussions in which team members can present findings so that empathy can occur. For example, if the MBTI is used, the team members can delve into their different personality types and share what it is like to interface with others regarding communication, decision-making, and conflict resolution. Such interaction builds self-awareness and further develops an appreciation for multiple perspectives.

Personality assessments form part of ongoing development, ensuring long-term value. They can lead to training programs, mentorship arrangements, and team-building activities. For instance, if an assessment shows that some team members prefer team environments. In contrast, others perform better if left alone, and leaders can use such knowledge to place employees in various projects strategically and better roles to maximize team dynamics and performance.

The second thing to realize is that personality assessment is a guidance tool, not a capability yardstick. For instance, organizations should avoid making decisions based on assessment results, such as hiring or promotion decisions. It is meant to be part of a wide evaluation process covering all performance metrics, skills assessments, and interviews. This would mean looking at an individual from a holistic point of view in terms of meeting the requirements of equity and inclusion.

Finally, the organizations must periodically reassess how well they deploy personality assessments. Soliciting feedback from those participating will give some indication of their perceived value and, therefore, of just how much personality tests successfully serve the stated purposes of those who apply them. Continuous improvement of the use of personality assessments is indispensable for making them even more relevant and effective.

2.5 Promoting Lifelong Learning and Growth

This would also help develop a continuous improvement and adaptability culture by promoting lifelong learning and growth. In today's fast-evolving work environment, learning new skills for reinventing oneself is critical. Staff members might encourage such a way of thinking by gaining workers access to numerous discovering possibilities: workshops, online training courses, mentoring programs, and seminars. Financial investment in staff members' advancement reinforces specific proficiencies and makes the companies efficient in reacting to sector changes and arising fads. This dedication towards knowing, for that reason, infuses a feeling of possession and empowerment within staff members, encouraging them to attain their specialist objectives for better payments to the company. It also includes motivating interest, introducing past officials to all company levels, and discovering possibilities to advertise a development society.

Companies ought to enable workers to feel secure to experiment, ask concerns, and share understanding without fear of failing. This might be done with regular comment sessions, jobs performed in cooperation, and online forums where concepts are traded. Acknowledging and commemorating finding success, regardless of how big or little, reinforces the worth of development within the company. By dedicating themselves to long-lasting discovery, companies continue to hone their affordable benefit while constructing a devoted and involved, positive, durable labor force to prosper in any future obstacle.

2.5.1 Celebrating Individual Contributions

Recognition of specific payments within the company will certainly produce a favorable job society, enhance spirits, and enhance total efficiency. The distinctiveness of ability and initiatives spent by people is recognized via acknowledgment, which validates one's effort and also assists in reinforcing a feeling of coming from and relevance in the group. Those staff members who are extra valuable for their payments often tend to be much more energetic, reveal inspiration, and be dedicated to their duties for much better efficiency and advancement. Official acknowledgment programs may be one of the most practical ways of acknowledging private payments.

They can be efficiency honors, employee-of-the-month programs, or unique states at group conferences. This enables an official to emphasize success and reveal business acknowledgment for team initiatives. Public acknowledgment motivates others to pursue quality and constructs a society where high efficiency is commended and copied. These acknowledgment initiatives must be comprehensive plus fair, ensuring that all staff members can be recognized for their distinct payments regardless of their function or period.

Besides official acknowledgment, specific payments can be commemorated with much less formal gestures. Straightforward gestures like a transcribed thank-you note from the supervisor, yell-outs in business e-newsletters, or acknowledgment at group gatherings can improve worker spirits. These individual touches are a foolproof means to reveal recognition and make them feel valued daily. The leaders ought to urge a society of peer acknowledgment in which the employee acknowledges various other participants' initiatives, bringing about additional sociability and partnership in the team.

Concerning private payments for parties, it is about acknowledging successes and picking up from failures and attempts. Urging a development frame of mind suggests valuing durability with initiative and with results. Organizations can ensure a protected atmosphere where one feels free to share experiences consisting of troubles towered above as chances for development. By commemorating progression and finding out trips, companies enhance the fact that each effective payment plays an essential component in the general effective payments of the group.

2.6 Case Study: Recognizing Strengths and Talents

Recognizing strengths and talents is extremely important to individuals and organizations that want to maximize their full potential and performance. One widely used tool for this purpose is the Gallup StrengthsFinder assessment, which companies like Accenture have used to tap their employees' strengths and better leverage them. Focusing on what people naturally do best allows an organization to create a culture of appreciation and engagement that will eventually affect productivity and job satisfaction.

This StrengthsFinder test helps any individual to identify a person's special talents. Whichever responses are provided to numerous questions denote one's innate natural talents and prioritize those talents into 34 possible talent themes. Those include but are not limited to, strategic thinking and relationship building, execution, and influencing. Knowing their strongest strengths will help employees recognize how they might contribute even more to the benefit of teams and the organization. Clarity enhances self-awareness, giving ownership in development and career choice.

The application of StrengthsFinder allows organizations to reap several benefits. For example, Accenture uses it to strengthen its teams by matching people against particular team roles. Employees given opportunities that better match their innate talents feel more motivated. There is better alignment where the work environment is in harmony with itself, team members complement each other in their skills, and collaboration is good. Organizations can tap into more diversified talent to drive innovation, hence attaining or achieving strategic initiatives.

Recognizing and celebrating strengths engender a positive organizational culture. Employees who feel valued for their contribution are most likely committed to their work and the organization's mission. Regular discussions of strengths encourage open communications and, therefore, collaboration as team members learn to appreciate the unique qualities each brings to the table. This recognition culture provides job satisfaction, leading to less turnover. Employees are much more likely to stay with an organization when it recognizes their strengths and invests in their future.

Identifying strengths through various testing methods, such as StrengthsFinder, strengthens work and emotional engagement in team dynamics. It also informs professional development.

Localized training can be developed to strengthen employees' identified strengths further, offering the greatest possibility for individual development. By focusing personal growth on business objectives, success for both employee and employer alike becomes a win-win environment.

2.7 Key Point Donald Trump's potential re-election in 2024

> **Economic Messaging:** Trump can emphasize his previous administration's economic accomplishments.

In this politically charged environment, effective economic messaging will help him reconnect with those stung by the economy's ebbs and flows. Former President Donald Trump can use his administration's prior economic successes to provide reassurance on the pressing concerns of inflation and job stability. By touting the more digestible benefits of tax cuts and deregulation during his presidency, he reminds voters of the economic growth behind his presidency. He builds a narrative that positions him as a champion of fiscal responsibility and a job creator.

> **Appeal to Emotions**
> Utilize emotional appeals to connect with voters on a personal level.
>
> **Focus on Key Issues**

> Identify and prioritize the issues that matter most to your base.

Perhaps the hallmark of Trump's administration was the unparalleled tax cuts that catalyzed economic growth, especially through the 2017 Tax Cuts and Jobs Act. This reduced corporate tax rates and provided tax relief for middle-class families. According to proponents, this engendered more consumer spending and investment. By highlighting these accomplishments, Trump reassures voters that his policies have historically been good for business, created jobs, and provided wage growth. This message could resonate much more with the electorate strangled by a rise in the cost of living and economic uncertainty: It brings hope based on past performance.

But to appeal to the spending-hurt, inflation-hit electorate, Trump must also talk about that. Inflation concerns practically every American because it cuts their purchasing power and raises day-to-day costs. With a concrete vision for price stability and job creation, he'll prove that he understands real people's economic anxieties. This might mean advocating policies that support energy independence, reduce supply chain bottlenecks, and adopt domestic manufacturing, which can ease inflationary pressures.

Second, Trump can discuss the need for deregulation in general, something he has at times described as an economic elixir. He might enlist the backing of small business owners and large corporations by attempting to lighten the regulatory yoke on businesses, enabling them to invest more heavily and expand operations. This is in keeping with the view that a freer regulatory environment nurtures innovation and brings jobs. By emphasizing this part of his economic platform, Trump may be framed as a candidate who cares for business and the worker.

He can also continue to enlist personal anecdotes and testimonials about how his administration's policies helped certain individuals and businesses. Real-life examples of job creation, business growth, and a rise in the standard of living will make his economic messaging more relatable and convincing. Secondly, a discussion of current administration policy and its impacts on the economy will draw a sharp contrast to reinforce his arguments for the return of his economic strategies.

Reference

1. Bible Gateway. (n.d.). What does the Bible say about pride? Retrieved from https://www.lwf.org/articles/the-sin-of-pride-in-the-bible#:~:text=Pride%20Brings%20Dishonor&text=%E2%80%9CWhen%20pride%20comes%2C%20then%20comes,(Proverbs%2029%3A23)

2. Harris, J. (2020). Pride theme in Pride and Prejudice. In Literary Analysis of Pride and Prejudice (pp. 45-60). New York, NY: Literary Press.

3. Gallup. (2021). StrengthsFinder assessment leadership profile essay. Retrieved from https://www.gallup.com/cliftonstrengths/en/strengthsfinder.aspx

4. Goleman, D. (2011). The brain and emotional intelligence: New insights. Retrieved from https://www.danielgoleman.info/books/the-brain-and-emotional-intelligence/

5. Kahn, W. A. (1990). Psychological conditions of personal engagement and disengagement at work. Academy of Management Journal, 33(4), 692-724.

6. Dweck, C. S. (2006). Mindset: The new psychology of success. New York, NY: Ballantine Books.

7. Seligman, M. E. P. (2011). Flourish: A visionary new understanding of happiness and well-being. New York, NY: Free Press.

8. Clifton, D. O., & Anderson, E. (2002). Strengths-based leadership: Great leaders, teams, and why people follow. New York, NY: Gallup Press.

9. Kahn, W. A., & Byosiere, P. (1992). Stress in organizations. In M. D. Dunnette & L. M. Hough (Eds.), Handbook of industrial and organizational psychology (Vol. 3, pp. 571-649). Palo Alto, CA: Consulting Psychologists Press.

10. Bakker, A. B., & Demerouti, E. (2008). Towards a model of work engagement. Career Development International, 13(3), 209-223.

11. Neff, K. D. (2011). Self-compassion: The proven power of being kind to yourself. New York, NY: William Morrow.

12. Luthans, F., & Youssef, C. M. (2007). Emerging positive organizational behavior. Journal of Management, 33(3), 321-349.

13. Wrzesniewski, A., & Dutton, J. E. (2001). Crafting a job: Revisioning employees as active crafters of their work. Academy of Management Review, 26(2), 179-201.

CHAPTER 3

Roar with Purpose: Setting Clear Goals and Vision

Introduction

Personal and professional development involves clearly defined goals and a well-oriented vision. This chapter deals with how intentional goal-setting and clarity of vision keep the fire in the belly of aspirations. It explores how individuals and organizations can unleash their potential by aligning their actions in a purposeful direction [1,2].

The whole chapter accentuates that a well-defined vision is like a compass guiding us through life and at work. It directs individual activities, enabling them to take tangible steps toward accomplishing his or her goals [3]. If vision is not well-defined, there is a good chance of getting lost, with movement but no sense of fulfillment. On the contrary, setting SMART (specific, measurable, attainable, relevant, and time-bound) goals means creating a structured pathway to success by breaking down the daunting journey into manageable steps.

This chapter shall examine the psychological and emotional benefits of setting goals. Scientists show that people with clear goals have more motivation and satisfaction [4-6]. Determining what I want to achieve helps clarify our priorities and gives us a sense of ownership and responsibility [7]. As I encounter problems and prospects, a clear vision and strategic plan allow us to make decisions more effectively, which would not conflict with the most important objectives [8, 9].

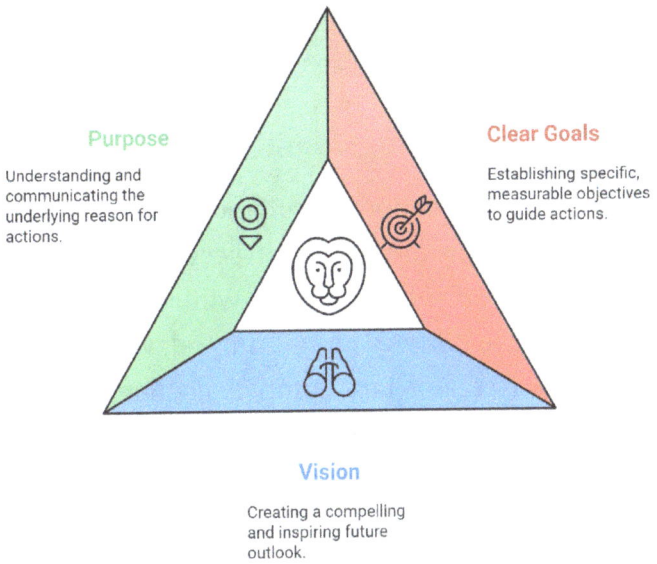

Figure 3.1 The importance of setting clear goals and having a well-defined vision

Besides personal anecdotes, "Roar with Purpose" uses examples from highly successful leaders and organizations that engagingly model goal-setting frameworks. These cases prove that a clear vision can mobilize a team toward one direction of unity, leading them to innovation [10]. The readers will understand more about the practical uses of goal-setting techniques through the narration [11].

As I journey through this chapter, let yourself ponder your vision and goals: Are they defined? Do they align with your core values and desires? By the end of the chapter, you will have the tools to define your vision and set meaningful goals, as well as the inspiration to roar with purpose toward your dreams. Let us begin this journey together to bring all of our aspirations into real life through the power of clarity and intention.

3.1 Defining a Compelling Team Vision

A compelling team vision adopts collaboration, motivation, and shared purpose within any group. It serves as a guiding star, showing the path to a collective goal while aligning individual aspirations with the team's intent. In today's dynamic work environment, where teams face complex challenges and shifting priorities, a well-defined vision can greatly improve focus and cohesion, making it easier for members to chart their work with clarity and intent.

It is impossible to stress the importance of a clear vision. This indeed clarifies major objectives and values; hence, it reduces ambiguity in day-to-day details. When team members understand the overarching goals driving their work, they will have priorities and can make informed decisions without going astray from the team's direction. Such shared understanding limits confusion and ensures that every effort is put meaningfully to use for the good of the entire team.

There are several key elements to writing a powerful team vision. The vision should be short and understandable in a sentence without jargon or complicated language. It should be impassioned, create excitement about the team's possibilities, and be relevant to the organization's goals. The other important aspect is inclusion: once team members are included in creating the vision, ownership, and commitment will fall into place because people are taken on board to decide what will happen with their team.

Defining the vision for a team requires the involvement of its members. This, therefore, needs deliberations aimed at ascertaining the core values and aspirations of the team. The inputs from these deliberations are then used to formulate an initial inspiring vision statement draft. For perfection to resound and be accepted by all, this draft requires sharing with the members for input. Once defined, the vision needs consistent communication and reviewing for relevance, while progress should also be celebrated. A well-articulated vision will inspire, engage, and unleash the mindsets of employees and teams toward a common objective.

3.2 Establishing SMART Goals

Setting practical goals is an essential ingredient in personal and professional success. The SMART framework is a structured goal-setting approach that offers much more clarity and focus. SMART goals are set so individuals and teams can create actionable plans to drive progress and accountability.

The first ingredient of SMART objectives is specificity. There must be a clear identification of the goal of what needs to be achieved. This includes answering who, what, where, when, and why. Then, the specific aim would be, for example, "I want to improve my sales," which would turn into "I want to improve my sales by 20% through targeting new clients in the technology industry." Specificity clears up what has to be done and makes defining the steps toward achieving it much more manageable.

Second, goals should be measurable to enable tracking of progress toward achievement and to know when the goal is reached. That is the establishment of criteria to permit measurement. Following the previous example of sales, a measurable goal would include the target quantifiable of increasing sales by 20%. In other words, using revenue figures or how many new clients one can get on board enables individuals and teams to monitor their progress and adjust toward achievement. This aspect of goal setting ensures motivation because one can always celebrate milestones.

The third ingredient is achievability, which emphasizes setting realistic goals. While one needs to challenge themselves, the goals must be achievable with resources, skills, and time available. An attainable goal identifies the potential obstacles and makes the target realistic. For instance, when a salesman is used to a traditional growth of 10% in sales year over year, increasing the rate to 20% may be overambitious unless substantially supported with strategy and resources. Setting achievable goals ensures motivation is maintained throughout, and discouragement is not an issue.

Relevance ensures that the goals align with broader objectives and personal values. Goals should matter to the individual or organization and fit within the larger context of what is being pursued. A relevant goal for a salesperson might be to increase sales in a specific sector because it aligns with the company's strategic direction or personal career aspirations. This alignment enhances commitment and focus, allowing individuals to see how their efforts contribute to larger objectives.

Figure 3.2 The Power of SMART Goals.

Finally, a goal must be time-bound, meaning there is a specific deadline for completion. This creates a sense of urgency and enables prioritization. The time-bound goal identifies when the results will be accomplished, for example, "I want to finish my sales training by the end of Q2." With a timeline, people can maintain momentum and strive, with consistency, toward meeting the goal.

Setting SMART goals is one of the most powerful systems for increasing personal and professional effectiveness. When objectives are specific, measurable, achievable, relevant, and time-bound, individuals and teams build clear, straightforward plans of action through which real progress is made. This format lays out clear objectives that motivate and engage more, adopting accountability and achievement. Grasp the SMART format and watch aspirations become reality, ushering success into any undertaking.

3.2.1 Aligning Individual and Team Objectives

Aligning individual and team objectives adopts a cohesive and productive work environment. When personal goals align with team objectives, it creates a unified direction that enhances collaboration, boosts morale, and drives overall success. This alignment clarifies expectations and empowers individuals to contribute meaningfully to the team's mission.

Alignment of individual and team objectives ensures that everybody works toward one goal. When team members understand how their work contributes to larger objectives, they are more likely to relate to a sense of mission. This will cultivate ownership and accountability, motivating them to commit fully to their role. Secondly, when these objectives are aligned, there will be little conflict in communication and decision-making because many misunderstandings arise when personal goals go against the team's priorities.

Clear communication channels are the backbone of achieving this alignment. Regular team meetings and one-on-one check-ins allow discussion of objectives, progress, and challenges. In these interactions, leaders should, with much repetition, remind the team of their vision and explain how an individual's goals fit into the whole. Collaboration tools and platforms make transparency possible by enabling team members to share objectives and track collective progress.

Another effective alignment strategy is facilitating goal-setting workshops. In such sessions, employees can team up to establish group purposes while indicating specific objectives that sustain those goals. This requires payment and develops ownership, considering that each participant is enabled to have a say in the group's instructions. Because specific objectives and group purposes are flagged off, it would be simpler to determine factors of harmony plus locations where assistance may be needed.

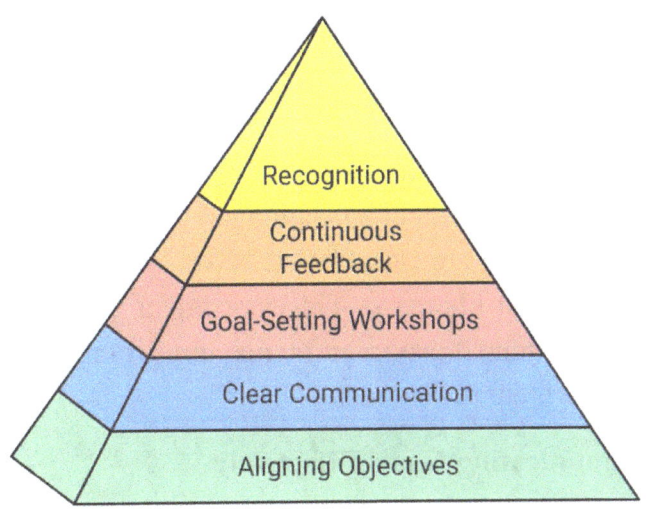

Figure 3.3 Aligning Objectives for Team Success.

Constant comments are an essential element of positioning that must be received in time. Jobs and situations transform, which implies that staff members are required to revisit their objectives consistently and make required modifications. Incorporating a response loophole allows real-time modifications and opens a discussion about areas of trouble and accomplishment. This maintains the specific course and strengthens flexibility within the group.

This can be even more inspired by identifying and commemorating specific payments towards the group's goals. Commemorating individual successes will certainly enhance the connection of private initiatives to the group's objectives, developing a favorable comments cycle that assists in great positioning. Groups can take on an acknowledgment society that assists in strengthening cumulative dedication to shared goals. The placement of private plus group goals is necessary for teamwork. It produces a feeling of unity and also drives people to interact towards typical objectives.

By developing clear interactions, accepting objective setup, motivating comments, and identifying payments, groups are well on their way to making certain that private desires coexist and enhance the usual objective. This placement enables an extra effective and involved group ambience important in promoting individual and business success.

3.2.2 Communicating Goals Effectively

Reliable, objective interaction is important to team effort and business success. It ensures everyone follows the exact same instructions and constructs common functions and responsibilities. The better the expression of objectives, the more likely employees will recognize their duties, be inspired, and work cohesively toward usual purposes.

Quality is vital when connecting objectives.

A well-defined objective ought to be uncomplicated as well as without obscurity. This includes making use of basic language as well as preventing lingo that might perplex staff members. Rather than stating, as an example, "We ought to enhance our operations", a more concrete and distinct objective would certainly be, "We are most likely to reduce task conclusion time by 20%, many thanks to presenting a brand-new task monitoring device. ". Such specificity helps team members understand what is expected from them and how they should contribute to such an achievement.

Communication through multiple channels ensures that the goals are well relayed. While the need for team meetings to discuss the goals is important, other supplementary modes of communication, such as e-mail, project management software, and visual means, help drive the message home. For example, presenting the goals more graphically, like in a chart or infographic form, makes such information appealing and accessible. Further, by pinning up these goals around shared physical and virtual areas, they constantly remind one of what the team is out to achieve.

The goals should be effectively communicated from the top and require active involvement from every team member. This should permit a two-way conversation wherein one can question and clarify or give inputs. This interaction will bring more comprehension, inspiration for ownership, and commitment to the goals. Leaders should permit an atmosphere wherein team members feel comfortable coming forward with their views and concerns and feel valued and included in this process.

Goals can't be static entities; they must be dialogical and reviewed. Revisiting goals in team meetings or check-ins helps keep them fresh and allows for adjustment when needed. This keeps accountability and provides various opportunities to celebrate progress and milestone achievements. When team members see their contributions impact, it reinforces motivation and commitment to shared objectives.

Figure 3.4 Effective Goal Communication.

Good goal communication cultivates alignment, motivation, and teamwork. The information provided should be clear through different channels, two-way communication should be encouraged, and goals should be revisited regularly. In such an environment, everybody is aligned and able to contribute to organizational success. Effective communication changes goals from simple desires into workable plans and charges the team toward objective accomplishment with purpose and energy.

3.3 Tracking Progress and Accountability

Any form of progress tracking and accountability is core to goal achievement in personal development and the team context. These practices ensure that individuals and groups stay in sync with their objectives and create a culture of responsibility and continuous improvement. Organizations can drive success through enhanced performance by implementing effective tracking and accountability measures.

Progress tracking is important to understand how far the individuals or the teams have come to realize their goals. It identifies what has been accomplished, what is outstanding, and where changes are needed. One can institute the KPIs so that performance can be measured. Suppose a team wants to improve customer satisfaction; it would measure metrics such as response time or customer feedback scores, which show trends and guide strategy adjustments. Ongoing review of these metrics keeps the team focused while offering quick identification of potential obstacles, thus enabling proactive solutions.

There are numerous devices and methods of effective tracking. Digital task administration software programs can give real-time information on success towards the objective, and spreadsheet control panels can do the same. Frequently, these energies provide a means of presenting the information visually to assist in recognizing patterns and patterns of information. Besides, regular check-ins can occur with official conferences or casual updates on progression, difficulties, and additional strategies. This ongoing dialogue ensures everyone remains accountable for their contributions and can pivot as needed.

Accountability helps individuals be responsible for their goals and commitments. When team members believe their contribution matters to the group's success, they are guaranteed to continue being engaged and involved. A clear definition of roles and responsibilities would be foundational steps toward accountability. Each teammate must know what is expected from them and how their work relates to the team's objectives. Accountability can be further pressed through regular feedback sessions, which provide opportunities not only for recognition but also for constructive discussions on areas of improvement.

An accountability culture can be developed when the atmosphere is conducive to open communication and respect for each other's views. It would be a leadership task to make the team members express their challenges and successes without being judged. This openness will build trust and strengthen collaboration as team members can support and share insights. Recognizing progress through team meetings, shout-outs, or rewards is another way to achieve accountability that would drive individuals to excel.

Progress tracking and accountability are vital in meeting your goals and developing a productive team environment. Effective tracking mechanisms, appropriate tool usage, and placing accountability within the culture will, in turn, drive a framework toward performance and success. Ultimately, it enhances the contribution of individuals and their teams toward developing ownership and commitment to achieve set objectives. In this way, monitoring and accountability are processes and a part of a good organizational culture.

3.3.1 Creating a Roadmap for Success

Creating a roadmap to success means adopting a strategic pathway that allows the setting of goals and concrete steps and allows one to follow the route for realizing one's desires. A well-structured roadmap would inspire clarity of vision and serve as a motivational tool that keeps teams moving toward their shared vision. With specific steps taken for building a full-scale roadmap, teams will increase their chances of success and alignment.

Crystallizing clear, specific objectives is the first step in developing a roadmap toward success. Objectives should align with the organization's vision and consider short-term and long-term perspectives. All stakeholders should be actively involved in setting clear objectives that reflect shared aspirations and priorities. By specifying what success will look like, the teams develop a common understanding to use as the basis for the roadmap.

Once objectives have been set, the next step will involve breaking them into actionable steps. All related tasks, milestones, and resources will be required for each particular goal. Then, every action should be clearly defined, and responsibility allocated to each team member. This much detail will clarify the expectations and create accountability within the team. Examples could be a new product launch, where specific steps would include market research, marketing strategy construction, and determining the launch date.

Creating a good roadmap will involve realistic timelines and milestones that indicate progress. Setting deadlines for every task and highlighting key milestones will keep the team motivated and on track. Milestones are checkpoints where teams can celebrate their progress and reassess whether they're moving in the right direction. For example, at the end of market research, a milestone to review findings can be done to refine the strategy before proceeding to the next phase. This structured approach enhances visibility while adopting accomplishment as milestones are achieved.

Figure 3.5 Achieving Success with a Roadmap.

Creating a roadmap is not a one-off activity but requires ongoing monitoring and adaptation. Here, there is a need for regular check-ins and reviews in light of progress realized, challenges arising, and necessary adjustments. Teams are encouraged to put in place means of monitoring and reviewing the outcomes of the roadmap against the objectives set out. Being open to pivoting by changing strategy when some of the strategies are not bringing about the intended results is crucial. This flexibility enables teams to meet various changes in circumstances and concentrate on their ultimate goals.

A well-defined roadmap to success guides individuals and teams in realizing their goals. The organization needs to develop a structured approach to enhance accountability by clearly stating the goals, mapping out actionable steps, setting timelines, and continuously monitoring progress. Ultimately, a roadmap focuses on achieving success, motivation, and teamwork so that individuals may work out challenges and share successes. In this way, developing a roadmap becomes indispensable for any undertaking producing useful output.

3.3.2 Incorporating Feedback Loops

Embedding feedback loops can help with continuous improvement and better performance. Feedback loops institutionalize gathering, analyzing, and acting on feedback from team members, customers, and partners in a very formal way. By systematically embedding feedback mechanisms in workflows, an organization would get closer to change adaptation, refining its strategies, and creating superior outcomes.

Feedback loops serve important purposes in organizations, including assessing progress and identifying improvement areas. Feedback from team members and stakeholders aids the organization in receiving clues on what works well and what needs changes. This continuous interaction leads to a transparent and collaborative culture since individuals will feel motivated to share their views and participate in a team's collective success.

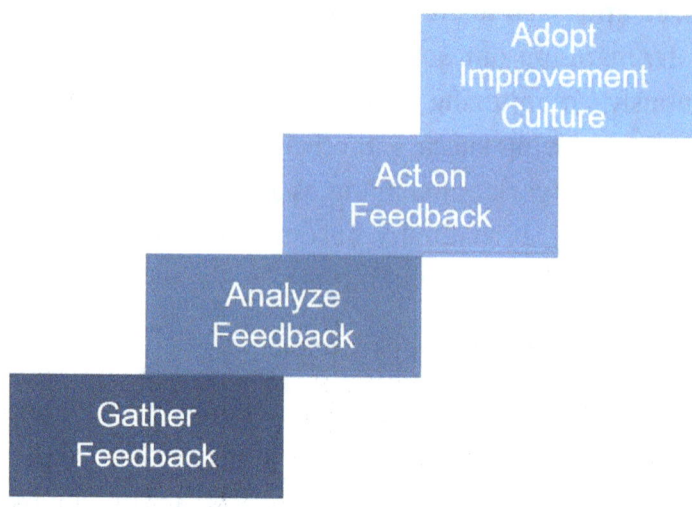

Figure 3.6 Achieving Continuous Improvement through Feedback Loops.

Further, feedback loops make one more responsible. When working in teams, if performance reviews are done regularly and feedback is considered, one will be more accountable for their contribution. Their sense of responsibility makes them work proactively, addressing problems and finding solutions. Thus, feedback loops help to create a dynamic environment where growth and innovation are valued.

This means that organizations must initiate a feedback design mechanism. These could be regular surveys, one-on-one check-ins, or team meetings centered on discussion and reflection. One needs to make certain that individuals have room to express what they feel without uneasiness over repercussions. Open-ended concerns may urge a more ingrained understanding, while specific metrics offer quantifiable information to be assessed.

Companies must also have clear systems for distilling and acting upon comments. This might include categorizing the comments into workable motifs and focusing on locations for renovation. Groups are required to assess the comments gathered, go over fads, and look for locations for enhancement. Concrete activity strategies have to arise from this, such that the comments attend to genuine circumstances coupled with leads to purposeful modification.

Integrating comments loopholes is likewise concerning embracing a society of continual improvement. Companies must motivate a mindset where responses are considered an important device rather than objections. Celebrating successes and acknowledging payments can strengthen this favorable point of view. Additionally, leaders must design responsiveness to responses, showing how to constructively approve and act upon input. When leaders request comments and reveal a dedication to improvement, it develops a fairly effective example for the remainder of the company.

Response procedures must be reviewed and improved to make response systems more efficient. To progress with groups and meet new obstacles, a company should voluntarily transform its systems to fulfill such requirements. Adaptability ensures that comments matter, along with the company finding out and expanding.

These loopholes can develop a society of constant enhancement and responsibility within companies. Setting up official devices for accumulating and assessing comments can aid the company in vibrant, welcoming input and advertising synergy. A continual enhancement society supports private and group efficiency plus placements companies towards transforming conditions for long-lasting success. Comments technicalities allow groups to pick up from the experience introduced and flourish in an affordable setting.

3.4 Adjusting Goals in Response to Change

In today's fast-moving and continuously transforming atmosphere, the capacity to transform objectives by adjusting to alter is vital for people and companies. Service, modern technology, and culture's assumptions change; therefore, flexibility assists in constantly maintaining one-upmanship over others. Identifying the requirement for adaptability and executing procedures for objective change permits groups to browse unpredictability while progressing toward purposes. Objective change emerges generally because exterior variables, such as market fads, consumer choices, and affordable characteristics, are uncertain.

For example, a business might establish enthusiastic sales targets based on present market problems to discover those problems transformed by a financial recession or technical interruption. In such situations, sticking to obsolete objectives can cause stress and disengagement among employees. Rather, this positive strategy of reassessing and straightening enables groups to preserve their concentration on achievable results that show the existing truth. In addition, interior variables such as group characteristics, source accessibility, and business concerns can likewise require objective changes.

A task that initially appeared possible might become illogical because of changes in group structure or source allotment. Identifying these modifications early and changing objectives as necessary ensures that groups can run efficiently and preserve spirits, as they are held to reasonable assumptions.

Companies ought to establish an organized testimonial plus alteration treatment to adjust objectives in action to alter effectively. This treatment starts with a routine reevaluation of the existing objectives, through which the groups can establish just how much has been covered and what needs to be serviced. These testimonials must go to pre-scheduled periods so groups can stay dexterous and preserve brand-new details.

Table 3.1 The key elements of adjusting goals in response to change.

Element	Description
Need for Flexibility	Recognize that external factors (e.g., market trends, economic conditions) and internal factors (e.g., team dynamics, resource availability) may necessitate goal adjustments.
Structured Process	Establish regular reviews of goals to assess progress and identify challenges. Involve all stakeholders in discussions to gather diverse perspectives.
Data-Driven Decisions	Utilize metrics and data during evaluations to inform adjustments. Base decisions on objective evidence rather than speculation.
Effective Communication	Communicate any changes to the team, explaining the reasons behind the adjustments to adopt understanding and alignment.

Celebration of Success	Recognize and celebrate milestones achieved, even small ones, to maintain morale and reinforce a culture of adaptability and resilience.

All stakeholders must provide their input during such assessments. This open communication allows team members to give their views and suggest changes where necessary. Using data and metrics in such discussions can provide objective evidence for decision-making, ensuring that any change effected is founded on solid grounds rather than speculations.

Once the adjustment is made, communication is crucial in bringing all team members onto the same page. Leaders must justify such adjustments in a way that shows how vital it is for its members to adapt to long-term success. Setting the context always helps team members understand the rationale behind the changes and builds a flexible, resilient culture.

Besides, successes, no matter how minute, derived through adjusted goals should be celebrated too. Recognizing progress creates a positive atmosphere and motivates the teams to stay focused amidst change. This renews morale and reminds people that adapting to changing times is a good thing, not a failure.

Setting goals, therefore, is adjusting to changed circumstances. In the present environment, flexibility, evaluation processes, and well-communicated changes are all vital components that individuals and organizations need. Only then can teams confidently venture into uncertainties. It keeps up the momentum for achieving objectives and encourages a resilient culture of innovation. In other words, the ability to change goals when circumstances change allows organizations to survive and thrive in today's competitive world and become/remain mission-centered and responsive to all stakeholders' needs.

3.4.1 Celebrating Milestones Along the Way

Any achievement regarding personal development, project implementation in teams, or organizational objectives is an important milestone in accomplishing goals. The acknowledgment of considerable achievements evokes morale and motivation among the team members. To that end, celebrations can serve a dual purpose in goal settings: an organization can turn positive culture into valuing progress and achievement through such celebration.

Milestone identification plays several roles. First, it reflects progress. Celebrations allow a team to step back, gauge how far it has come, and further the linkage between effort and accomplishment. In long-term projects, such reflection can be priceless since the route to the final objective often appears impossible. Highlighting interim successes may help a team maintain momentum and a sense of direction.

It bonds the team together whenever a milestone is celebrated; people come to celebrate their success, which may be a way of building bonding and shared purpose. This bonding experience brings people closer together on the working team as they progress toward shared goals. Such celebrations bring in memories that motivate at times of difficulty and remind everybody that things have moved and may continue moving well.

Considering the many goals pursued, these milestones can be many things. This can mean finishing key phases, certain metric achievements, or launching a product in a project setting. In personal development, milestones can be about achieving certain skill levels or finishing several training sessions. Small victories and bigger achievements should be identified and celebrated regardless of context because they are important for the overall journey.

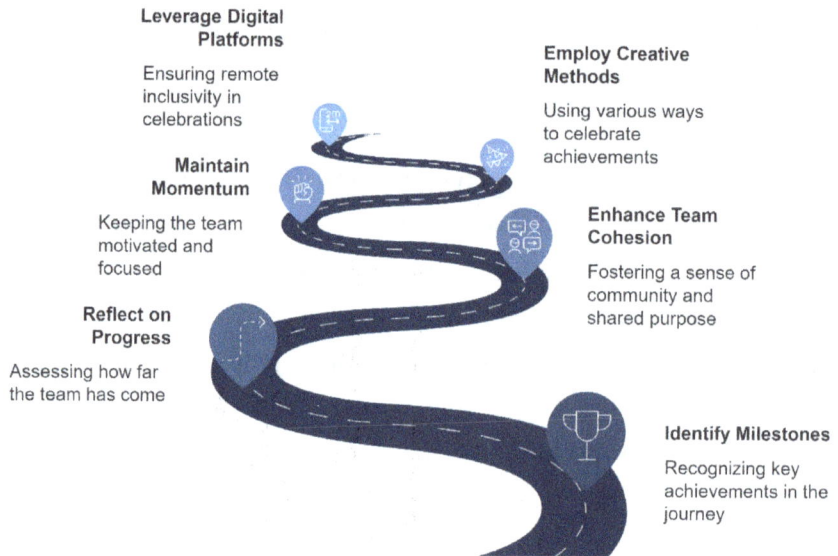

Figure 3.7 Celebrating Milestones in Achieving Goals.

Organizations might desire to commemorate turning points in several imaginative methods. Something as basic as group lunches or shout-outs at conferences might permit staff members to recognize the success of their success. Various other joyful techniques include group getaways, honors, and a cork-kick event where tales and experiences connected to the trip are shared. Gaming or themed occasions can additionally include enjoyment to make the events more unforgettable and interesting.

Digital systems can additionally be leveraged to commemorate turning points outside of in-office communications in a digital or cross-breed setup. This is feasible with online acknowledgment boards, video clip messages, or online events that ensure all employees feel consistent regardless of the area. This maintains interaction throughout the group since individuals have various choices about the event.

Furthermore, it is very important to commemorate the journey to building inspiration, enhancing team effort, and enhancing society's success. Commemorating development permits groups to go back and examine success while preserving energy towards the best objective.

Imaginative celebration approaches ensure that all staff members feel valued and that their payments are identified. Eventually, these parties will note great success and produce a favorable environment for urging a connection between development and partnership. Accepting sports events can make the path to success much more fascinating and satisfying for all involved.

3.4.2 Engaging the Team in Goal-Setting

This is a standard business routine. However, it aids individuals in collaborating better, improves inspiration amongst team members, and shows that the company is straightened. Establishing objectives with employee involvement might make them extra dedicated to attaining those purposes. This method reinforces partnerships and leverages a variety of viewpoints to achieve even more purposeful and functional outcomes.

This serves several critical purposes: involving the team in goal-setting strengthens the message that every member's input has value. Where there is an avenue for contributions of ideas or insights, individuals feel valued and heard-inclusivity that raises morale and builds a positive team culture where everyone is vested in the outcomes. Also, team engagement in setting the goals can lead to establishing more realistic and attainable objectives since members will share their expertise and experiences, giving some context to what is achievable.

Secondly, personal goal setting with the group's interaction advertises openness and placement. When objectives are established collaboratively, there is an understanding of exactly how the specific adds to the better purposes established by the company. Such alignment reduces misunderstandings and puts everyone on the same page to achieve a common purpose. When team members understand their role in the light of bigger goals, they are most likely to show motivation and focus in realizing such goals.

Leaders should implement several key strategies to engage the team in the goal-setting process effectively. First, produce a collective setting where open discussion is urged. Assisting in conceptualizing sessions or workshops lets staff members share their concepts easily. Leaders can position assisting concerns to promote conversation, such as "What do you think should be our key emphasis this quarter? "or "What difficulties do you expect, and how can we resolve them?

An additional effective strategy is to utilize evaluation or comment devices that allow team members to specify a choice or concern anonymously. This can assist in collecting more extensive understandings, particularly for those who need to be much more vocal in team setups. In integrating these comments, leaders can include the group's point of view right into the last goal-setting procedure.

Whatever the collection objectives, functions, and obligations for liability need to be clarified. To assist staff members with their jobs, involve them in specifying each participant's payment. When individuals understand what is expected of them and how their initiatives align with the group's objectives, they will go out of their way and continue to be dedicated to that duty. Additionally, normal check-ins and development updates must be included as a component of the involvement method.

These touchpoints allow staff members to review development, share obstacles, and commemorate successes. This recurring discussion enhances the joint nature of the goal-setting procedure and permits modifications as required. Interacting with a group in goal-setting is one powerful method that fuels partnership boosts inspiration, and guarantees business positioning. An extra comprehensive environment—a location where every person's voice is heard—allows leaders to create objectives that are much more appropriate and sensible.

Collective workshops, comment devices, and clear duty meanings can construct group possession and responsibility.

Eventually, it's all about driving efficiency and embracing a favorable group society where payment and team effort matter. Welcoming a joint procedure of establishing objectives permits groups to understand and construct a common feeling of objective and dedication.

3.5 Using Visual Tools for Goal Clarity

Visualization devices boost quality, conceptualization in objective setup, and administration. Converting complicated suggestions and goals right into aesthetic styles assists a company in connecting its objectives extra effectively. It places all staff member on the same web page, permitting them to recognize their payment towards those purposes. Aesthetic devices make details extra decipherable and interactive, making objective setup extra interactive and straightforward.

Among the most prominent advantages of aesthetic devices is their capacity to share information in the shortest amount of time. Because the human mind is hardwired to refine aesthetic details much quicker than messages, graphs, charts, and schematics reveal progression, emphasize partnerships, and represent timelines. For example, a Gantt chart graphically displays project timelines and dependencies so team members can see the flow at one glance. Clarity like this minimizes misunderstandings and strengthens focus, as individuals can see how their work contributes to the big picture.

Visual tools ensure participation and engagement. Teams making visual representations of their goals, like mind maps or vision boards, will be more involved. This team effort allows creativity, allows the expression of thoughts visually, and fortifies one's commitment to one's goals. This idea, prompted by visual tools, can make goal-setting an active rather than passive interactive and dynamic process, automatically triggering motivation and enthusiasm.

Other visual tools could enhance the clarity of goals: mind maps for effective brainstorming and organization of ideas about a central goal, allow teams to explore related objectives and activities expansively in an organized manner; flowcharts portraying processes and workflow, which help the team understand the steps toward their goals; and dashboards for real-time visualization of data to review progress and KPIs at one glance.

Infographics are another effective means of interestingly communicating complex information. They have the potential to summarize objectives, methods, and results using captivating infographics supported by a combination of graphics, text, and data. This helps with understanding and is a valuable reference to which team members can refer throughout the project.

Effectively implementing visual tools involves knowing the goals and determining what tools best represent them. Training sessions help team members become familiar with visual tools and techniques so everyone feels comfortable using them. Freedom of creativity and flexibility in developing visual tools are essential to enable team members to express their uniqueness.

Visual tools should continually be updated periodically to reflect a change in goal or increase in progress. This continuous commitment to maintaining clarity makes the visual tools relevant and valid. The teams must also develop a repository for the visual tools in the center that all members can easily access.

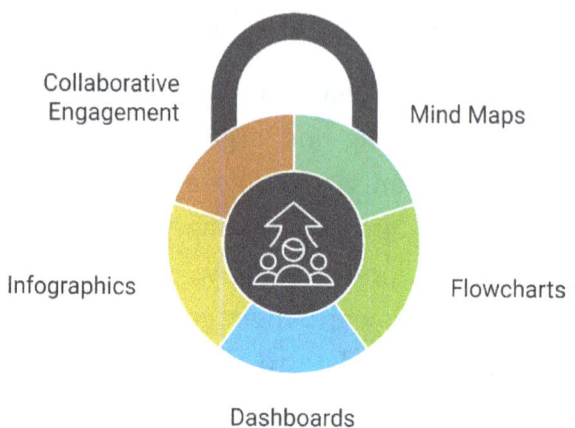

Figure 3.8 Visual Tools for Goal Clarity.

It clarifies goals and greatly enhances team clarity, engagement, and alignment. Goals should be translated into visuals; this way, the organization can communicate the objectives to the teams and ensure the latter is invested in achieving these objectives. From mind maps to dashboards, teams can use a few visual tools to suit their needs best. In other words, visual aids simplify the ostensibly convoluted process of goal setting in an active interaction, whereby limitless potential may be realized in actualizing objectives.

3.5.1 Ensuring Transparency in Progress Reporting

Progress reporting brings transparency, advancing trust, accountability, and cooperation within teams and organizations. Openly communicating progress creates consistency in an environment where the team feels informed, valued, and integrated. This creates an enabling environment where motivation can grow, and teams are empowered to identify challenges and successes together for better outcomes.

Reporting is critical not only because it builds trust among team members but it also provokes teamwork. When group members are informed of each other's progress, problems, and successes, they feel more involved with the decision-making process. A sense of belonging encourages members to contribute positively to discussions and problem-solving. The benefit of transparent reporting is that misunderstandings are reduced, and there will be less conflict because everyone has a uniform understanding of the expectations placed on each member and what each person is doing.

Transparency also ensures accountability. When progress is better shared, team members will likely own their responsibilities. Knowing their contributions are visible, individuals are encouraged to commit further to their respective tasks and ensure follow-through on promises. Accountability improves each member's performance and reinforces the effectiveness of the whole.

Organizations should ensure transparency in reporting through several means. First, regular reporting-probably weekly or bi-weekly updates-should be set up where team members may report against the set targets, challenges that were faced in addition to, and what they plan to do next. Such meetings should be designed to permit open dialogue and questions, enabling everyone to have their say. This real-time update on the progress of individuals and teams may be facilitated through collaborative tools and platforms.

Another fruitful strategy is developing visual dashboards that depict the KPIs and other metrics on progress. These should offer the team a representative glance to monitor progress so performance against goals is easily visible. Visual elements like charts and graphs facilitate comprehension and interest, so team members may judge where they stand vis —-vis their objectives.

Transparency can be achieved when the leaders encourage a culture of open communication. It should start with the leader, showing them where they are and how it's going. By sharing their successes and setbacks, leaders encourage team members to normalize discussing challenges and build collaboration toward solutions.

Apart from this, channels for feedback must be established. Team members should be able to give their opinions on progress reporting and offer suggestions for improvement. Regular feedback makes reporting processes more relevant and valuable for the group's emerging needs.

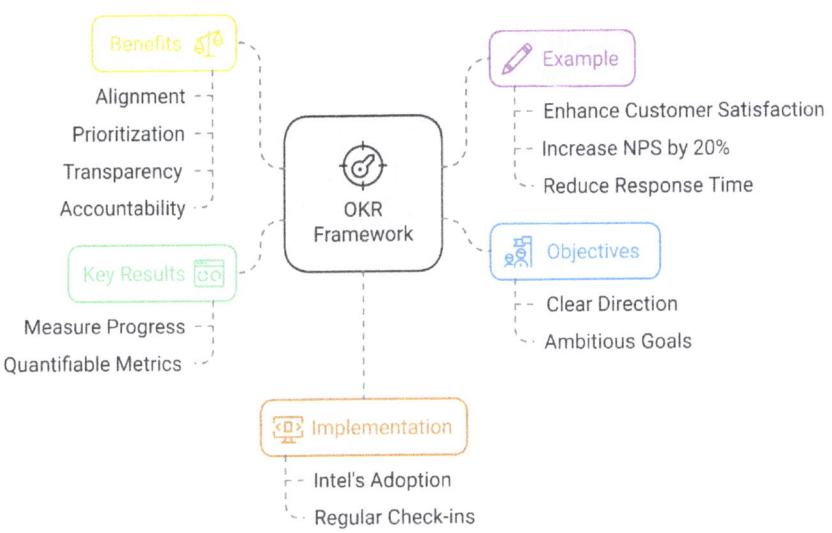

Figure 3.9 Setting clear goals and a compelling vision.

Progress reporting is one of the essential habits one could instill into teams to ensure trust, accountability, and true teamwork. Organizations can make team members feel informed and engaged by implementing regular reporting mechanisms, using visual tools to display information, and holding open communications. In this way, not only will the performance of every individual be improved, but also that of the team, with shared responsibility for their collective success. As teams work through their objectives, embracing transparency in progress reporting leads to better collaboration, driving superior outcomes for the organization.

3.6 Case Study: Setting Clear Goals and Vision

Today, success in the competitive business world is driven by setting clear goals and a compelling vision for any organization that desires success. One of the practical frameworks gaining momentum for this alignment is the OKR methodology, which was made famous by Intel. OKRs depict a systematic way of goal-setting and adopt transparency and accountability in teams so that organizations might roar with purpose in pursuing their objectives.

OKR is a goal-setting framework that helps organizations outline their objectives and the results achieved in the process. Two parts constitute its core framework: the objective part, which needs to be qualitative to provide direction, and the key results part, which must be quantified by metrics measuring movements or achievements of the same objectives. This dual nature of the structure enables teams to set high goals but keep success measured clearly.

For example, a technology company may aim to " improve customer satisfaction." The aligned vital results would be increasing the NPS by 20% and decreasing customer response time below 24 hours. The OKR system crystallizes the objective and measurable results of the effort so that everyone can understand the direction of the effort.

One key benefit of the OKR framework is that it aligns team goals with higher-level corporate objectives. In the case of Intel, OKRs aligned every part of the company's efforts toward common goals and drove them all to work together to achieve the same strategic vision. This goal alignment is essential for large corporations, where miscommunication quickly stops the momentum. It gives teams a clear idea of their role in attaining the big-picture mission.

For this reason, the OKR methodology also favors team effort prioritization. "Groups can concentrate on several minimal goals, which is crucial to avoid weakening initiatives throughout many campaigns. In this way, companies can accomplish much more in crucial locations for success. Various other important facets of the OKR structure urge openness and liability. When purposes and essential results are shared openly, companies can produce an open setting where everybody understands what others are dealing with.

Such openness sustains cooperation and also aids staff members in supporting each other in attaining their objectives. Where development shows up, one is most likely to feel responsible for their payment, resulting in higher interaction and efficiency. Intel's fostering of OKRs personifies this liability society. Ingratiatingly, routine check-ins are urged to see exactly how points are going, go over difficulties, and make required changes. Such a step-by-step procedure ensures that the groups are straightened and situations or new details can quickly transform. Well-set objectives and also an eye-catching vision provide companies with the ability to win in a competitive market.

As shown by Intel, the OKR structure successfully aligns group purposes with firm objectives while embracing openness and responsibility. OKRs enable organizations to create focused workforces that roar with purpose in pursuing their objectives. Embracing this structured approach improves performance and encourages a culture of collaboration and shared success that catapults the organization toward its long-term vision.

3.7 Key Point Donald Trump's potential re-election in 2024

> **Immigration Policy:** Advocating strict immigration controls, which resonates with voters concerned about border security and national safety.

In light of the 2024 presidential elections, Donald Trump's probable candidacy centers on just a few angles that sink deep into his base. The most significant points of his platform revolve around immigration policy, especially his support of strict immigration control, which appeals to a large portion of the electorate concerned with security on our borders and safety for our nation.

The call for rigid immigration policies has primarily characterized Trump's presidency. His administration implemented laws such as the construction of a wall at the border to reduce illegal immigration and implement immigration laws. Both were framed in the context of national security and jobs for Americans, which many voters still like.

> **Leverage Outsider Status**
> Position yourself as an outsider challenging the political establishment.
>
> **Repetition for Impact**
> Use repetition to reinforce key messages and slogans.

Trump has reiterated these policies in the run-up to the 2024 elections on grounds of law and order. He portrays himself as a protector of American sovereignty, where unregulated immigration can lead to economic instability and threats to public safety. Along with a rigid migration plan, Trump charms those residents who consider boundary safety crucial and are also worried about criminal offenses connected to unlawful migration.

He additionally uses a migration plan to show how he resolves the state of mind of a crucial component of the American selection. According to surveys, many citizens believe that migration is just one of the most essential concerns, specifically with expanding criminal activity and financial unpredictability. "His fans frequently feel that the government needs to use up these concerns, making them intend to choose prospects encouraging them to act.

Moreover, Trump's unsupported claims bordering migration use wider motifs of nationalism and identification of national politics. By mounting migration as a danger to American worth and security, he charms citizens who feel their social identification is under siege. This messaging has shown efficiency in setting up his base and drawing in unpredictable citizens who focus on safety and security. While there is substantial recognition of Trump's migration plans, powerful resistance does exist.

Doubters explains his hardline placement as ruthless and progressively pointless in taking care of refined migration facts. Instead, an extra well-balanced reform equivalent in safety, security, and humanitarianism should be advertised. As the political election strategies, among the crucial difficulties for Trump, is exactly how to appear in this separated landscape: to secure his base while soothing much smaller citizens, most of whom have much more understanding of migration plans may aid guide.

Furthermore, the political setting dynamically alters, and financial, healthcare, and weather problems can move councilors' interest rates. Trump's capacity to focus on migration while addressing other melting problems will determine his destiny in the 2024 political election.

Donald Trump's re-election opportunities substantially depend upon his migration plan. With the inflexible migration controls he promotes, he talks with citizens for whom boundary safety, security, and nationwide security are serious concerns, utilizing a story that speaks directly to their worries.

Attempting to remain successful in this selecting calculus, Trump's obstacle will certainly be keeping the interest of his base while dealing with a more comprehensive range of citizen issues. The migration plan remains a crucial column of his political election technique in his re-election project, along with an extra substantial discussion of national identification, safety, and security in America.

Reference

1. Pausch, R. (2008). The last lecture. Hyperion.

2. Doerr, J. (2018). Measure what matters: Online goals and results. Portfolio.

3. Doran, G. T. (1981). There's a SMART way to write management's goals and objectives. Management Review, 70(11), 35–36.

4. Collins, J. C., & Porras, J. I. (1996). Built to last: Successful habits of visionary companies. HarperBusiness.

5. Covey, S. R. (1989). The 7 habits of highly effective people: Powerful lessons in personal change. Free Press.

6. Buzan, T. (2006). The mind map book: Unlock your creativity, boost your memory, change your life. Penguin.

7. Kaplan, R. S., & Norton, D. P. (1992). The balanced scorecard: Measures that drive performance. Harvard Business Review, 70(1), 71–79.

8. Schwartz, D. (2014). The art of team alignment: How to create a team that works together. Wiley.

9. Stone, D. (2013). The feedback loop: A guide to understanding how feedback can help you grow and succeed. CreateSpace Independent Publishing Platform.

10. Zenger, J. H., & Folkman, J. (2019). The extraordinary leader: Turning good managers into great leaders. McGraw-Hill.

11. Goleman, D. (2011). The brain and emotional intelligence: New insights. More Than Sound.

CHAPTER 4

Courageous Conversations: Mastering Communication

Introduction

Communication brings together, in one thread, all relationships-personal, professional or of a teamwork nature. The intent of Chapter 4 is to look at various skills and strategies necessary for negotiating difficult conversations with clarity and confidence. [1, 2] Courageous conversations can be defined as those critical dialogues in which honesty, vulnerability, and respect merge for people to discuss difficult topics, iron out conflicts, and get closer [3].

Courageous conversations are needed more than ever in increasingly fast-paced and polarized environments [4, 5]. Misunderstandings that should be dealt with could escalate into major conflicts, and clear communication may sometimes lead to frustration and disengagement among team members [6]. This chapter should give the reader ammunition to engage in this dialogue appropriately and ensure their thoughts and feelings are aired while listening to and understanding others [7].

I will go through some important concepts: emotional intelligence, active listening, and how to make an environment for safe dialogue [8]. This way, the readers will understand the meaning of communicating their opinions confidently and respectfully while being open to others' thoughts. In addition, this chapter will bring on some helpful hints for overcoming anxiety and discomfort during difficult conversations because, as the common saying goes, a problem should be confronted rather than avoided [9].

Next, I'm going to discuss feedback in courageous conversations. While constructive feedback is the only way to grow and improve, it often involves sensitive topics. Learning to give and receive feedback is an important aspect of creating a culture of safety and collaboration where individuals feel valued and heard.

Chapter 4 concludes with the overriding message that mastering communication is not about speaking better but is equally about developing courage for tough conversations. Using real-life instances, sensible techniques, and reflective tasks, viewers will certainly be motivated to go on and their convenience areas towards the transformative power of enduring discussions that could raise individual connections, enhance group characteristics, and contribute to a much more open and comprehensive business society.

4.1 Understanding the Importance of Communication

The indispensable ability of reliable interaction underpins success in every location of life. It's important in individual partnerships, expert setups, and social communications that a person should, as well as empathetically, share one's ideas, sensations, and suggestions. Recognizing the relevance of interaction boosts communication amongst individuals and constructs a joint and efficient environment within groups and companies. Interaction is everything about attaching.

It develops the foundation of any partnership where a specific can share requirements and experiences and develop connections. The trust fund, a crucial component in any healthy and balanced connection, is embraced with open and straightforward interaction. When individuals feel listened to and recognized, they will likely be more freely verbalized, share their ideas, and function efficiently with each other. This link sensation is essential in individuals with specialist setups, given that great relationships generally imply greater contentment and efficiency.

The key to teamwork in any professional setting is effective communication. Clear communication allows team members to align objectives, roles, and expectations. The free flow of information enables the teams to make informed decisions, solve problems efficiently, and innovate together. Poor communication may engender misunderstandings, conflicts, and low morale. Open dialogue inculcates a culture of adopting collaboration and laying the grounds for creativity and productivity to thrive.

Problem-solving also involves effective communication. When problems arise, articulating the issues and listening to different perspectives is extremely important. Effective communicators can look at problems from multiple angles, synthesize information, and build comprehensive solutions. An organization can tap into the collective intelligence of its workforce by adopting open discussions and valuing everyone's contribution to arrive at more effective and innovative solutions to problems.

Communication lies at the core of employee engagement and motivation. Leaders' clear and transparent communication regarding goals, expectations, and feedback will bring team members closer to their work and enable them to understand how their contribution matters. On the other hand, regular communication from leadership will make the employees valued and informed, thus boosting morale and motivation. Lack of communication brings feelings of isolation and disengagement, resulting in lower productivity and higher turnover rates.

Conflicts necessarily arise in relationships or any other organization. Communication helps ventilate conflicts constructively. When feelings are openly and respectfully communicated, misunderstandings and differences of opinion are ironed out before they blow out of proportion. Communication skills allow an individual to assert their feelings and negotiate solutions while respecting another individual's feelings. Good communication will lead to healthy relationships and harmony on the job.

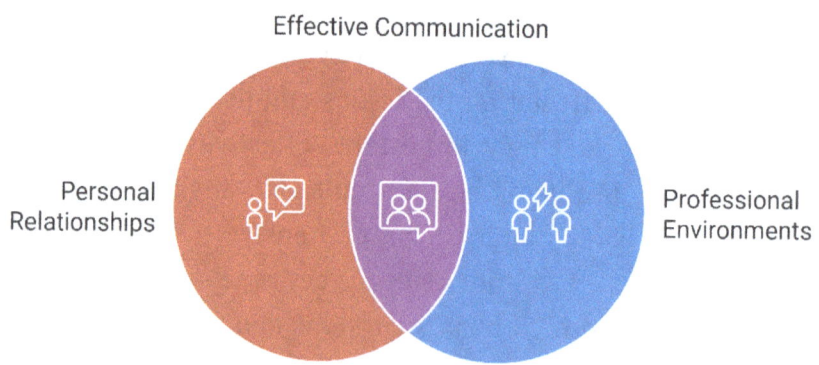

Figure 4.1 The Power of Effective Communication.

Understanding the value of communication will lead to personal and professional success. Communication develops far better relationships, encourages collaboration, offers more problem-solving capability, increases engagement, and resolves many conflicts. Trust, openness, and productivity will build up as individuals and organizations focus on effective communication. Mastering the skills of communication means, in the end, not just a means of information exchange but building bridges toward meaningful interaction and enduring success.

4.2 Techniques for Active Listening

Lively listening is the most vital communication attribute because it provokes understanding, builds trust, and develops personal and professional relations. As opposed to passive listening, active listening encompasses an all-around engagement in responding thoughtfully. Active listening techniques can be effectively imparted to individuals to incorporate more depth and meaning into their interactions.

The first step of active listening is paying attention to the speaker. That means removing distractions like phones, computers, or other tasks and paying attention to the conversation. It also means showing interest in nonverbal ways, such as nodding and using eye contact. This acts as respect towards the speaker, and you will automatically learn all that is shared.

Both verbal and nonverbal affirmations denote that you participate in what is being said. Simple words like "I see," "I understand," or "Go on" may encourage the speaker to continue sharing. Body language, such as leaning slightly forward or tilting your head, signals that you are interested and attentive. Such gestures create a supportive environment where the speaker feels valued and heard.

Feedback is part of active listening. Sometimes, paraphrasing or summarizing what you've heard the speaker say can help confirm understanding and permit the speaker to clarify a misunderstanding. For example, "Let me make sure I understand. I hear you saying that you're frustrated with the deadlines for the current project." This method shows that you're paying attention and will permit further conversation.

Active listening involves much openness of mind. Try not to formulate your opinions or responses while the other person speaks; rather, listen to what the other has to say completely before responding. That means setting aside preconceived opinions or biases and being open to new ideas. You deferred judgment and made the speaker feel free to say whatever was on his mind, probably leading to an honest and productive conversation.

Once the speaker has spoken their mind, it is time to respond appropriately. Your response has to relate to what the speaker said and show you understand what was being said. It could be in the form of seeking further explanations or giving your view respectfully. Responses deepen the conversation and connect you with the speaker even more.

The basis for active listening is empathy. Attempt to understand how the other feels—that doesn't mean you have to share a point of view. Acknowledge feelings as a way to validate experiences and connect. The simplest responses, such as "That sounds like a tough time" or "I can see why you'd feel that way," can do much to show empathy and support.

Following up after a conversation can reiterate active listening and the importance of the conversation. Regarding discussions with specific issues or concerns, check in later with the speaker about the progress of the matter. This will show that you care about their well-being and will strengthen the relationship, building trust with time.

Figure 4.2 Enhancing Active Listening Skills.

Mastering active listening techniques will help in effective communication and building relationships. One can substantially improve one's listening skills by standing, displaying interest, giving feedback, delaying judgment, responding if necessary, showing empathy, and following up. These techniques help create a trustful and open atmosphere where more meaningful interactions and deeper connections can occur. Therefore, active listening develops personal growth ability, enhances relationships, and creates better collaboration in the professional arena and personal life.

4.2.1 Navigating Difficult Discussions

Moving through tough conversations successfully involves one of the major skills required across personal and professional perspectives. Conflicts, constructive feedback, sensitive topics- whatever may be the reason for having difficult conversations, conducting them with clarity and sensitivity can make or break any relationship or result. Herein are some of the most important tips to successfully navigate those tough conversations. Preparation is necessary in approaching your challenging discussion. Take a minute to clarify your goals and consider the bottom lines of your message. Prepare for the other individual's responses and put yourself in their shoes. This anticipation will certainly help mount your message thoughtfully and avoid shocks that may show up throughout a conversation.

Accumulating pertinent realities or instances can reinforce your placement and highlight quality. The outcomes of any tough discussion can be significantly different depending upon the location in which it happens. Select a personal neutral location in which both fit. A safe environment encourages candid actions and decreases defensiveness. Start the discussion favorably by recognizing your purpose in talking pleasantly and your need to listen to and recognize one another.

When reviewing aching topics, your language can raise or diminish stress. Use "I" declarations to share your sensations and viewpoints without seeming accusatory. For instance, rather than claiming, "You constantly disrupt me, "attempt "I feel disappointed when I'm disrupted. This strategy concentrates on your experience rather than criticizing the other individual, which can foster an extra useful discussion.

The trick to any challenging discussion is to pay attention proactively—program rate of interest by nodding your head, making eye contact, and using singing statements. Rewording what the other individuals are stating allows them to recognize that you heard them; after that, you can clear up and recognize each other. You can confirm sensations and viewpoints, producing a considerate environment where open discussion can happen securely.

Feelings can run warm in difficult discussions. Nonetheless, it is of the utmost requirement to stay tranquil and structured. Take deep breaths, talk with a company, and articulate to reveal self-confidence and control. If you feel overloaded, stop the conversation briefly. Remaining tranquil aids, you assume plainly and give thoughtful feedback instead of acting quickly out of aggravation or rage.

Figure 4.3 Strategies for Navigating Difficult Discussions.

Instead of dwelling on the problem or placing blame, direct the discussion to resolution. Work together with the other party to determine shared interests and potential concessions. This future-focused approach creates a sense of partnership and invites both sides to be invested in the solutions. Reframing the situation in terms of collaboration can turn a negative conversation into one that's positive, leading to greater understanding and a resolution.

Sometimes, debates get either too hot or too emotional. It is good to feel when it is time to step back. Suggest taking a break if the conversation reaches a deadlock or becomes emotionally overwhelming. This pause allows both parties to gather their thoughts and approach the discussion with a fresh perspective later.

Arguably, tough conversations offer an opportunity that is very important for solidifying relationships and urging more openness. Preparing in advance, ensuring a safe space to have tough conversations, utilizing "I" statements, listening actively, keeping calm, redirecting to the solution-focused talk, and knowing when to take a time-out gives one the confidence and empathy needed to enter tough conversations. Subsequently, these would adopt constructive discussions, aid conflict resolution, and increase mutual understanding-all, leading toward better personal and professional lives.

4.2.2 Giving and Receiving Constructive Feedback

Constructive feedback is a necessary motive in both personal and professional life to adopt growth and improvement. It is a healthy tool that effectively helps one recognize one's strengths yet knows where one fails. However, its successful delivery and reception determine the effectiveness of feedback. When done correctly, constructive feedback can strengthen relationships, boost motivation, and cultivate a culture of continuous learning.

Constructive feedback should be specific. Generalized statements only confuse and annoy the recipient; specific examples provide clear actions to take. Instead of "You need to do better," for example, the more constructive feedback would be, "In your report, some key details were missing. That did tend to make things less than clear." This points out the problem while showing the way. Also, using the "sandwich" method of feedback delivery helps buffer the criticism between positive comments, builds a person up before and after the critique, and makes the criticism easier to digest. This helps with receptivity and maintains a supportive atmosphere by keeping the tone respectful.

Receiving constructive criticism is always challenging, as it points out areas where one should grow. However, one must be open to feedback. Emotional reactions aside, feedback is a great opportunity for development. If an individual remains open, he can learn and advance from the insights someone else gives him. Also, if the feedback needs to be clarified or more critical, one should be able to ask for an explanation to create a more constructive discussion. And questions like, "Can you elaborate on that point? This will help in ensuring a better understanding and encourage further discussion.

How to effectively engage in constructive feedback for growth?

Giving Feedback   **Receiving Feedback**

Focus on specific behaviors and supportive delivery   Maintain an open mindset for reflection

Figure 4.4 Constructive feedback is essential for adopting growth and improvement.

Therefore, giving and receiving constructive feedback is part of the culture needed to enhance personal and organizational growth. Through open communication and mutual respect, a person will create an enabling environment where feedback is not necessarily anxiety but considered a wellspring of value. Such culture builds better individual performances while securing stronger team dynamics, promising motivation and productivity within a certain working group. In other words, the secret to unleashing potential and adopting continuous improvement lies in mastering the art of feedback.

4.3 Encouraging Open-Ended Questions

Open-ended questions are among the strongest communication tools imaginable. They permit deeper conversations and safer, more contemplative responses. Unlike yes/no-type questions, open-ended questions cannot be answered with just a simple yes or no; rather, they invite elaboration and exploration. This nudges people to engage each other and ultimately connect. Helping others ask open-ended questions will enrich discussions throughout private and professional life.

Open-ended questions adopted critical thinking and creativity; respondents expressed thoughts, feelings, and experiences in their own words. Let me illustrate this: if you ask, "What do you think about the direction our project is taking? "people are encouraged to provide an opinion and insights, whereas, in a closed question, they confirm or deny a statement. This type of question leads to an open door of information, whereby the questioner can understand the other person's view. Furthermore, party concerns might provoke the individual to assess and determine their drives plus presumptions, bringing their feedback much more extensive than the shallow degree.

In individual connections, broad concerns can substantially improve interaction along with links. They allow people to share tales, experiences, and feelings, embracing affection and counting on it. For example, ask, How did you feel about that experience? Welcomes the other individual to dig into their feelings with ideas, advertising an extensive understanding between events. This method reinforces connections and urges energetic attention as people must take note of the reactions and involve meaningfully.

Open-ended questions work well in a specialist setup for group conferences, meetings, and efficiency testimonials. Leaders can enable their staff members to share their viewpoints and problems and make them feel welcome by making certain everybody matters and is being paid attention to. For example, if there is a conceptualizing session, it can be specified," What obstacles do you predict with this method?"

"It will certainly urge staff member to share their sights, offer reasoning that may bring about a cutting-edge remedy, and use a joint analytical strategy. Besides, in efficiency evaluations, open-ended inquiries like " What objectives do you wish to accomplish in the coming year? Enable staff members to take possession of their growth and also share goals. However, dealing with locations must be carried out equitably and unbiasedly. It encourages synergy between staff member and their supervisors. Nevertheless, it might reveal the toughness and weak points in a staff member's efficiency and assist with setting goals for the year listed below.

Individuals can adopt a culture of open-ended questioning through several techniques. First, practice active listening and show genuine interest in the responses. This encourages others to elaborate on their thoughts and feelings. Furthermore, modeling open-ended concerns in discussions can motivate others to do the same. Phrasing concerns to start with "What," Just how," or "Why" normally leads to a lot more extensive solutions. Producing a secure and helpful setting is essential; when individuals feel comfortable sharing, they are more likely to participate in much deeper conversations.

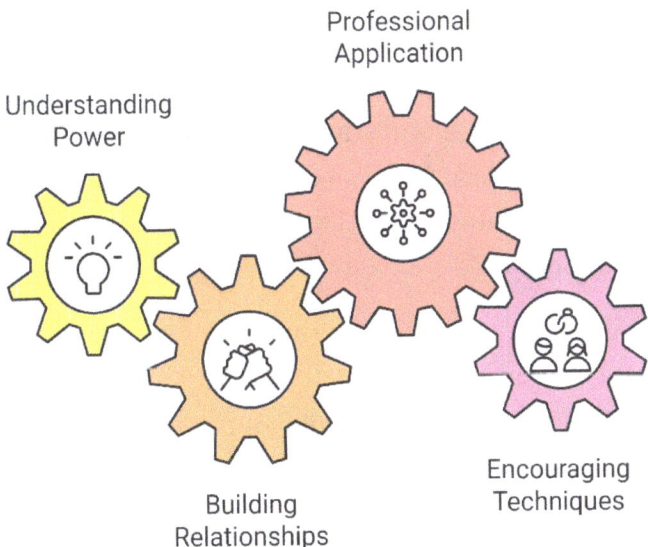

Figure 4.5 Enhancing Communication with Open-Ended Questions.

It urges open-ended inquiries, drawing out much healthier communications and far better partnerships. Attempting to make an area feel comfy in one's skin, as well as voice ideas and sensations, will eventually reveal raised understanding, teamwork, and bonding. From individual to specialist discussions, an open-ended concern transforms the expectation of a discussion to make individuals go deeper. Eventually, it assists in producing much healthier discussions, resulting in individual development and far better connections.

4.3.1 Managing Emotions During Conversations

Handling one's feelings throughout a discussion is a salient ability in any offered communication that substantially supports reviewing delicate or questionable subjects. Feeling is essential when interacting and analyzing messages; it confirms that communications can be created properly by controlling our psychological actions. It is a crucial ability essential at individual plus specialist degrees where reliable interaction affects understanding, partnership, and resolution. Handling feelings throughout a discussion begins with recognizing the psychological circumstances or subjects most likely to elicit one's sensations.

Identifying these triggers permits people to prepare for psychological responses and reply more attentively. For example, if a topic often tends to incite disappointment or anxiousness, recognizing this in advance can aid in establishing methods to keep one's cool. Strategies such as deep breathing, favorable self-talk, or the requirement to count before responding can provide room to recognize their sensations and select a much better reaction.

Energetic attention develops the basis of psychological control throughout communications. Listeners will certainly comprehend the scenario and also their side concerning their viewpoints and sensations, making it much easier to reduce their psychological reactions. During active listening, one should pay attention to the spoken words and other non-verbal cues like the tone of voice and the speaker's body language. Being all-inclusive stirs a more empathetic response, thus minimizing feelings of defensiveness and frustration. Showing interest in the other person's viewpoint puts them in a relationship based on respect and openness, reducing emotional discussion fallouts.

Emotional Intelligence is the subset of social intelligence that involves the ability to monitor and understand one's feelings and the feelings of others. EI can greatly improve communication effectiveness, especially in difficult conversations. Individuals with high emotional intelligence maintain composure, empathize with others, and respond appropriately to emotional cues. It means awareness of one's emotional condition and how that can impact the conversation to make it less one-sided and more rational. Self-awareness and reflection will enhance one's emotional intelligence over time.

A safe and supportive environment always allows for the emotional handling of conversations. People will be more forthcoming and constructive in their responses if they feel they will not be at risk from others for negative judgment or retribution. You can work toward setting this sort of environment as a conversation partner by using respectful language, showing regard for the feelings of another individual, and being in the mood to listen rather than interrupt. Trust and respect can be encouraged within an atmosphere where all parties are at ease; hence, emotional escalations could be reduced and more productive discussions entertained.

Sentiment monitoring in discussions is important in increasing interaction and boosting connections. Ending up being notified of what triggers feelings, paying attention to energy, using psychological knowledge, and establishing a security area are methods to browse tough conversations quicker and coupled properly. Such steps will enhance people dynamics and present a society of open discussion and regard. Taking care of feelings throughout discussions is necessary for individual growth and producing useful connections at an individual and specialist degree.

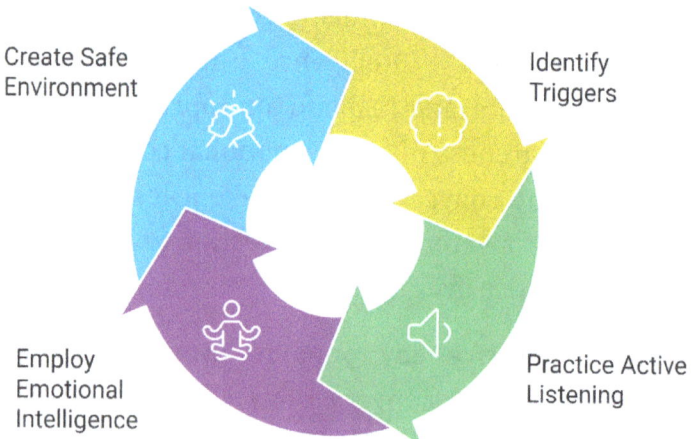

Figure 4.6 Cycle of Emotional Management in Conversations.

4.3.2 Establishing Communication Norms

Interaction standards are vital for a healthy, balanced, effective environment in individual relationships, work environments, or neighborhood setups. They establish the approved policies and assumptions for how individuals will communicate with each other. Well-defined standards promote a team to advertise considerate discussions, enable much better collaboration, and reduce false impressions of each other. In this way, reliable interaction patterns can be put down for smooth communications and assist in developing a society of visibility and inclusiveness.

Interaction standards consist of different elements of communication: intonation, action, time approach of interaction, and also sort of responses. As an example, a work environment standard might be that upon job conclusion, employees ought to send comments within 48 hrs of conclusion to keep a constant enhancement society. A household might likewise develop a standard of regular conferences where concerns or issues can be shared in a calm and considerate setting. These standards are those that, when specified, lead to a clear understanding of assumptions amongst the team participants and, therefore, extra reliable and also unified communications.

Normally, establishing the standards of interaction includes all events. The result is normally finer since it makes individuals feel listened to and valued, leaving them with some possession of the developed standard. This can be done by holding conversations or workshops where employee share their point of view with choices relating to interaction. By permitting the criteria to be affected by varied points of view, teams can develop regulations that show the demands as well as worths of all participants, therefore guaranteeing a better likelihood of adherence and also dedication.

While being clear may be one point, being open and adaptable should be protected. Groups maintain altering, and brand-new obstacles might need altering interaction standards to make them appropriate and suitable. As a result, it is an excellent concept to revisit the standards regularly and make modifications to ensure that they remain to meet the team's requirements. Inspiration of recurring comments from employees concerning just how well the developed standards offer urges a continual society of enhancement and versatility; interaction methods transform with characteristics.

Developing interaction standards likewise entails advertising liability amongst team participants. Every person must recognize their duty to promote these standards and agree to attend to any actions that drift from them. Developing a refuge for useful comments permits people to hold each other answerable without anxiety about the problem. For example, if a staff member constantly disturbs others throughout conferences, the team needs to resolve this action pleasantly and synergistically. Responsibility will certainly be established within teams to stay with pre-defined standards that boost basic interaction efficiency.

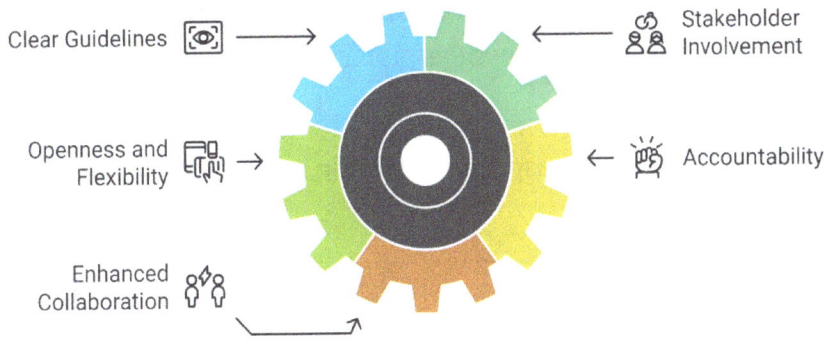

Figure 4.7 Building Effective Communication Norms.

Interaction standards are important to developing regard and efficiency within an atmosphere. Teams can develop an influential interaction society by establishing clear policies that consider all celebrations' viewpoints and motivate visibility, adaptability, and responsibility. These standards add to better interpersonal connections and guarantee better cooperation, technology, and general fulfillment within the team. After all, the time and effort one invests in communicative norms set the ground for bettered interpersonal relations and teamwork, which, in turn, create room for improved performance of tasks at personal and professional levels.

4.4 Utilizing Nonverbal Communication Effectively

Non-verbal communication helps to a great extent in portraying and interpreting details obtained from daily interactions. It includes everything from facial expressions to posture, gestures, and eye contact. Understanding and using appropriate non-verbal communication accurately will promise better interpersonal relationships, reduce misunderstandings, and result in a more interactive communicative environment. Being conscious of the non-verbal cues will also help the sender ensure that the intended message is clearly and appropriately communicated.

Table 4.1 Outlines key aspects of utilizing nonverbal communication effectively.

Element	Description	Tips for Effective Use
Facial Expressions	Convey emotions such as happiness, sadness, anger, or surprise.	Maintain a relaxed face; smile genuinely; be aware of your expressions.
Body Language	Includes posture, gestures, and overall body movements.	Use open gestures; avoid crossing arms; lean slightly forward to show engagement.
Eye Contact	Indicates attentiveness, interest, and sincerity.	Maintain appropriate eye contact; avoid staring; be sensitive to cultural norms.
Gestures	Hand movements that emphasize or clarify verbal messages.	Use gestures to illustrate points; ensure gestures are culturally appropriate.
Posture	Reflects confidence and openness; communicates engagement.	Stand or sit straight; avoid slouching; align your body with the speaker.
Proxemics (Personal Space)	The physical distance maintained between communicators.	Respect personal space; adjust distance based on context (formal vs. informal).
Tone of Voice	The pitch, volume, and pace of speech convey emotions.	Vary tone to match the message; avoid monotone delivery; speak clearly and at a comfortable volume.
Touch	It can convey warmth, support, or power dynamics.	Use touch appropriately (e.g., handshake); ensure consent and comfort.

The importance of nonverbal communication cannot be understated; often, it is more about what was not said. Studies have shown that as much as 93% of communication may be nonverbal, and major chunks rely on body language and tone of voice. For example, a warm smile may denote friendliness and openness, whereas crossed arms could imply defensiveness or unease. By aligning verbal messages with nonverbal signals, communicators create trust and clarity while carrying out the interaction; this reduces the possibility of misunderstanding.

It includes facial expressions, posture, eye contact, and gestures. Facial expressions are the most potent in communicating emotions. A smile can show happiness, while a frown might indicate concern or disapproval. Body language involves posture and gestures, inviting engagement or signaling withdrawal. Open body language, such as uncrossed arms and leaning slightly forward, may indicate receptiveness and interest. Eye contact establishes a connection; proper eye contact shows that a person is attentive and honest. Understanding such non-verbal cues enables a person to relate better and communicate more emphatically.

Individuals can practice a few techniques to develop their skills in communicating nonverbally. First is self-awareness; reflecting on how one's nonverbal cues might be perceived can facilitate more intentional communication. Second, observing the nonverbal signals of others provides great insight into their emotions and reactions. Practicing active listening, maintaining eye contact, and leaning in can help reinforce engagement and comprehension. In addition, it is always important to adapt non-verbal communication according to the context of the interaction. For example, formal contexts require restraint in personal disposition, while informal situations allow for fairly relaxed dispositions.

The ability to effectively use non-verbal communication consolidates interpersonal interaction by building more meaning into interactions. Facial expressions, body language, eyes, and gestures will all support a consistent message if a person connects their verbal message with non-verbal cues, making awareness and adaptation to an acquired skill. Non-verbal communication provides desired benefits in personal and professional life and reinforces an empathetic environment. Ultimately, finding a command of nonverbal communication will be imperative for good relations in an ever-shrinking world, wherein meaningful interactions and increased levels of cooperation can be forthcoming.

4.4.1 Creating Safe Spaces for Dialogue

Safe spaces are the foundation for open communication, trust, and understanding among individuals in various contexts, from personal relationships and workplaces to community settings. A safe space encourages people to share their thoughts, feelings, and concerns without fear of judgment or repercussions. Thus, creating a safe and respectful environment allows groups to engage in meaningful dialogue that can lead to collaboration, conflict resolution, and personal growth.

A safe is a setup where one discovers welcome, assistance, worth, and regard for the person. Individuals can share their experiences and sights in such an atmosphere, understanding that they will be listened to and thought about. This is among the specifying principles when the subjects of conversation entail delicate topics: race, sex-related orientation, mental health, and wellness, as well as office concerns to which individuals might feel prone. Developing safe areas will certainly enable sincere discussion, much deeper links, and a better understanding among individuals.

Numerous aspects are needed to create a retreat for discussion. Initially, ground policies need to be developed. Such regulations should urge regard for privacy and attention. Individuals may accept that they should not disrupt each other and should proceed with open minds. Articulated ground regulations pleasantly establish the tone for interaction and help avert false impressions.

Another essential ingredient is energetic assistance. An excellent mediator might regulate the discussion to guarantee that all voices are listened to and stress is handled. The company might additionally manage the circulation of discussion, identify and confirm individuals' feelings, and help create a comprehensive environment by motivating quieter participants to share their ideas and delicately reining in leading voices. Thus, involvement is well-balanced.

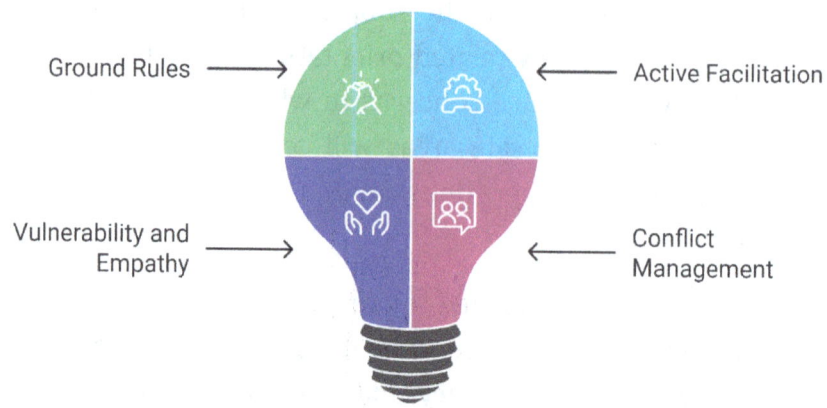

Figure 4.8 Elements of Safe Spaces for Dialogue

The area additionally needs to develop susceptibility and compassion among individuals. Motivating individuals to share experiences will certainly build greater compassion and understanding. Assistance can model susceptibility by sharing individual tales and pointing out feelings that might occur, which can urge others to do the same. One more crucial means to construct deepness in discussion with the neighborhood is the method of understanding, paying attention to recognizing the audio speaker instead of creating feedback.

Problems might occur in any discussion; resolving them favorably within a retreat is crucial. Developing a procedure for handling differences can aid in keeping a considerate ambiance. Individuals must be urged to reveal their viewpoints steadily and come close to problems as possibilities for development and understanding. By refocusing problems, teams can change prospective divisiveness into richer conversations, resulting in better understanding and service. They are the rooms where security is developed for discussion and open interaction, enabling purposeful links between people.

Teams do this by establishing borders, motivating useful conversations, being susceptible and understanding towards each other, and resolving disputes favorably. This will certainly make all individuals feel valued coupled with value in this room; such areas embrace partnerships and specific development, coupled with understanding amongst participants. Eventually, purchasing refuge for discussion will certainly be essential in taking on a much more comprehensive and thoughtful culture where varied viewpoints can be shared and comprehended.

4.4.2 Documenting and Following Up on Conversations

Recording and adhering to it is necessary for both professional and individual experiences. These procedures enhance interaction by capturing the main points discussed, activities to be taken, and dedications made. Efficient paperwork and follow-up approaches will equip officials and groups by establishing responsibility, decreasing misconceptions, and developing better partnerships. Discussion paperwork offers rather several beneficial applications.

Initially, it develops a document of subjects gone over that can be described later. This will be useful in expert setups where a conference might include complex subjects, choices, and activity products. Making notes throughout discussions aids individuals in making certain all celebrations bear in mind the bottom lines, plus straighten them with what was gone over. Documents also aid in tracking task progression, making clear duties, and raising group openness.

Documentation can also be an important tool in conflict resolution. In dispute cases, documented proof of who said what can clear up misunderstandings and provide context to decisions. It acts as a reference point for all parties involved, limiting the potential for misunderstandings that could lead to further conflict.

Individuals must write the conversations systematically if they are supposed to do it correctly. A person should first determine what to record: the topics discussed, decisions taken, activity assignments, and their due dates. Writing notes in clear sections allows individuals to review and refer to them more easily. The use of bullet points or numbered lists enhances clarity and readability.

Table 4.2 The aspects of documenting and following up on conversations.

Aspect	Description	Best Practices
Importance of Documentation	Provides a written record of discussions, decisions, and action items.	Capture key points, decisions, and responsibilities.
Conflict Resolution	It helps clarify misunderstandings and provides context.	Maintain a clear record to reference during disputes.
Effective Strategies	Organize notes into clear sections for easy reference.	Use bullet points, headings, and numbered lists.
Technology Utilization	Leverage tools for real-time documentation and collaboration.	Use note-taking apps, shared documents, or project management software.
Follow-Up Role	Reinforces accountability	Send follow-up emails summarizing

	and ensures action items are completed.	discussions and next steps.
Maintaining Momentum	Regular check-ins encourage accountability and progress.	Schedule periodic updates on action items and project milestones.
Building Relationships	Demonstrates value for contributions and encourages engagement.	Acknowledge input and provide updates to enhance trust.
Personal Conversations	Ensures clarity in family discussions and shared decisions.	Document key agreements and follow up to keep everyone informed.

Another successful strategy is document processing with the help of technology: note-taking apps, project management software, or shared documents will ensure that contributions are in real-time and everyone possesses updated information. Again, this ensures maximum output because team members can track updates and changes in real-time.

Follow-up is equally essential to documentation immediately after a conversation. This reinforces accountability and ensures that action items are accomplished. Sending an email or message summarizing the key discussion points and next steps in the follow-up can clarify and strengthen commitments made during the conversation. It also keeps the parties involved in what was discussed and considered, and by doing so, one shows professionalism and attention to detail.

Second, follow-ups can retain momentum on current projects or initiatives. Regular follow-up on action items cultivates a sense of accountability and keeps others informed of progress. Practice maintains a communicative and collaborative atmosphere where views are supported in their struggle to meet deadlines and achieve goals.

Documenting and following up on conversations build better relationships. When people feel their contributions are noted, and an action plan is coming from them, they are more likely to be motivated and interested. A sense of responsibility further develops trust and respect among team members, which turns a group into a practical working team that can create a positive work environment.

Document vital discussions in personal relationships, such as family meeting decisions or planning important events, with everyone on the same page. Following up with discussions enforces how vital the debate is and each person's thoughts.

Documentation and further follow-up with conversations are essential to improve communication, accountability, and relationship-building. By effectively capturing key points and ensuring action items are covered, one can reduce misunderstandings and build a culture of collaboration. From personal or professional standpoints, this creates transparency and trust, hence more productive and meaningful interactions. Investing time in inscribing and following up improves the quality of the outcome and relations among people, laying a foundation for success and further teamwork.

4.5 Facilitating Group Discussions

Group discussion facilitation is a crucial skill that helps immensely in effective communication, collaboration, and decision-making among the team. A good facilitator guides the conversation, ensures all voices get heard, and allows the group to discuss complex subjects. Facilitators can increase engagement, creativity, and achievable results by creating an inclusive, structured environment. The facilitator's primary job is to keep the discussion moving while remaining neutral. This involves structuring the agenda, defining rules guiding the debate, and keeping the pace. A facilitator must stimulate involvement with every member to allow quiet persons to express themselves and moderate dominant persons. In balancing participation, the facilitator levels the field so that many more perspectives emerge, leading to richer discussions.

At the outset, every group discussion needs to establish ground rules to help team members interact respectfully and constructively. These would certainly consist of standards of energetic listening, such as not disrupting others and being thoughtful. A guideline might specify the degree of privacy needed so participants feel guaranteed concerning sharing without effects. In doing this, the facilitator produces such standards with involvement from the team, possession, and duty from individuals, which are the type to make the conversation a lot more efficient. One of the most crucial abilities of a facilitator in team conversations is promoting engagement among all team participants.

Conciliators can use numerous strategies throughout a conference to generate actions consisting of flexible concerns that urge more representation and exploration. Rather than asking, " Do you settle with this suggestion? "a mediator could ask," What are your ideas on the feasible problems of this technique? " Such inquiries require fuller reactions and allow each to make a distinctive payment.

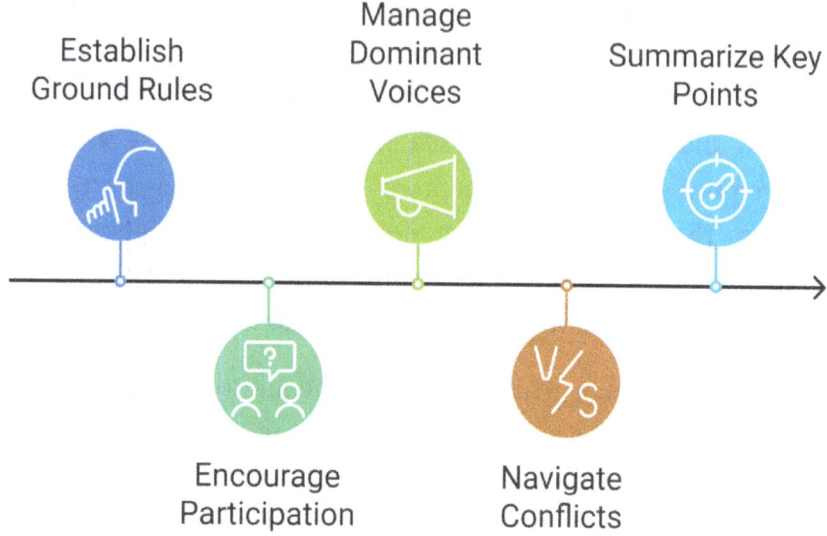

Figure 4.9 Facilitating Effective Group Discussions.

Additionally, the round-robin sharing strategy will certainly allow each individual to contribute. The facilitators can use small conversations or breakout sessions to facilitate small, intimate conversations that reconvene into a huge team. This might help individuals feel much more comfortable sharing their ideas, producing a vibrant and appealing discussion. With any team conversation, there is bound to be some dispute or distinction of point of view.

The art of promoting exists in how constructively the neck and neck are taken care of. Distinctions of viewpoint ought to be recognized differently, along with conversation that is helpful. The facilitator can assist in reframing the problem right into a chance for expedition and understanding by motivating individuals to ponder other individuals' understandings. Summarizing the bottom lines plus looking for commonalities helps to de-escalate stress and keep the discussion efficient. Throughout closure, the mediator must summarize the increased bottom lines, choices, and activities determined throughout the conversation.

This assists in enhancing the conversation's results and ensures that the individuals leave with an understanding of their actions. Requesting comments relating to the conversation procedure makes it possible for facilitators to discover future campaigns. The mediator embraces a favorable environment, motivating recurring interaction by thanking individuals for their payments and recognizing their initiatives.

Assisting team conversations is important for better group interaction and cooperation. By establishing guidelines, motivating engagement, handling disputes, and efficiently shutting conversations, the mediator can guarantee a vibrant atmosphere within which important discussion and decision-making occur. Eventually, proficient assistance leads to much better group partnerships and increased success. Therefore, efficient assistance goes to the heart of the team effort.

4.5.1 Leveraging Technology for Communication

Along with the boosting rate in today's world, modern technology has become necessary for everyone or for companies to connect with others. New electronic ways of interaction have brought about a large change in how people attach, communicate, and interact with others. On the great use of such innovations, support towards interaction effectiveness, partnership, bridging geographical voids, and renovation in connections coupled with performance will certainly be attained. Innovation has substantially streamlined interaction procedures.

Email, immediate messaging, and video clip conferencing facilitate fast information exchange and allow one to overtake coworkers, customers, and companions despite the distance. Think about Slack or Microsoft Teams, where real-time messaging and document sharing are sustained, enabling rapid responses as opposed to hold-ups that may be anticipated from even more traditional interaction methods. These devices allow arranged discussions with networks and strings to track conversations and discover appropriate details quickly.

Besides, organizing devices like Calendly or Doodle make it much easier to arrange conferences without all the boomerang and onward movement that typically comes with locating a time that fits all parties concerned. Incorporating these modern technologies into the day-to-day process frees up the person's time to concentrate on his core jobs, therefore raising general performance.

One more location where modern technology plays a vital function remains in cooperation. Cloud-based collaboration with platforms such as Google Workspace and Microsoft 365 can allow several users located in different geographical parts of the world to collaborate on the same document, spreadsheet, or presentation. Such real-time collaboration increases workflow efficiency and promotes team spirit because the members can provide their ideas and feedback more quickly.

Project management tools like Trello, Asana, and Monday.com organize teams' tasks, deadlines, and responsibilities management. These platforms also increase transparency and accountability in team performance, as team members can see one another's progress and contributions. Such collaborative technologies will help organizations create a well-rounded and active workforce.

One of the most significant advantages of technology in communication is that it bridges the gap between geographical locations. Nowadays, groups are typically created by individuals from various areas and time areas. Many thanks to video clip conferencing devices like Zoom coupled with Microsoft Teams face-to-face conferences aid in maintaining individual discussion group interactions. Doing this properly is essential in structuring partnerships and obtaining depend amongst the staff members, which leads to boosted partnership and, hence, group characteristics.

Additionally, social media sites and specialist networking websites such as LinkedIn have made it easier for individuals throughout boundaries to connect with others and trade concepts, suggestions, or business possibilities. Such systems permit experts to expand their networks and expose themselves to varied viewpoints, improving their understanding and urging technology.

While innovation provides many advantages for interaction, it also creates obstacles that should be addressed. Info overload can happen when people are pestered with messages throughout numerous systems, resulting in improved quality and performance. To alleviate this, companies must develop clear interaction standards that specify which devices to use for certain functions and how to take care of notices efficiently. Moreover, dependency on innovation burglarizes individual calls, a vital component in a partnership structure. Where feasible, a correct equilibrium between electronic and face-to-face interactions is essential for undamaged connections.

At the same time, innovation has made interaction vital in modern-day culture. Technology helps people and organizations communicate more effectively through efficiency, cooperation, and bridging distances. However, I should be aware of the challenges of digital communication. Setting proper rules and balancing technology and personal interaction will help leverage technology for better communication and improved relationships in personal and professional contexts.

4.6 Case Study: Mastering Communication

In today's fast-moving and, at times, polarized world, courageous conversations are about creating an environment where challenging topics can be discussed, tough feedback given, and diverse opinions shared constructively. A popular model that comes to your aid in this context is "Radical Candor" by Kim Scott. Companies like Dropbox have this technique working for them, leading to transparency, accountability, and trust-flowing relationships, with some key results: stronger relationships and higher team output.

The philosophy of Radical Candor relies on two fundamental values: caring personally and challenging directly. It stresses the value of genuinely respecting coworkers while being able to inform them of the truth. Scott splits the method of interaction into four quadrants: Radical Candor, Ruthless Empathy, Manipulative Insincerity, and Obnoxious Aggression. When individuals express their minds plainly and straight yet reveal a real concern for the receiver's welfare, this scenario shows Radical Candor.

The objective of Radical Candor is not simply to give comments but to open a room where the group feels risk-free in sharing their suggestions and problems. This triggers a society where individuals are welcome to promote and test the standard and also expand with each other. When a company masters this interaction design, these obstacles damage and supply space for a more comprehensive and interesting labor force.

Specific skills must be honed for people to have courageous conversations effectively. Chief among these is active listening. This means giving all attention to discussions, acknowledging the contribution of others, and responding appropriately. When participants feel heard, they open themselves more readily to genuine dialogue.

In addition to this, giving effective feedback is clear and specific. People must be straightforward with the behavior or issue instead of being general or soft in one's critiques. For instance, other than saying, "You need to improve," it would be more pragmatic to say, "In the last project presentation, I noticed your key data was missing, and our credibility suffered because of this fact." Such clarity makes the receiver understand the issue and builds an accountable atmosphere.

Empathy is crucial in brave conversations. Honesty must be coupled with compassion, and feedback must be given to value the recipient's feelings. People open themselves up to safe dialogues if they are approached with empathy regarding difficult discussions. In other words, one takes cognizance of emotional clues and adopts an appropriate conversation style concerning the situation and the person concerned.

Second, leaders can model courageous conversations by showing their vulnerability: sharing their challenges and inviting feedback from others empowers team members to share their own. Openness like this strengthens relationships and reminds everyone that they are all in this together, learning from and improving continuously.

Engaging in courageous conversations can be daunting because individuals always fear conflict or backlash. The organization should lead the way in encouraging a culture of openness and growth to break this resistance down. Good, regular communication sessions with training on how to resolve a conflict will help team members navigate challenging discussions. Scheduling time for casual check-ins will also help normalize open dialogue. When team members share experiences and challenges routinely, tough conversations become more accessible when needed.

Courageous conversation is an essential component of acquiring communication skills at a personal and professional level. Persons and organizations can facilitate openness, trust, and accountability by utilizing such models as Radical Candor. Emphasize active listening, empathy, and feedback clearly, and team members can conduct meaningful dialogues, relate better, and collaborate more. In this present time, where effective communication has become even more important, the art of courageous conversations needs to be absorbed into personal growth and organizational success.

4.7 Key Point Donald Trump's potential re-election in 2024

> **Populist Appeal:** He continues to position himself as a champion of the working class, appealing to voters disillusioned with traditional politics.

As the presidential election of 2024 nears, populist appeal seems increasingly to be one of the key components of Donald Trump's likely reelection bid. Over time, he has adopted a position as the protector of the working class that profoundly appeals to voters who feel disillusioned by more traditional political establishments. It is populist; it's central to his campaign strategy along many dimensions because it appeals to the concerns and frustrations of several demographic groups, especially those who feel their voices have gone unheard.

Trump's campaign messaging was one of proximity to the working class: he was an outsider, sympathetic to the plight of ordinary Americans. He has continuously stressed work styles and wages, rising with the financial possibilities of Blue-Collar America versus what he calls pretentious Washington political leaders. This story resounds with citizens who feel excluded by globalization and technical adjustment, which, at times, has cleaned away tasks in standard markets.

> **Create a Sense of Urgency**
> Frame issues in a way that encourages immediate action from supporters.
>
> **Use Controversy Strategically**
> Embrace controversy to keep the conversation focused on you.

This market emphasis highlights an inbuilt disappointment with the present state of events. His base commonly watches Trump as a leader who has been and will continue to test developed standards and support plans prioritizing American employees. Populist unsupported claims do reward in galvanizing a faithful base that feels encouraged by his message of financial nationalism and security. In this context, the aspect of expanding disappointment with conventional political numbers would be significant.

Standard political leaders must be in contact with their facts within the country plus working-class areas of the nation. Trump's outsider condition plus readiness to interfere with recognized political standards make his re-election prospects enticing amongst these people who need adjustment. His method is a substantial discrepancy from the several Democratic and Republican prospects, possibly with even more typical designs that stop working to attract today's vote and hunger for a much more connected-to-the-people leader.

Furthermore, Trump's dependence on social media sites and direct networks allows him to bypass the conventional media filter and reach his fans directly. This method corresponds to his outsider approach and constructs a feeling of area amongst his bases. Several values his honesty in addressing questionable concerns and have combined this with his allure as a leader who does not wait to test political accuracy.

Trump reinforces these words with actual concentration on real issues that matter to his base: immigration, trade, and law and order policies remain at the center of his campaign appeal. With promises of maintaining tight immigration policy and American manufacturing, he appeals to voters susceptible to job security and national sovereignty. These and his tough-on-crime and public-safety platform provide quite an appealing platform to those anxious about societal changes.

What adds to his populist appeal is that Trump can frame his opponents as members of the political establishment. By portraying Democratic candidates as representatives of a system that has failed ordinary Americans, he positions himself effectively as a champion of the people, ready to fight for their interests against an allegedly corrupt elite.

Donald Trump is preparing for his possible re-election in 2024, and the mainstay of his campaign strategy is populist appeal. He stands for the working class and tries to resolve the problems of those citizens who feel disappointed so that they support him in an election struggle and indecisive electors' dream of change. In this polarized political environment, dissatisfaction with traditional politicians and the ability to connect with ordinary

Americans may play the most fateful role in the process that awaits Trump's campaign. It remains to be seen whether this will be enough for his re-election, but his emphasis on populism no doubt helps shape the narrative of the upcoming election.

Reference

1. Singleton, G. E. (2014). Courageous conversations about race: A field guide for achieving equity in schools. Corwin Press.

2. McCoy, L. P., & Thein, A. H. (2021). Navigating courageous conversations: A guide for educators. Teachers College Press.

3. Scott, K. (2017). Radical honesty: Be a kick-ass boss without losing your humanity. St. Martin's Press.

4. Stone, D., Patton, B., & Heen, S. (2010). Crucial conversations: Tools for talking when stakes are high. McGraw-Hill.

5. Gorski, P. C. (2019). Brave spaces: A new way to talk about race. Stylus Publishing.

6. Brown, B. (2018). Dare to Lead: Brave Work. Tough conversations. Whole hearts. Random House.

7. Brown, B. (2015). The power of vulnerability: Teachings of authenticity, connection, and courage. Sounds True.

8. VitalSmarts. (2019). The importance of active listening in difficult conversations. Retrieved from https://www.vitalsmarts.com

9. Kahn, W. A., & Byers, A. (2020). The art of difficult conversations: How to engage in tough discussions. Harvard Business Review.

CHAPTER 5

Leading by Example: The Power of Authentic Leadership

Introduction

With increasing complexity and speed of change, the call for authentic leaders has never been louder. Chapter 5 discusses the transformative power of authentic leaders in organizations and society. Authentic leadership arises from honesty, integrity, and self-awareness, which form the foundation whereby leaders command trust and loyalty from their followers. This chapter will examine how leaders possessing such qualities adopt a positive work environment and drive meaningful change and innovation.

In other words, authentic leadership can be defined as an approach in which a leader is true to oneself and related to values, beliefs, and actions [1-4]. It varies from the traditional ways of being authoritative or leading through charisma, mainly focusing on establishing genuine relations with team members [5-7]. They actively build an atmosphere where individuals feel valued, heard, and empowered to contribute to the common cause. This chapter looks at the defining characteristics of the authentic leader, such as vulnerability, humility, and emotional intelligence, and how these traits provide the foundation necessary to activate effective leadership.

The chapter also points out the importance of leading by example. An authentic leader realizes that actions will always speak louder than words. Through the behaviors and values they model to others, leaders facilitate a culture of accountability and commitment [8-10]. This section, therefore, tries to bring to light some practical examples of leaders who have displayed authenticity in their leadership practices, which has greatly boosted employee engagement, morale, and organizational performance [11-13].

This chapter, therefore, intends to discuss the advantages of authentic leadership and also touches on challenges leaders face in the tough art of maintaining authenticity in high-pressure situations. It considers the tension between being true to oneself and becoming socialized by the organization's and its stakeholders' needs [14]. An authentic leader navigating these could retain resilience and inspire others around him.

Overall, "Leading by Example: The Power of Authentic Leadership" persuasively reminds one that effective leadership is not about the results but building trust and a sense of belonging among team members. In their effort and struggle to flourish within the fast-changing competitive environment, organizations will find the principles of authentic leadership serving as strategic roadmaps for creating a culture characterized by transparency, collaboration, and shared purpose. The chapter invites the readers to contemplate their leadership practices and how they might embrace authenticity to become effective leaders.

5.1 Defining Authentic Leadership

Authentic management is a modern-day partnership principle of leading that includes truthfulness, openness, and principles in leaders. Whereas most timeless and conventional management versions rely on regulating authority plus control, genuine management consists of the leader's "real self" and the demand to establish count on plus top-notch connections with fans. This principle has obtained energy recently, specifically within conversations regarding exactly how companies look to adjust much better to significantly complicated together with vibrant atmospheres. At its core, genuine management is secured by self-awareness.

Genuine leaders deeply recognize their worth, stamina, weak points, and feelings. This self-awareness aids them in leading with stability and clarity, deciding to align with their core ideas. Genuine leaders allow others to do the same by adhering to themselves and fostering an atmosphere of visibility and sincerity within their groups. An additional critical feature of genuine management is relational openness. Genuine leaders guarantee that interaction networks are constantly open and employee responses are welcomed.

They produce an atmosphere where individuals can share without really feeling evaluated. Such openness advances trust funds in partnerships, advertises cooperation, and promotes advancement since individuals, coupled with varied understandings, are valued.

Furthermore, genuine management is started on moral plus ethical premises. Genuine leaders will never leave the best reason when essential options are risky. They take an interest in the best interests of their members and society in general, through which social responsibility is performed. The ethical grounds create trust and loyalty in followers because they understand their leader stands for what is right and fair.

Authentic leaders embrace vulnerability, too. They believe in sharing their experiences, including challenges and failures, which humanize them and help them bond with their team at a deeper level. By showing one's imperfections, authentic leaders can make others feel comfortable enough to share their struggles, thus creating a more caring and resilient environment for the whole team.

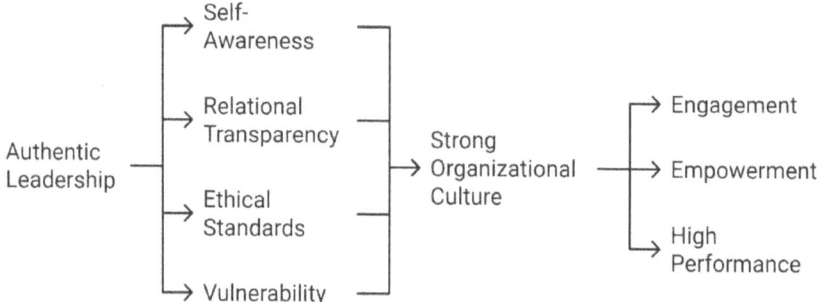

Figure 5.1 Authentic leadership is a contemporary approach to leadership.

Besides adding to that, the effect of authentic leadership spills beyond the individual relationship into developing a profound organizational culture of nurturing high levels of engagement and empowerment, leading to high performance. Leaders who act authentically provide an exemplary role model for conduct, inspiring team members to align their actions with the organization's values. This will probably lead to job satisfaction, morale, and feelings of belonging in the workplace.

5.2 Demonstrating Integrity in Action

Integrity is an essential component of outstanding leadership, and it plays a significant role in building trust within teams and organizations. Putting integrity into practice integrates words with action, makes ethical choices, and then lives morals day in and day out-morals that remain consistent even when times get tough. Leaders with integrity create a culture of accountability, which is the kind of culture in which individuals are free to be themselves and go on to achieve greatness.

The primary ways leaders show integrity involve honesty: communicating the truth, sharing information, or providing constructive feedback. For example, a leader who shares openly about successes and failures is a model for transparency and promotes authenticity among team members. If employees witness their leaders accepting mistakes or acknowledging areas of weakness, they're more apt to be comfortable owing to their challenges. This approach advances a culture where learning and improvement are valued more than blame and fear.

Besides honesty, ethical decision-making is also critical in the manifestation of integrity. Several leaders face moral challenges that place them between what is convenient and suitable. Leaders affirm their integrity through a continuous choice for ethical solutions. The leader who, in every instance, would want to see resources distributed according to the dictates of fairness, even when it is easy to cater to special cases, sets an example before the entire organization. It strengthens trust and builds a reputation for the organization.

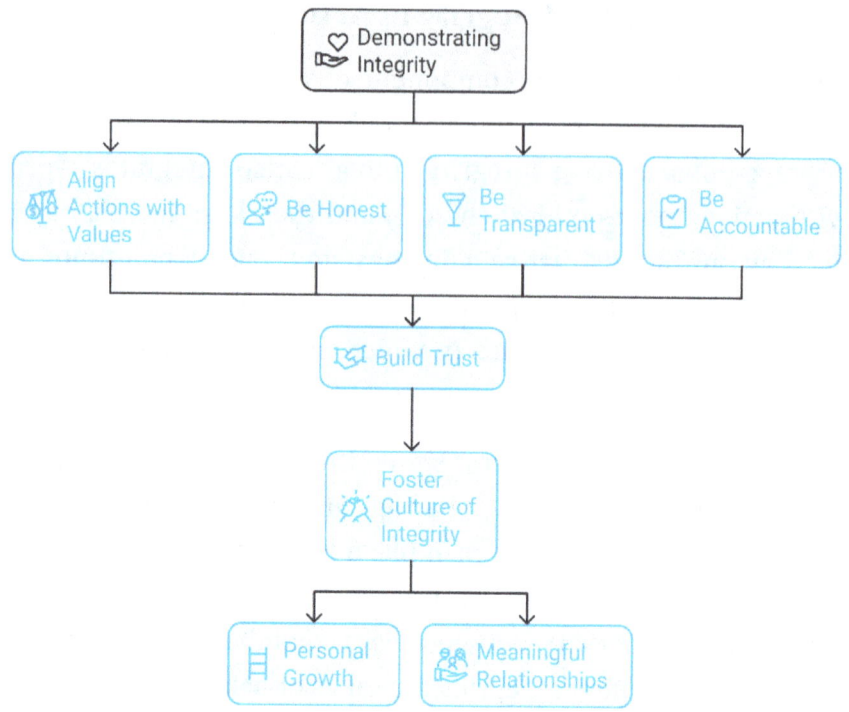

Figure 5.2 Integrity is an essential cornerstone of effective leadership.

Accountability is involved in integrity action. Leaders must be responsible for their actions and choices and those of team members. That will lead to admitting mistakes, taking responsibility for results, and implementing corrective measures when called for. When leaders model accountability, they inspire their teams to follow suit, creating a ripple effect that enhances overall organizational performance. Accountability becomes a collective value when a leader accepts their mistake in a project and collaborates with their team to find solutions.

Demonstrating integrity also involves maintaining confidentiality and members' trust in leaders. When employees share personal insights or sensitive information, the leader should safeguard such information. Protecting confidentiality demonstrates that leaders are concerned about protecting their team members and respect each member's integrity. This helps establish a positive relationship where open and honest communication is used as a foundation; team members feel valued and understood.

Integrity is demonstrated in the consistency of the leader's behavior. A leader with integrity keeps values the same regardless of the audience or situation. Consistency in behavior and decision-making cements credibility and fortifies trust. People are more likely to rally around a leader who demonstrates consistency in their values, which brings cohesion and drive to the team.

5.2.1 Sharing Personal Stories and Experiences

Sharing experiences and stories is a powerful tool in communication and leadership. It builds bonding, develops trust, and promotes empathy between individuals, personally and professionally. By sharing their stories, leaders make themselves human and provide insight into who they are, what motivates them to work, and the challenges they face. It builds relationships and provides an atmosphere for people to share stories.

Sharing personal stories enables one to connect on a deeper emotional level. Stories can transcend barriers and resonate with listeners, allowing them to relate to the speaker's experiences. For example, a leader sharing a difficult project can paint a picture of the fight and struggle involved in achieving success; therefore, the experience is relevant to team members who may have faced or are facing similar challenges. Such a shared understanding builds empathy and reinforces the knowledge that 'everyone has problems,' rendering support.

Figure 5.4 Sharing personal stories and experiences.

Besides, personal stories can be life-enhancing teaching tools. They put things into perspective with real-life examples, enhancing understanding and retention. When the leader shares his experience, he may illustrate essential lessons and insights not easily expressed in abstract concepts. For instance, a leader talking about some failure he has experienced might point out what went wrong and what was learned, turning these insights into useful insights to guide the audience's decision-making. This storytelling approach makes the message more engaging and instills a sense of resilience and adaptability among team members.

Besides, sharing personal experiences will help to provide authenticity in leadership. The more leaders share about their processes, triumphs, and setbacks, the more trust is built into them. Workers are bound to relate more to a leader with vulnerability and openness. All this will create an environment where all members feel safe expressing their thoughts and emotions, boosting collaboration and innovation. If workers feel they make a rewarding payment, they will feel completely associated with their tasks.

Another favorable impact of sharing individual tales is the chance to motivate and inspire others. Leaders who share their trips can inspire their groups by revealing how difficulties can be eliminated and describing how feasible individual development is. For example, a leader who has browsed considerable life difficulties might motivate others dealing with such troubles to stand firm and locate remedies. This motivational element of narration can develop a feeling of function in a specific person, allowing him to have difficulty achieving his objectives and welcome the obstacles as opportunities for development.

Lastly, sharing individual experiences can construct group communication. Sharing one's tale amongst participants will bring a sensation of coming from plus add-on. This method might damage silos and also urge partnership since people come to be much more purchased each various other's success. Groups comprehending each other's histories and experiences are much better outfitted to function sympathetically, boosting interaction and partnership.

5.2.2 Admitting Mistakes and Learning

Owning up to one's blunders aids in individual and specialist growth. In the modern-day world, which is significantly pressured to be successful, confessing mistakes has become hard. Nonetheless, accepting blunders is vital to installing a finding out society and a resistant one. When leaders and people honestly confess their blunders, they assist in positive discussion and development in themselves and the individuals around them.

Admission of blunders ensures self-contemplation coupled with knowledge. Now, one can recognize what failed and why it did, and it would certainly be credited to the specific elements that triggered the blunder. This process of reflection enhances self-awareness and equips individuals with the insights needed to avoid similar pitfalls in the future. For instance, a manager who recognizes that having mismanaged a particular project can deconstruct the decision-making process for important lessons to help drive future strategies effectively.

Besides, allowing oneself to show mistakes will create a transparent and trusting team and organization. When leaders model this vulnerability by admitting mistakes, their team members can feel safe enough to recognize them. Openness invites sharing thoughts and ideas for doing something different that is needed for psychological safety. In such an environment, team members are more likely to take risks, innovate, and collaborate by understanding that through mistakes, growth opportunities arise rather than failures that need punishment.

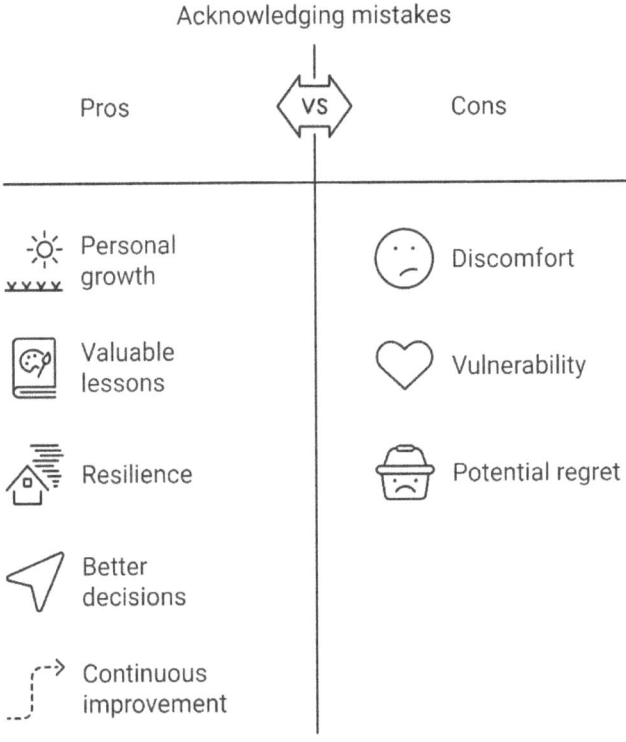

Figure 5.4 Comparison admitting mistakes is crucial to personal and professional growth.

Besides, acknowledgment of committed mistakes can strengthen relationships. By admitting mistakes, the leaders humanize themselves and become closer to their teams. Subordinates appreciate honesty and authenticity, which eventually can raise their loyalty and commitment. For instance, if the CEO shares frankly about some strategic mistake and the aftermath consequences for the company, he builds trust with the employees by showing that to lead does not mean to be perfect, but to be responsible and to learn from one's mistakes. This helps build a unified bond of unity and belonging where team members are connected by reflecting on past experiences.

Learning from errors also affords a proactive approach toward problem-solving. Rather than sitting on failures, individuals and teams could focus on developing solutions and strategies to get better. This shift in overview transforms the obstacles into possibilities for discovery in the spirit of durability and flexibility. Think about a sales group that tries to break down a failed project and promptly see what fell short to reverberate with consumers, coupled with educating a different strategy for future efforts. Where the blunders are considered tipping rocks instead of stumbling blocks, companies are far better off developing a society of constant renovation.

In addition, approving dedicated mistakes functions as a procedure of understanding, which assists in enhancing companies. Companies welcoming a discovering society advertise technology and adjust to an ever-changing atmosphere. Sharing experiences and lessons picked up by staff members develops a usual shop of expertise and experience that can profit companies. This would certainly not just enhance private efficiency but likewise drive business success.

Blunders need to be acknowledged and discovered for individual and professional advancement. Through introspection, exposure, and relationship-building, individuals can transform mistakes into favorable understanding.

Additionally, companies can build cooperation, development, and durability by developing a society where errors are commemorated as possibilities for development. A non-aversion to identifying and learning from mistakes symbolizes reliable management and is important to a healthy and balanced office makeup. The technique assists in enhancing people and enables cumulative success and progression.

5.3 Encouraging Transparency and Openness

Transparency and visibility are essential to constructing trust fund collective connections and development in companies today. For a company to be clear, it needs to be open to choices and procedures coupled with info; to be open, the ambiance should be secure for sharing concepts, problems, and comments. These concepts develop the foundation of reliable communication and genuine interaction, resulting in an extra vibrant and resistant business society.

One of the most vital advantages of openness is that it constructs rely on the group. If the management shares info honestly around, for instance, business objectives, obstacles, or decision-making procedures, they feel answerable and a component of something. Workers can trust leaders even further when they know honesty is shared within each line of communication, the loop, and their contributions and work matter. This will form a fundamental basis for relationships in teams where trust will advance cooperation and lessen the chances of friction.

Moreover, transparency encourages employee engagement. When team members understand why certain decisions are made and feel well-informed about the general direction the organization is taking, they will be more invested in their work. Generally, the more engaged employees tend to be the more motivated, productive, and committed to organizational success. This means that organizations that keep their workforce informed about progress in key strategic goals may inspire employees to actively contribute to achieving those goals because they feel their contributions are part of a broader context.

Encouraging openness in the workplace also allows psychological safety to flourish. When people feel safe speaking, sharing, and conversing about challenges without risk of criticism or persecution, they are even more creative. This atmosphere allows divergent perspectives to emerge, leading to more innovative solutions and superior problem resolution. Such a situation would involve team brainstorming regularly, where all ideas are valued, promoting ownership and inclusiveness, which, in turn, drives better results.

Further, transparency and openness form the essence of any workable feedback mechanism. Wherever the leaders instill open interaction, it creates more drive among the team members to give constructive feedback, which is a path to continuous improvement. Creating a feedback loop allows each organization to learn from the real-time insights of people closest to the work and make changes to processes, products, and services. A society that values comments as a development device ensures responsibility along with assistance in establishing people and groups.

Second, openness in decision-making procedures lowers problems and enhances partnership. When all staff members recognize which procedure choices are made, the likelihood that they will certainly feel prevented or omitted is minimized. Open interaction concerning decision-making standards develops an assumption of justice and equity in the group. This practice is most critical when change or uncertainty is experienced, as transparency will reduce anxiety and resistance to change, allowing transitions to occur more smoothly.

Finally, organizations with a reputation for transparency and openness find themselves as potential and attractive employers in the competitive labor market. Many staff members expect to discover an atmosphere where they can share an open society based on stability and honest habits. An online reputation for business openness interests the most effective skills that share such worth and bring about an extra connected and fully committed labor force.

5.3.1 Upholding Ethical Standards

Promoting moral criteria is fundamental in private and business degrees. Values overview activities and choices that will certainly be profoundly valuable in the here and now, extremely active and adjoined globe. Ethical standards guide people's actions with integrity, equity, and respect for others. Ethics within an organization inspire trust and enable the firm to have a good culture and reputation in the marketplace.

Commitment to integrity means honesty and transparency in all dealings, including customers, employees, or stakeholders. Leaders who lead by example in integrity signal to the teams that ethical conduct is not just compliance but a part of the values system. When employees see their leaders applying ethics in practice, even in difficult situations, they will likely take similar behaviors. This develops a society where honest decision-making ends up being the order of business, and even more responsibility plus depend on can happen.

Additionally, moral requirements can be kept if the company's worth and concepts are well understood. A company's audio code of principles overviews staff members concerning appropriate actions and decision-making treatments. The code should specify the staff members' assumptions and offer instances of dealing with a moral problem that might develop in the office. Educating and continuous conversations concerning principles and specifications instill values, guaranteeing that all workers remain in sync with the company's objective and vision.

An additional essential facet of maintaining values is infusing duty with a society of responsibility. The company must offer an atmosphere where staff members can talk and articulate their worries concerning activities or methods they might find dishonest. Hotlines or idea boxes could provide anonymous reporting devices. It develops a society of sincerity and visibility, boosting trust among individuals who can report dishonest habits without revenge. This enhances the honest structure of the company.

Companies must also understand that meeting moral requirements goes beyond plain adherence to regulation. Regulation must be complied with; however, moral conduct calls for doing more than the minimum. This requires representation of choices that affect workers, clients, the area, and the atmosphere. For example, businesses that participate in company social duty show respect for moral criteria by taking the campaign to progress societal excellence and ecological sustainability.

Moral management is additionally an essential facet of preserving high standards. Leaders who focus on principles in decision-making and communication produce an environment where moral habits grow. They need to promote the significance of principles, exercise values themselves, and highlight that long-lasting success relies on the sustainability of honesty in the company. Acknowledging and compensating them for being moral additionally mounts this dedication to urge others to act according to the values established by the company.

5.3.2 Promoting Consistency in Behavior

Advertising uniformity in habits is vital to being an excellent leader and making certain businesses successful. Uniformity constructs trust funds to boost interaction and provide security in which individuals feel safe and can run at their finest. Where there is uniformity in the habits of management and company assumptions are established as standards for activities and choices that can generate a unified and efficient society within the work environment.

The key to promoting consistency is the congruence between words and actions. It behaves in ways consistent with what has been said and articulated regarding values and principles. In promoting a vision or set of values and doing nothing to act in concert, leaders immediately violate their credibility and break trust among team members. For instance, if a leader preaches teamwork but consistently minimizes collaborative work because the leaders consistently reward individual contributors, mixed messages get communicated, and one of several actions could occur: confusion or disengagement. This way, the leaders keep showing their values through behavior and set the standard by which others will review their achievements.

Consistency of one's actions facilitates communication within teams. When leaders consistently communicate expectations and give feedback on performance, the team members have great clarity about their responsibilities and requirements. This reduces ambiguity in their roles and helps them align with the organizational goals. This regular check-in or transparency in communicating performance expectations creates a supportive environment where team members are more likely to feel supported and meet or even exceed expectations. Consistent communication also creates a feeling of belonging because one knows what should be done and how it should be done according to the institution's norms and culture.

Another positive side of encouraging consistency is that it builds an organizational culture of stability. Behaviors and practices, if consistently reproduced, behaviors and practices create predictability, which can be appealing in a frantic and uncertain world. When employees know what to expect from their bosses and colleagues, they are more likely to feel secure and confident in their contribution. That stability can engender job satisfaction and lower turnover rates, as employees are more likely to stay where they are wanted and understood.

Besides, consistency in behavior allows for accountability through the organization's levels. Leaders who design constant habits anticipate the very same from others. Additionally, this responsibility is embedded in staff members' minds when they see their peers hang on to the same criterion. A society of liability suggests high efficiency and instills possession within individuals given that they recognize their payments matter, which they belong to something more significant.

Furthermore, motivating uniformity might enhance decision-making procedures. Leaders who deal with the same requirements and concepts when deciding to improve justice and equal rights. Choices made by leaders whose technique is considered regular are relied on by workers, which can reveal that choices were made based upon well-known standards, not individual inclinations or approximate judgments. Such uniformity increases spirits and enhances dedication to business objectives.

5.4 Inspiring Others Through Passion and Commitment

Motivating others with interest and also dedication is a vital element of management. Hence, leaders who show a genuine love for their work and a solid dedication to their reason develop an environment that influences and stimulates others. This transmittable power will certainly impact the group's characteristics, establishing an atmosphere of quality for all involved.

The inspiration of others flows from deep within a leader through their ability to communicate vision clearly and conventionally. Passionate leaders articulate their vision and goals in ways that will surely resonate with the teams. This emotional connection helps individuals visualize the bigger picture, understanding how their efforts will go toward creating organizational success. Suppose one likes to narrate the story behind any particular project or initiative passionately. In that case, he can light a spark in the team members' minds, who then put in a lot of energy and imagination. And people tend to give more when they feel their work connects them to something larger than themselves.

Besides, commitment is an important factor in motivating others. For instance, an excellent example of being committed as a leader is working hard, putting in extra hours, and sacrificing oneself for others. Such unwavering commitment by the leader sends the right signals to employees that their effort has been recognized and the company deserves their dedication, too. For instance, committed leader faces obstacles and see their people through hardships; they are committed and loyal. Employees are inspired to mirror this commitment, cultivating a strong work ethic and shared purpose.

Table 5.1 Summarizes the key aspects of inspiring others through passion and commitment.

Aspect	Description	Impact
Clear Vision	Leaders communicate their goals with clarity and conviction.	Leaders communicate their goals with clarity and conviction.

Demonstrated Commitment	Consistent dedication through hard work and support during challenges.	Builds trust and loyalty, encouraging a strong work ethic.
Recognition of Achievements	Acknowledging both big and small successes publicly.	Advances a culture of appreciation, motivating continued effort.
Encouragement of Innovation	Creating a safe space for brainstorming and idea-sharing.	Inspires creativity and risk-taking, leading to innovative solutions.
Authentic Storytelling	Sharing personal experiences and struggles to connect with team members.	Enhances relatability and trust, motivating others to pursue their passions.
Building a Supportive Culture	Adopting an environment where team members feel valued and empowered.	Increases engagement and commitment to organizational goals.
Empowerment	Encouraging team members to take ownership of their roles and contribute ideas.	Cultivates initiative and responsibility within the team.
Emotional Connection	Connecting the team's work to a larger purpose or mission.	Strengthens commitment and enhances job satisfaction.

Inspiring others also means celebrating achievements-large and small. Suppose the leaders appreciate their team's hard work, instilling a culture of recognition within them to strive for excellence. Celebrating milestones recognizes the team's efforts and keeps the fire inside them burning for future projects. For instance, a manager who goes out of his way to highlight the achievements of a team in meetings or publicly creates pride and camaraderie. Such practice makes the people interested and committed because they know their contributions count.

Besides, passion and commitment may drive innovative and creative initiative within teams when leaders create scope for experimentation and the generation of new ideas. It inspires people to think out of the box and take risks. The passionate leader provides a safeguarded environment for brainstorming and collaboration where team members feel free to share their ideas. This openness can lead to groundbreaking solutions and improvements as employees feel empowered to contribute their unique perspectives. When a leader is excited about innovation, the culture breeds creativity, and people become more concerned with the organization's future.

Furthermore, passionate and dedicated leaders often relate personal stories and experiences to which team members can easily relate. By being vulnerable and authentic, they connect with others beyond professional lines. This can make one more relatable as people work for and with someone they trust and are loyal to-not because one is a figure of authority but also because one genuinely cares about the employee's well-being and success. It demonstrates that when leaders begin to share their journeys with ups and downs, they open up for them, too, to follow their passions and commitments.

5.4.1 Building Credibility with Your Team

Building credibility within your team is critically connected to better leadership, creating a culture of trust, collaboration, and high performance. Credibility is the foundation of strong relationships, which affects how team members consider their leader's decisions, guidance, and intentions. Since leaders have built up credibility, they have allowed their teams to give their all in their roles, which enhances productivity and improves organizational success.

Preceding all of this is the issue of consistency both in words and actions. Leaders should behave in a way consistent with their values and commitments. Whenever leaders promise something, they should deliver. For example, if leaders pledge to give feedback or support regularly, they must ensure that it happens consistently. This dependability gives the team members confidence in their leaders, knowing they are reliable and committed to their growth. On the other hand, unpredictable behavior establishes suspicions that weaken the position of the leader such that it becomes difficult for team members to have confidence in the leader's decision-making. Another essential ingredient of credibility involves transparency. Clear information about happenings, actions, and decisions from the leaders creates transparency that allows for a supportive environment. Leaders enable team members to participate in decision-making by being transparent about specific actions' challenges, successes, and reasonability. This adopts ownership and belonging among employees, who invest in their work and the organization's goals. For instance, if the leader discusses the problems with the team and asks for their input on solving them, it shows respect for what they have to say and credibility as a collaborative leader.

Competency is another critical ingredient in gaining credibility. Leaders should demonstrate competency and proficiency in guiding teams. That does not mean leaders must be knowledgeable in all things, but at least in the related aspects concerning their team's area of work. Leaders who address challenges with informed solutions and valuable insights enhance their credibility. Apart from that, a leader who can say that he doesn't know everything and seeks assistance or expert opinion has humility and a commitment to lifelong learning, which furthers his credibility.

Another essential ingredient in enacting credibility is active listening. When leaders take the time to listen to their team members, their concerns, ideas, and responses, that means they consider them. This approach makes leaders better understand their team and builds a culture of openness. Regular one-on-ones or team check-ins are great ways to check in with the team members, understand their issues, and let them know that leaders care about their success. When employees feel heard, they're more likely to give respect to and build trust with their leader.

The other thing is building credibility, which will be paramount as the team members' contributions are acknowledged and valued. When leaders ensure accountability by celebrating the achievement of individuals and teams, such actions reinforce appreciation among members within the institution for further performance. Such acknowledgment should be insignificant; a word of many thanks throughout conferences or scrawling success notes down in group interactions can do a lot. When leaders continuously commemorate their groups' initiatives, they are worth success, building on their reliability.

5.4.2 Balancing Authority and Approachability

Unproductive management preserves authority while being friendly and ready for a favorable, effective job atmosphere;

leaders need to regulate regard and job self-confidence in their task functions yet continue to be obtainable and relatable to their staff members. If done right, leaders will certainly construct dependability and commitment and, because of this, enhance group efficiency and business success.

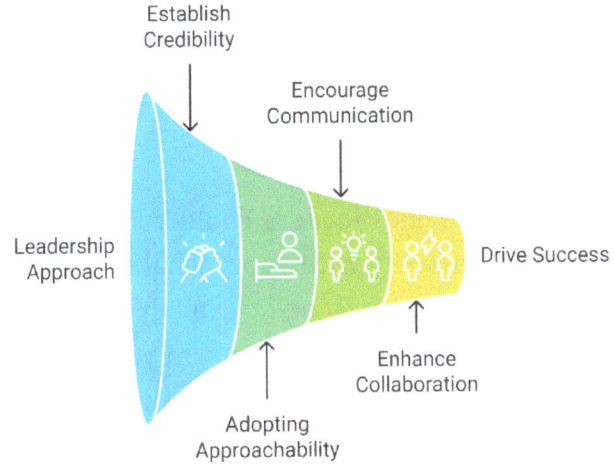

Figure 5.5 Balancing Authority and Approachability.

The authority facet of management can be released by providing instructions for deciding and establishing responsibility. Leaders are therefore anticipated to establish objectives, specify duties and also make certain that the group observes the criteria together with plans set. Regarding the workout of authority, an excellent leader must show experience and make decisions on issues that refer to business purposes plus well-specified tasks. There is something more vital: when leaders connect vision and assumptions with confidence, they construct complacency and clearness in their groups, something rather important if they function cohesively.

Authority needs to be more of a method that is heavy on authority, which produces a society of concern and disengagement in which team members are daunted to share suggestions or worries. This is where approachability comes in. The approachable leader lets team members feel comfortable sharing their thoughts, questions, and feedback. Approachability ensures open communication, which is crucial for collaboration and innovation. Employees who believe they can talk freely without any aftershocks will most likely give valuable insights and be more engaged.

Here are several strategies leaders could consider in balancing their command of authority with approachability. They will need to practice being supportive by being available for the team. This means being available and reaching out to your team members. Regular check-ins, open-door policies, and informal interactions will help break down barriers and get people talking. The fact that the leaders take the time to connect with their team personally underscores that they value the contribution and welfare of the latter, which, in turn, enhances trust and approachability.

Great leaders also know the art of listening actively. When leaders listen to the concerns and ideas of each team member, they make them feel that their insight is valued. This helps them make decisions and justifies their approachability, too. Thus, it allows employees to feel more secure under their leader's authority and to work with motivation toward one common goal.

Transparency in decision-making is another way of balancing authority and approachability in leadership. Leaders who explain why things are done a certain way help the team members understand the greater good. Openness breakthroughs are important because the group recognizes that the leader is worth the group's input rather than simply complying with orders. Workers who recognize why points are made are far more likely to sustain choices instead of doing what they are being informed about, and subsequently, this boosts the leader's authority. It is additionally important for leaders to design humbleness. Admitting errors coupled with the level of sensitivity drastically opens up opportunities for approachability. Revealing that leaders are not the best and that they can learn from what happens sets an environment of constant improvement amongst peers. This modesty makes employees comfortable discussing their concepts or issues because they comprehend the leader's point of view and that he will certainly not evaluate them.

Leading efficiently entails using an equilibrium between authority and approachability. Proficiency and decision-making, visibility to interaction, and an affable nature guarantee leaders the development of a favorable and effective workplace. Such an equilibrium depends on a teamwork initiative and encourages team members to reveal their complete participation in their jobs. In this respect, leaders will be far better placed to guide their groups toward success by developing a society of regard and technology.

5.5 Mentoring Future Leaders

It attracts present leaders, as well as companies preferring proceeded development as well as technology. Significant individual coaching establishes abilities, self-confidence, and an ability pipe that will drive a company's objective. Spending time, as well as sources via the mentoring connection, equip skilled leaders to, even more, encourage the future generation with a society of continual understanding plus management advancement. Mentoring issues are leading and sustaining experts throughout their trips.

That implies developing solid partnerships based upon counting on where advisors share understanding, experiences, and understanding. Their function is to encourage the mentees to take the campaign seriously and create management designs. A great consultant pays attention to mentees, attempts to comprehend their desires, and assists with dressmakers according to private demands. This tailored technique aids mentees in browsing obstacles and taking possibilities, inevitably constructing their self-confidence and proficiency. Some vital benefits of mentoring future leaders focus on understanding and ability transfer.

The advisor might provide an understanding of the sector, business methods, and management techniques that barely pick up from official education and learning or training. Such real-life experiences and discovery conversations simultaneously prepare the consultants to furnish the mentee with hands-on abilities, making them much better decision-makers and trouble solvers. The advantage of this understanding transfer is that it helps the mentees. Additionally, it enhances the company since a skillful labor force efficiently fights obstacles and creates originalities.

Additionally, mentoring develops a sense of belonging and involvement with the organization. When leaders take time to invest in the development of future leaders, the organization values talent development. Talent development demonstrates a commitment that can contribute to employees' higher morale and longer retention. Mentoring relationships establish networks of support in which mentees can learn about and connect with other professionals across the organization for varied perspectives. This collaborative environment enhances knowledge sharing and develops a culture of teamwork, which contributes to a more coherent organizational culture.

The added benefit of mentoring future leaders is identifying and developing high-potential talent. In mentorship, leaders can identify those who are very promising depending on their qualities as potential leaders and willingness to learn. This early identification would enable the organizations to invest in the focused development of such people through training programs, leadership positions, or special projects. Such training would provide a steady supply of qualified leaders who could take up key positions whenever necessary.

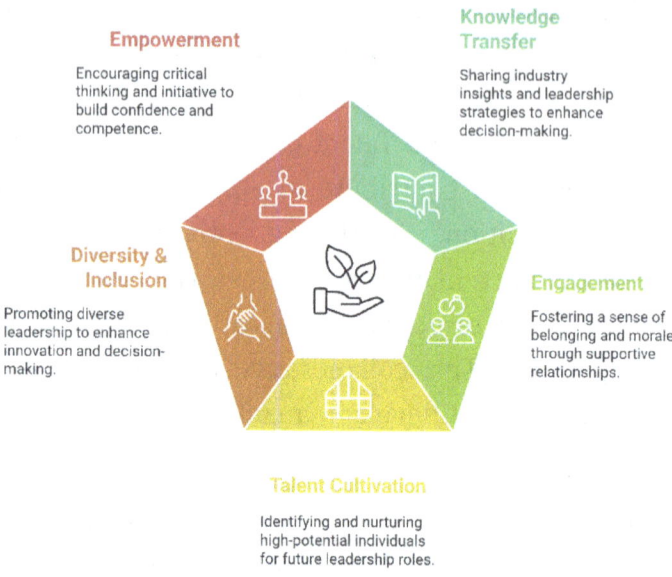

Figure 5.6 Mentoring future leaders is vital for current leaders and organizations.

Apart from that, mentoring provides a route to diversify leadership. While leaders mentor different groups, they serve as catalysts in breaking barriers and creating opportunities for groups usually underrepresented in active leadership. The commitment to an inclusive organizational culture results in better decision-making with an element of increased innovativeness. Diverse leading teams bring multiple perspectives and experiences that could drive creativity and enhance problem-solving capabilities.

Conclusion Organizations will only realize a long-term impact when mentoring the next generation of leaders. As experienced leaders invest in developing the talent base of emerging leaders, they will help transfer crucial knowledge, more engagement, and build a diverse pipeline of capable leaders. Effective mentoring relationships enable people to grow professionally and personally with greater confidence and skills. In how mentorship becomes a priority amidst increasingly multilayered challenges and opportunities, the ways to raise the next generation of leaders better prepared to drive business success and innovation will be shaped. The commitment to mentoring empowers people and nurtures the whole organization to leave a legacy in developing and perpetuating leadership excellence.

5.5.1 Creating a Legacy of Leadership

Creating a leadership legacy is not just about personal success but rather an enduring impact that shapes the future of other generations of leaders. A strong leadership legacy comprises values, principles, and practices instilled by the leaders in their teams and organizations. The legacy guides current operations and provides a foundation for sustainable growth and development. By purchasing the growth of future leaders, developing a society for which an excellent company can stand, and modeling core worths, today's leaders can make sure that their impact will certainly live well past their period.

Truthfully, at the core of leaving a long-lasting management tradition is a dedication to the advancement of others. For leaders who comprehend that establishing ability and releasing the perspective in individuals is a long-lasting tradition, this takes coaching, training, and development chances. By providing time together with sources to establish its future leaders, today's leaders aid in producing a causal sequence past their periods. For instance, a leader who helps the trip for employees proactively develops an advising society of partnership with others, urging them to do likewise. Management expertise and worths waterfall down; advancement makes certain a solid skill pipe. Business society is an additional crucial consideration in establishing management tradition. Leaders are an important societal factor that controls acting, making choices, and connecting within companies.

Leaders institutionalize worths such as stability, responsibility, variety, and advancement, which clarifies how employees engage and deal with each other. A favorable society advertises staff member interaction and fulfillment, bringing in and preserving premium ability. This is where leaders, by regularly living these worths, enable individuals to feel valued and encouraged to offer the best feasible payment, strengthening the tradition they want to leave. Developing a management tradition is additionally regarded as a good example of principles and moral decision-making.

Leaders who lead with a concentration on values and stability develop sensations of trust in their staff members and their regards. Making honest options is also difficult, as it reveals that leaders will certainly do what is right, not what is very easy. The tradition of an honest structure supplies assisting concepts for future leaders who will certainly use the instances established by their predecessors as they encounter difficulties and obstacles. The tradition of moral management gives the company trustworthiness and a preserved society of dependency on and obligation.

Besides, development, together with versatility, is what one requires to leave a management tradition. In the here-and-now globe, where fast modifications happen, a company must be adaptable and open to getting originalities. Development and experiment develop a certificate to assume and transform in different ways. Structure an atmosphere where advancement is commemorated warranties that leaders allow companies to flourish upon facing brand-new obstacles. This tradition of versatility prepares the future leader for durability and ingenuity to browse whatever unpredictability might come next.

Finally, the management trip can be noted and handed down through its paperwork and sharing. In this procedure, leaders would certainly introspect into their experiences, successes, and lessons found to make a collection of understanding for future generations. This might be with mentorship programs, management training sessions, or composed representations shared within the company. Leaders influence others to proceed with their job-plus concepts by expressing their worth and vision, guaranteeing their tradition expands and affects the companies much past the separation day.

5.6 Case Study: The Power of Authentic Leadership

Genuine management is a high-impact strategy focusing on openness, honesty, and an authentic connection with fans. In companies where leaders use genuine management, count on, regard, and energetic involvement, grow. Among the most reputable instances of genuine management is Howard Schultz, previously Starbucks's Chief Executive Officer. His take care of workers' well-being and reasonable sourcing enabled Schultz to show how leading by instance can deeply affect the company and its society.

Howard Schultz signed up with Starbucks in 1982 as Director of Retail Operations plus Marketing. His vision changed Starbucks from a tiny coffee bean store to an effective, international shop café sensation. At the core of Howard Schultz's management society was a deeply held sentence: a firm's success and success collaborate with its employees' well-being. He has described Starbucks staff members as companions, a title that reveals his promise to produce extensive products and make them possible for society. The basis of Schultz's genuine management was worker well-being.

He understood that delighted, including staff members, relate to pleased clients; therefore, he presented plans where the requirements of the Starbucks companions were vital. On-job advantages like medical insurance supply alternatives and paid adult leave were also supplied to part-time employees. This dedication to staff members' well-being enhanced spirits and drew in a fully committed labor force that felt valued and valued. Schultz's genuine management expanded past worker connections into moral sourcing and company social obligation. He thought companies had to show their respect for the culture and the atmosphere. He executed the principles exercised in Starbucks by guaranteeing that it generates coffee fairly and partnering with farmers to offer a practical cost coupled with sustainability. This dedication to moral sourcing was what customers were searching for in brand names that straightened with their worth. Schultz was clear regarding exactly how Starbucks sourced its items, collecting the clients' trust and loyalty—enhancing the brand name's track record as socially accountable. Most significantly, Schultz's design was defined by open interaction.

He sought staff comments and urged the voicing of viewpoints and concepts. This method encouraged the companions and produced a society of cooperation and technology. Through genuine management, Schultz showed that the objective of a leader is not to regulate but to produce an atmosphere where everybody's voice is listened to and valued.

Schultz's management was likewise checked through tough times, specifically throughout the 2008 financial downturn. Instead of turning to discharges, he purchased staff member training and advancement, thinking that a solid, competent labor force would be a much better place at Starbucks for healing. This choice showed his dedication to his companions and his ideas in their capacity. By focusing on worker advancement, he kept spirits and prepared the business to be more powerful post-recession. All the instances of Howard Schultz in Starbucks personify the power of genuine management much better. He has a mixed society of shared count-on-plus regard with a dedication to worker well-being, values in sourcing, and open interaction.

Schultz motivates his companions and customers by leading by example, while his credibility in management has driven both business success and social change. His legacy reminds us that great leadership is not all about the bottom line but about making a difference in people's and society's lives. Through authenticity, leaders inspire others to be likewise, creating a new generation of leaders who want to make a difference.

5.7 Key Point Donald Trump's potential re-election in 2024

> **Cultural Issues:** Leveraging cultural and social issues, such as education and freedom of speech, to mobilize conservative voters.

Donald Trump's would-be re-election campaign now involves deep cultural and social issues that strike the core of conservative politics as the presidential election 2024 approaches. Major talking points are on education, speech, and the general happenings of the cultural landscape. By framing these issues as what conservative values mean to him, Trump seeks to galvanize supporters and further strengthen his position within the race.

Other relevant and discursive cultural issues Trump will likely use include education. Debates on the contents of the curriculum, parental rights, and school choices are central to American life. Many conservative voters are increasingly concerned with what they think is indoctrination in public schools, particularly those lessons on gender identity and critical race theory, among other progressive reforms in education. In this domain, Trump can make himself a robust parental rights and educational reformist to press for parents' voices in their children's education. He can activate conservative voters passionate about education reform by championing school choice initiatives and supporting policies that put traditional values first in the classroom.

> **Build a Strong Coalition**
> Form alliances with key groups to broaden your support base.
>
> **Highlight Successes**
> Regularly showcase accomplishments to build credibility and trust.

An additional essential social concern is freedom of speech, which his base anticipates him to act on. Likewise, several traditionalists feel that their points of view are significantly censored in the general public room via social networks and in the mainstream media. Trump can maximize that, generally establishing himself versus what he calls "political accuracy" and censorship. He can stimulate citizens who think their legal rights to cost-free expression are intimidated by sustaining plans that progress free expression and slamming regarded prejudices in media and modern technology. The position additionally speaks to his core fans and interests a larger group of individuals worried about civil liberties.

Besides this, a lot more basic social anxieties the Trump project can accentuate consist of a seeming undercutting of standard worths and enhancing appeal of dynamic ideas. In this regard, he is inclined to mix assistance amongst those who feel disaffected by transforming times by mounting himself as representing American patriotism and household worth. This message reverberates in SUV locations where most citizens worry about modern plans' effect on their areas.

The undoubted plus is that Trump can work with voters emotionally and culturally. His rhetoric sometimes sounds more like an appeal to the remembered version of America and a call to the electorate for restoration to simpler, more cohesive times. He is mobilizing those who feel something is missing in the current political climate and is willing to turn up and give a reason for his candidacy.

This, in essence, means that Donald Trump's 2024 re-election campaign will be very pegged on using cultural and social issues to mobilize conservative voters. He feels related to his base when discussing education issues, free speech, and protecting traditional values while gaining new followers. As those cultural dynamics continue to evolve, it would be Trump's job to render such issues into an appealing narrative of patriotism and individual rights. Ultimately, the cultural zeitgeist is where Trump wants to plant himself as the leading figure of the conservative movement on his path to winning re-election.

Reference

1. Avolio, B. J., & Gardner, W. L. (2005). Authentic leadership development: Getting to the root of positive forms of leadership. The Leadership Quarterly, 16(3), 315-338.

2. Ilies, R., Morgeson, F. P., & Nahrgang, J. D. (2005). Authentic leadership and eudaemonic well-being: Understanding the effects of authentic leadership on follower outcomes. The Leadership Quarterly, 16(3), 373-394.

3. Walumbwa, F. O., Avolio, B. J., Gardner, W. L., Wernsing, T., & Peterson, S. J. (2008). Authentic leadership: Development and validation of a scale. Journal of Management, 34(1), 89-126.

4. Harter, S. (2002). Authenticity. In Handbook of positive psychology (pp. 382-394). Oxford University Press.

5. Goffee, R., & Jones, G. (2000). Why should anyone be led by you? Harvard Business Review, 78(5), 62-70.

6. Kouzes, J. M., & Posner, B. Z. (2002). The leadership challenge: How to get extraordinary things done in organizations (3rd ed.). Jossey-Bass.

7. Luthans, F., & Avolio, B. J. (2003). Authentic leadership development. In K. S. Cameron, J. E. Dutton, & R. E. Quinn (Eds.), Positive organizational scholarship (pp. 241-258). Berrett-Koehler.

8. Brown, M. E., & Treviño, L. K. (2006). Ethical leadership: A review and future directions. The Leadership Quarterly, 17(6), 595-616.

9. Neider, L. L., & Schriesheim, C. A. (2011). The authentic leadership inventory (ALI): Development and empirical tests. The Leadership Quarterly, 22(6), 1130-1144.

10. George, B. (2003). Authentic leadership: The quest for a moral compass. The Harvard Business Review, 81(1), 1-9.

11. Avolio, B. J., & Luthans, F. (2006). Building the leader's vision. Journal of Leadership & Organizational Studies, 13(1), 10-25.

12. Gardner, W. L., Cogliser, C. C., Davis, K. M., & Dickens, M. P. (2011). Authentic leadership: A review of the literature and implications for future research. The Leadership Quarterly, 22(6), 1120-1145.

13. Eagly, A. H., & Carli, L. L. (2003). The female leadership advantage: An evaluation of the evidence. The Leadership Quarterly, 14(6), 807-834.

14. Schultz, H. (2011). Onward: How Starbucks fought for its life without losing its soul. Rodale Books.

CHAPTER 6

Adopting Resilience: Navigating Challenges Together

Introduction

In today's complicated and hectic world, browsing obstacles robustly is necessary for efficient management. Chapter 6 confirms durability as an individual characteristic and a cumulative ability to check how it reinforces groups and companies. Durability makes it possible for leaders together with their groups to adjust to recoup and prosper in misfortune, developing a society of willpower as well as cooperation [1]

This chapter highlights the significance of durability in today's vibrant setting, where consistent modification and obstacles appear unexpectedly. Financial variations, technical disturbances, and social distress are some situations where leaders frequently deal with situations [2]. Standing company yet ingenious ends up being very crucial [3]. Strength is not nearly birthing the influence; it's everything about accepting modification and utilizing that as a chance for development and advancement. The chapter highlights that the most effective method of establishing strength remains in a sustaining group setting. When leaders model and assist in opening lines of interaction, they develop a society that equips employees to share difficulties and work together on remedies [4].

This additionally advertises analytical ability in groups and helps develop a feeling of trust fund and sociability among participants [5]. Groups browsing with difficulties can make it possible for a common feeling of function, coupled with substantial dedication for overcoming the probabilities towards recognizing common objectives [6]. It additionally deals with useful techniques for group strength, such as developing a development frame of mind, versatility, and accessibility to tension administration sources [7]. Leaders are motivated to develop an atmosphere worth picking up from failings and commemorating successes, regardless of dimension [8]. This will certainly assist in developing self-confidence and versatility in their groups to manage future obstacles.

6.1 Understanding Team Resilience

Group durability is the ability to climb again, start picking up from obstacles, and arise more powerfully. It's cumulative efficiency among participants to sustain each other, keep favorable expectations, and concentrate on their objectives when faced with misfortunes [9]. Recognizing team strength calls for evaluating variables that add to it, characteristics enforcing it, and approaches leaders can use to generate a resistant society amongst groups.

At many standard degrees, group durability relies on favorable social partnerships and a feeling of coming from. Recognizing that your colleagues will certainly encourage and offer one's requirements plants a togetherness that will drive unity when times are challenging [10]. Count on is grown in an open, communicative setting with common experiences and regard. Groups that have used energetic structure tasks also urged comments to ensure that the last can feel that they can conveniently share concepts and their problems [11]. The sensation of safety increases their risk-taking actions, which aids the participants in sustaining each other with such turbulence- a particular strength component. Flexibility is one more critical rule in group durability.

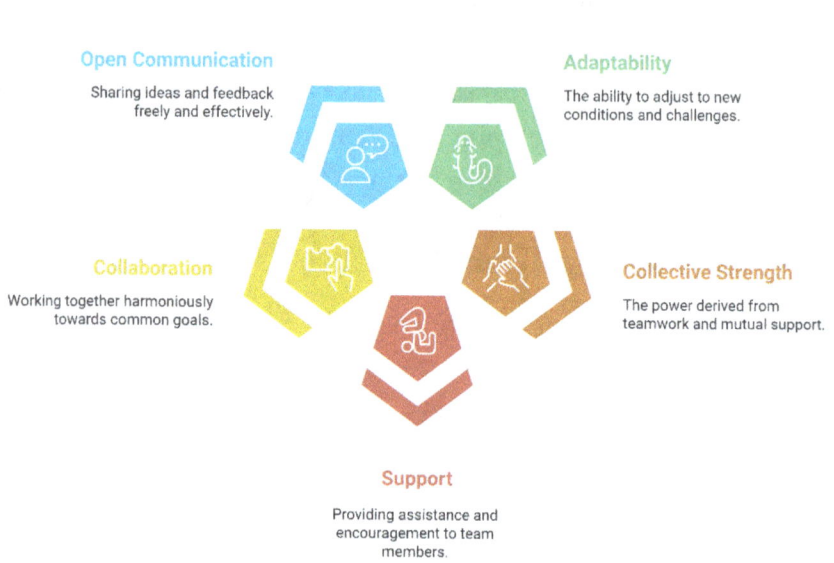

Figure 6.1 Team resilience is an essential quality that enables groups to navigate challenges.

Among the trademarks of durable groups is their capacity to transform towards altering scenarios. This versatility originates in a developed way of thinking where the participants consider obstacles as possibilities for understanding and renovation instead of difficult obstacles. The leaders themselves can motivate this frame of mind by embracing a society worth trial and error and commemorating successes and failures. Through rewording troubles such as finding chances, groups can function towards adaptable analytics and construct general strength.

In addition, efficient management assists in structuring group strength. Leaders self-model strength to motivate their groups to reveal a comparable mindset. This might materialize in remaining tranquility throughout stressful circumstances, preserving a favorable expectation, and being solution-focused instead of problem-oriented. On top of that, leaders give sources plus sustain to assist the groups in handling tension and obstacles. This can be educated in taking care of stress and anxiety, accessibility to psychological wellness sources, or offering chances to facilitate offered for staff members to recover along with the show.

An additional essential ingredient in group strength is interaction. Normal communication and open conversation about troubles and successes will keep the place undamaged. Leaders need to encourage visibility by permitting employees to reveal their sights and anxieties and share assumptions. This free circulation of interaction produces a joint atmosphere where the employees think they can effectively help address the problem. Additionally, acknowledgment and celebration of little triumphs reinforce spirits and construct the idea that a team of individuals can make it through misfortune.

An additional hallmark of group strength is variety in its make-up. Variety brings various viewpoints together with life experiences to improve analytics with originalities. As one feels valued for a unique payment, this will certainly require more participation to sustain each other through bumpy rides. It deserves to be remembered that leaders can take actions to proactively advertise inclusiveness, making certain that every voice is listened to. This will certainly assist in strengthening the strength of the group.

6.2 Identifying Potential Challenges Ahead

Companies should proactively recognize possible obstacles to overcome such unpredictability in today's dynamically transforming setting. Comprehending these prospective difficulties will absolutely assist leaders and groups in producing means to guarantee strength and versatility. This aggressive technique prepares the ground for unforeseen interruptions and equips the company to take possibilities that might emerge from difficulties. Besides that, technical interruption is among the crucial worries for companies.

As innovation rapidly changes, organizations need to adjust to every brand-new device, system, and procedure that continues to change. This likewise suggests handling arising innovations and also making personnel completely educated and furnished to use them. Failure to approve the change in modern technology minimizes competition and constructs inefficacy. From time to time, leaders should review their technological landscape and invest in various training and development programs to enable their teams to grasp innovation.

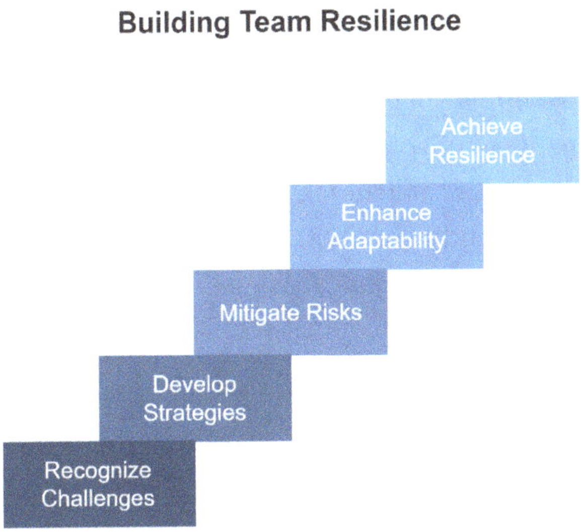

Building Team Resilience

- Achieve Resilience
- Enhance Adaptability
- Mitigate Risks
- Develop Strategies
- Recognize Challenges

Figure 6.2 Organizations must proactively identify potential challenges.

Another huge challenge arises through changes in the working population. The evolution of remote work, gig economies, and changing expectations of employees have completely changed how people used to work. Organizations need to address employee engagement, retention, and work-life balance challenges. As employees increasingly seek flexibility and purpose, leaders must develop a culture supportive of well-being and professional growth. Surveys and feedback sessions will enable the organizations to be on their toes to deliver on employee needs and expectations and effect timely changes in policy and practice.

Other factors that potentially threaten the survival of organizations are economic fluctuations. Economic instability influences consumer behavior, supply chains, and business stability. The leaders need to check feasible financial indications and fads affecting their procedures. Backup preparation, diversity in supply chains, and monetary gains will certainly assist companies in avoiding financial disturbance. Constructing a strong stakeholder partnership involves providers and clients bringing understanding and other assistance during hard times. Social and also social concerns are progressively arising as prospective obstacles for companies.

Problems such as variety, equity, and addition (DEI) are crucial for embracing a favorable social work environment. Companies that stop working to resolve these problems might deal with reputational dangers, lowered worker spirits, and problems bringing in leading skills. Leaders ought to focus on DEI campaigns and produce an atmosphere where all staff members feel valued as well as consistent. Firms can be strengthened by making the society of incorporation component them with routine training and open discussions on social proficiency.

Furthermore, a company should plan for ecological difficulties related to environmental change and sustainability problems. With better customer recognition, companies are progressively obligated to their eco-friendly impact. Leaders ought to analyze their company's methods for renovation, such as lowering waste, enhancing power performance, and sourcing lasting products. Sustainability lowers threat yet likewise boosts brand name credibility and consumer commitment.

Last, psychological health and wellness, as well as well-being, have become several of the most crucial obstacles in today's job life. Stress for work-life equilibrium and various other outside stresses distinguish staff members' performance and spirits. Therefore, companies must take campaigns over psychological wellness seriously, providing for demands like therapy, anxiety monitoring programs, and versatile working. With a society that sustains psychological health, durability is advertised amongst workers as they make every effort in difficult times.

6.2.1 Developing Problem-Solving Skills

Problem-solving is important for personal and professional life in today's hectic and complex globe. Functional analytic activities allow one to manage obstacles, make informed choices, and perform remedies that produce outcomes. Problem-solving abilities can boost performance and convenience, whether as an individual or in a group.

Table 6.1 The development of problem-solving skills within a team.

Skill Area	Description	Methods for Development	Expected Outcomes	Examples of Application
Critical Thinking	Analyzing information and evaluating options.	Workshops on logical reasoning and analysis.	Enhanced ability to assess situations objectively.	Case studies and real-life scenarios for analysis.
Creative Thinking	Generating innovative ideas and solutions.	Brainstorming sessions and creativity exercises.	Increase innovation and diverse solutions.	Idea generation sessions for new projects.
Decision-Making	Making informed choices based on available	Training on decision-making frameworks.	Improved ability to make timely and effective	Use of decision trees and pros/cons

	data.		decisions.	lists.
Collaboration	Working effectively with others to solve problems.	Team-building activities and group projects.	Strengthened teamwork and shared problem-solving.	Group problem-solving workshops.
Adaptability	Adjusting strategies based on changing circumstances.	Role-playing and simulation exercises.	Greater flexibility in approach to challenges.	Crisis management drills or scenario planning.
Analytical Skills	Breaking down complex problems into manageable parts.	Training on data analysis and interpretation.	Improved ability to understand and tackle complex issues.	Analyzing data sets to identify trends.
Communication Skills	Effectively sharing ideas and solutions with others.	Workshops on effective communication techniques.	Enhanced clarity and understanding in discussions.	Presenting solutions in team meetings.
Feedback Utilization	Learning from feedback to improve problem-solving approaches.	Regular feedback sessions and peer reviews.	Increased self-awareness and continuous improvement.	Implementing feedback in future projects.

The advancement of analytic abilities greatly requires the fostering of important reasoning. Essential believing includes objectivity in evaluating details and the supposition of alternating perspectives, along with inspecting the credibility of debates. It, therefore, supports a wondering about society that concerns presumptions, choices, and results that might emerge. Essential believing can be allowed via brainstorming sessions, mind mapping, and decision-making structures.

Such strategies help the individual break a complicated issue into smaller parts that are simple to recognize and pursue. One more important active ingredient is organized tissue generation. The procedure for fixing an issue or creating an imaginative remedy for some specific trouble is frequently carried out in several actions: issue interpretation, info event, prospective services generation, service examination, and application of the most effective. By adhering to a structured strategy, people are shielded versus intricacy and can ensure they have thought about every feasible angle. Therefore, urging groups to adopt this organized approach is bound to generate even more thorough evaluations and exceptional results.

Second, creative thinking is vital for problem-solving. It allows thinking about imaginative remedies and doubting the normal method of doing things. To improve imagination, a company must create an open setting where staff members do not hesitate to offer their concepts without concern or objection. Thinking, role-playing, and situation evaluation work methods to promote imaginative reasoning. Motivating varied groups to work together boosts imagination, given that various histories and perspectives commonly cause even more inventive remedies.

Psychological knowledge considerably enhances problem-solving. Individuals with high psychological knowledge comprehend their feelings and the feelings of others, which aids them in better navigating social relationships when dealing with tough scenarios.

Such understanding can promote reliable interaction, teamwork, and problem resolution. Training programs to boost psychological knowledge will certainly help people manage tension, show compassion towards associates, and preserve a favorable perspective during damaging problems. The various other crucial component in problem-solving is strength. In particular, resistant individuals can better manage troubles and consider obstacles as possibilities for renovation.

Structure durability requires the growth of a favorable state of mind, welcoming versatility, and learning from one's failings. A company can assist by sustaining a perspective that discovers via testing where blunders belong to the success foundation, not failure. Offering sources for managing tension and sustaining work-life equilibrium likewise adds to specific strength.

Lastly, problem-solving abilities will certainly be combined with continual understanding. In today's fast-evolving setting, staying updated with the latest happenings in one's market, brand-new modern technologies, and ideal methods is crucial. Encouraging employees to pursue professional development opportunities, attend workshops, and network enhances problem-solving capabilities. A lifelong learning culture is created, ensuring the teams stay agile and better equipped to handle challenges.

In all, problem-solving skills development encompasses developing critical thinking, creativity, emotional intelligence, resilience, and the commitment to lifelong learning. The more capable individuals are of these competencies, the more capable an organization will be to surmount various challenges and drive innovation. Good problem-solving skills mean individual success and that teams and organizations are strengthened to deal with continuous change.

6.2.2 Encouraging a Growth Mindset

As psychologist Carol Dweck says, the growth mindset is to believe that talents and abilities can be developed through dedication and effort, learning from them. A fixed mindset would see abilities as static and unchangeable. Individual and organizational mindsets centered on growth offer more possibilities for resilience, innovation, and continuous improvement. Through establishing this kind of assumed, leaders can encourage their groups to come close to obstacles, pick up from failings as well as accomplish exceptional success.

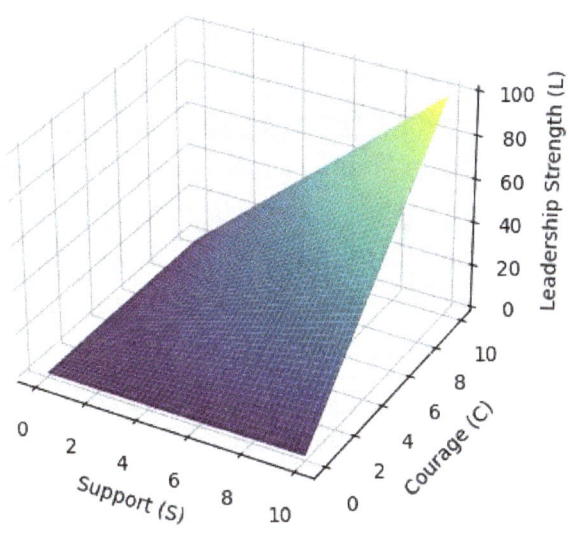

Figure 6.3 3D Visualization of Lionhearted Leadership.

One of the most vital methods to instill a development state of mind is via language in interactions. Leaders must communicate that initiative and determination, not skill or capacity, aid in understanding passions. Recognizing effort, resourcefulness, and perseverance in hardship instead of inherent skill is more suitable. For example, instead of stating, "You're doing wonderful work," one can state, "I value the initiative you're giving this task. This talks about accomplishment together with maintaining them making every effort. Reorientating language by doing this sustains a developed way of thinking, which the capability creates in time.

$$L = S \times C \quad (6.1)$$

Management Stamina (L) boosts when there is significant group Assistance (S) and also a high degree of Guts (C) to encounter obstacles. Bordering on your own with "lions" (solid, encouraging people) improves your management capacities while staying clear of "hen scrape" (unfavorable impacts) takes into consideration higher emphasis as well as toughness. This formula personifies the significance of lionhearted management: constructing a durable and enduring atmosphere with shared assistance. An additional essential location of motivation towards an acquisitive mindset entails permitting security for testing. They must feel secure to take threats and make blunders without unfavorable effects. The company can attain this via open conversations, thinking about failings as possibilities for discovering instead of in reverse actions.

Leaders need to design the ideal habits via conversations of their individual experiences in which they have run into failing, plainly meaning what has been picked up from those circumstances. Normalize it: Teams will certainly want to attempt brand-new plus extra difficult points if the understanding procedure is stabilized. The 2D line story reveals management toughness differs with assistance when Courage is taken care of at 5. It can readjust the taken care of the worth of C to see how various degrees of Courage impact the connection.

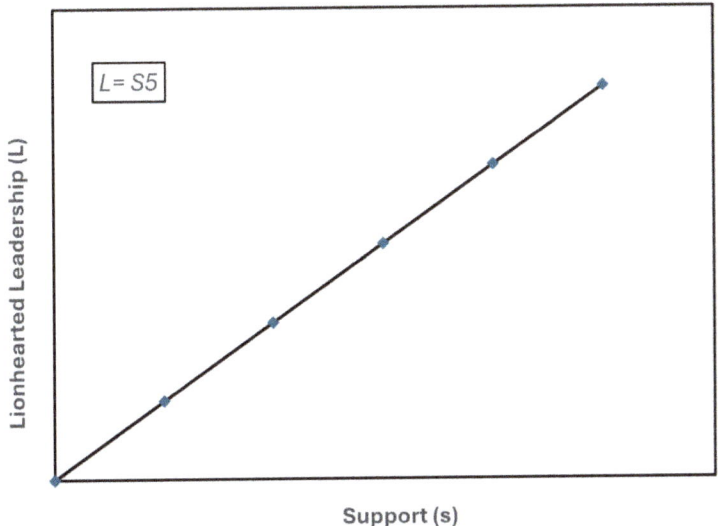

Figure 6.4 2D Visualization of Lionhearted Leadership.

This would also entail embracing a development way of thinking via specialist growth opportunities. The firm must purchase training, workshops, and coaching programs to improve ability growth and understanding of development. Urging staff members to seek brand-new experiences enhances capacity and the reality that development is a trip. In sustaining long-lasting discoveries, society can be instilled to drive people to look for brand-new obstacles and improve their experience.

Normal comments are a vital element of advertising a development state of mind. Constructive comments assist people in comprehending their toughness, along with locations for renovation, and assist their growth. Leaders must concentrate on giving details and workable understandings instead of unclear analyses. These targeted comments permit people to establish clear objectives and track their development, enhancing the idea that they can boost with initiative and technique.

Additionally, peer comments enable a common discovering area in which participants restate the development courses of others. Development needs likewise to be commemorated to urge more development in the frame of mind. The company should identify together and highlight specific and group success despite just how little. Acknowledgment enhances the suggestion that initiative leads to renovation and also success. Commemorating turning points develops a favorable comments loophole, inspiring people to proceed with pressing their limits plus pursuing quality.

6.3 Creating Contingency Plans

Disagreement preparation is among the essential danger monitoring tasks that allow companies to prepare for disturbances or occasions they might not be prepared for. This strategy is taken proactively to minimize the results of situations permitting businesses to suffer procedures throughout harmful situations. Preparing for prospective obstacles plus their clear reactions will naturally make a company extra durable and constant in times of chaos. The first step in preparing for backup entails a complete danger evaluation.

Companies need to recognize all inbound dangers that might create disturbance in procedures due to all-natural catastrophes, cyber protection violations, disruptions in the supply chain, or abrupt adjustments in market problems. The evaluation will certainly entail assessing each recognized threat's chance and possible influence on the company. Leaders can concentrate their preparation initiatives by focusing on these dangers to guarantee sources are set aside successfully versus one of the most considerable dangers. When the dangers have been determined, prospective backup approaches should be described for every situation.

This ought to consist of clear duties and duties amongst staff members, interaction methods, and actions to reply to each recognized danger. For instance, the backup strategy might include the safety and security treatment for staff members, the moving of procedures, and the backup lines of interaction in the event of dangers related to all-natural catastrophes. Specifying such procedures permits companies to act promptly and effectively in a dilemma.

The second thing is that involving stakeholders in the preparation procedure is very important. Encouraging workers, administration, and outside companions provides an incorporated method to backup preparation. The stakeholders will certainly have something to use regarding threat recognition and structure reduction methods. Possession and duty are encouraged when staff members are handled board throughout the backup preparation. Evaluating and fine-tuning backup strategies is additionally critical.

Normal drills and simulations can assist companies in assessing their strategies' efficiency and determining locations for renovation. These workouts confirm reaction techniques and train staff members on their functions throughout a dilemma, guaranteeing that everybody is prepared to act definitely. Comments from these drills ought to be used to upgrade and boost the action strategies, enabling companies to adjust to transforming situations and arising dangers.

Backup interaction is a vital aspect of any provided backup strategy. Organizations must define networks for information sharing throughout a situation to ensure all stakeholders are educated and involved. This establishes a situation interaction strategy explaining how details flow amongst staff members, clients, and the general public. Openness in interaction on schedule aids in constructing self-confidence and avoids false information. This method can preserve spirits and self-confidence throughout bumpy rides.

Companies should also understand that backup preparation is not a single initiative but a recurring procedure. As the interior plus outside settings alter, so does the contingency plan. Routine evaluations and updates would keep the strategies fresh and effectively workable. Most importantly, a society of preparedness can be taken on within a company, making it possible for positive danger administration to take care of unpredictability conveniently.

6.3.1 Promoting Stress Management Techniques

Handling tension effectively makes it possible for specific wellness and ensures business performance in today's fast-paced and requiring globe. High degrees lead to fatigue, lowered efficiency, and a hostile office environment. Consequently, advertising reliable methods for dealing with tension is of utmost significance in embracing a healthy and balanced work environment that permits the provider to flourish. Equipping people with better methods and approaches to deal with stress will certainly boost general business spirits, performance, and retention.

Education, learning, and recognition are some of the most efficient means to urge tension administration. A company can use training workshops or sessions on how tension signs and symptoms occur and how they can impact a person's psychological and physical wellness. Programs that show numerous anxiety administration approaches, such as mindfulness, time administration, and leisure workouts, can be covered. Informing workers regarding signs and symptoms, a measure of tension and coping reaction, will allow them to start handling their tension degrees.

Mindfulness and reflection are currently extensively acknowledged as one of the most reliable tension factors. By urging workers to exercise mindfulness, they will certainly become much more knowledgeable about themselves and their feelings. These basic methods consist of deep breathing exercises, assisted images, or reflection, which can be conveniently integrated into a hectic workday. The company can likewise supply workshops on mindfulness or silent locations to loosen up together with a mirror.

Organizations can help workers cultivate a feeling of tranquility and emphasis by promoting a society that values mindfulness and decreases anxiety. Time management is another important part of anxiety reduction. Bad time management can cause frustrating work and enhanced stress. Organizations can supply training on efficient time management methods, such as focusing on jobs, establishing reasonable target dates, and transforming jobs into workable actions.

Performance devices and strategies, such as the Pomodoro Technique or time-blocking, can be urged as methods by which staff members can enhance their job routines. By advertising better time management, organizations can reduce workers' sensations of bewilderment and improve their ability to satisfy their obligations. Physical well-being is likewise directly connected with handling tension. Motivating normal workouts can considerably lower degrees of anxiousness coupled with associated comorbid problems.

Additionally, companies can encourage staff members to exercise daily by advertising health and fitness campaigns, such as team workouts, strolling conferences, or obstacles. Additional benefits, like membership in various gyms or fitness applications, may drive people to care for their bodies better. As has been said many times, a healthy body has a healthy mind. Therefore, exercise is also important in stress regulation.

The workplace culture should support the effective management of stress. Communication and a sense of community may allow an employee to feel valued and understood. Organizations should encourage team-building and socializing activities that build employee connections. This can likewise develop uniformity and assistance for staff members by supplying a system for sharing experiences and difficulties. When staff members can review their stressors without judgment, they will likely look for aid and use tension management sources.

Ultimately, companies need to sustain the demand for work-life equilibrium. Authorizing workers to establish limits between work and personal life dramatically minimizes anxiety levels. It might be available in the form of versatile working plans, such as working from home or adaptable hours, which aid them in figuring out their duties at both ends much more favorably. Organizations that show concern for work-life equilibrium value their staff members' well-being, which develops task satisfaction and commitment.

The leaders must also create anxiety-monitoring strategies to promote a healthy and balanced workplace. Education and learning in mindfulness, time management, physical well-being, and open interaction will certainly help staff members manage their tension levels. An encouraging society and the valuing of work-life equilibrium will boost this procedure. Financial investment in the administration of anxiety advantages private workers and has architectural ramifications for business success and strength.

6.3.2 Learning from Past Challenges

Discovering from past difficulties accumulates durability, technology, plus continual renovation. Any tiny or large failure consists of time for representation and discovery. Previous failings can hence be examined to review what failed, which can assist companies in determining weak points, penalty modification procedures, and producing strategies that guarantee much better efficiency in the future. This positive position lowers the possibility of reappearance and creates a know-plus versatile society.

The vital advantages of learning from previous obstacles entail establishing an extra durable business structure. When groups review previous troubles, they can generate an understanding of what failed and why. Such understanding permits companies to fix hidden problems with interaction, source appropriation, or critical preparation. A firm that experienced supply chain disturbances throughout a situation might perform an extensive testimonial of its partnerships with suppliers or its logistical plans.

As a result, a company can recognize weak points where extra backup preparation can be incorporated, enhancing future strength to comparable problems. Learning from previous problems aids in breakthrough responsibility within a firm society. When companies discuss failings and why they took place openly, it produces a feeling of safety in sharing experiences without blaming. This sort of openness would certainly improve sincere discussion and shared problem-solving. Groups can equally assess what failed, relying upon varied viewpoints to conceptualize functional options. This type of common discovery will reinforce teams' partnerships and enhance a typical improvement fix.

Besides enhancing durability coupled with responsibility representation of previous obstacles can be a motorist of technology. Frequently innovative options are born from getting rid of numerous barriers. Assessing previous problems enables companies to recognize opportunities for development and renovation. For example, a modern technology business dealing with grievances due to a pest software program launch may collect cross-functional groups to redesign its screening procedures. This will certainly result in dedication to discovering and establishing new techniques, items, or solutions that will certainly assist in addressing the first issue, boost top quality, and ensure client complete satisfaction. Recording lessons learned from a previous difficulty gives the basis for an understanding that can be used to make future choices.

Systems must be established to record understandings from job retrospectives, post-mortems, or comment sessions. Paperwork will certainly offer the basis for future jobs, coupled with campaigns to attract their lessons and ensure that historical understanding is readily available to groups. These can be incorporated into training products plus onboarding to notify brand-new staff members of understandings that may improve their understanding of prospective mistakes and ideal techniques.

Ultimately, leaders give the setting, allowing positive understanding from previous obstacles. Leaders design reflective methods and urge open conversations concerning obstacles to establishing the tone within a company. Celebrating an understanding of obstacles even more verifies that failing is not an endpoint but a one-step path to development. Leaders can ensure an organized technique for filtration and enhancement by executing normal evaluation sessions where groups analyze their efficiency despite previous difficulties.

6.4 Building a Supportive Team Network

The endurance of an encouraging network within any company can go a long way toward improving cooperation, spirit, and efficiency. A helpful network assists in producing an atmosphere where staff members feel valued and encouraged to offer their finest work. This network constructs a favorable work environment and allows people to expand directly and skillfully.

Motivating open interaction has been just one of the first steps in constructing a helpful network among the participants. This is based on openness and depends on where people can share their suggestions, difficulties, and comments without judgment. The leaders are anticipated to use excellent communicative techniques; for example, paying attention diligently and offering positive comments establish the group's speed. Regular check-ins, team meetings, and informal get-togethers can let team members express themselves and connect personally. Indeed, the feeling of belonging and cooperation could be supported in organizations by creating an environment where every voice can be heard.

Additionally, it is important to promote team-building activities. These activities may include professional development, outings, or even problem-solving. Activities like these help team members bond with each other through mutual trust. These team-building activities engage them with colleagues in different roles, where they come to know and understand each other. If an opportunity is given to develop personal relationships among individuals, they are more likely to stand by each other at difficult times, which makes them highly resilient. Chances are that mentorship and peer support will also make a great difference in building a support network of the team members. Team development and knowledge sharing become possible when novice members are teamed up with senior ones. Mentorship enforces a learning culture by requiring individuals to ask questions and seek help without facing the consequences. Secondly, peer support groups are also an advantage that enables team members to share experiences and discuss challenges and successes. These initiatives encourage personal development while, at the same time, bonding among team members is enhanced. Recognition plus recognition are vital parts of the group assistance system. That is, recognition of payments elevates spirits and inspiration immediately. Thus, the leader needs to supply acknowledgment programs via normal events of the success of people together with groups. Tiny acts of thankfulness, such as shout-outs throughout conferences, will certainly go a long method in confirming positivity or customized thank-you notes.

Identifying initiatives constructs a society of thankfulness where staff member sustain each other in their ventures. Likewise, developing a mentally secure atmosphere to develop an assistance network is crucial. Staff members ought to feel positive that sharing ideas, asking inquiries, and attempting brand-new points will not cause adverse repercussions. Leaders ought to develop an environment of emotional safety and security where discussing errors coupled with failings is motivated as possibilities for additional knowing, not putting blame. When team members know they can take risks and learn from experiences, that is the most proper atmosphere for collaboration and innovation.

Finally, promoting diversity within a team makes the support network sound and tight by bringing together different ideas and experiences. It leads to creativity and innovation due to differing ideas from different backgrounds. Every organization should strive to provide a welcoming environment in which the culture of all team members is valued and respected. It adds value to the team and upgrades the quality of the entire organizational culture.

6.4.1 Recognizing Signs of Burnout

Burnout is the state of emotional exhaustion, physical tiredness, and mental fatigue caused by excessive prolonged stress. It may arise in all situations but is most prevalent in the job environment because people are expected to deliver quality services continuously. Identifying signs of burnout is paramount to the concerned individuals and organizations, as timely treatment helps to stem further deterioration in health and output. Knowing these signs is important as it helps leaders create a supportive environment that puts the mind at the forefront by promoting a healthier work-life balance.

The majority of individuals who deal with burnout experience chronic fatigue. Burned-out people have said they feel sapped of energy and life, even with adequate time to rest. This persistent situation can lead to lower levels of productivity and problems focusing on work. Employees may need help engaging in work or maintaining the same level of enthusiasm and motivation. Looking at this fatigue as a warning sign of burnout will help address the issues for proper support.

Another unmistakable sign of burnout is increased irritability or emotional instability. Burnout might frustrate him, change his moods, and even make him cynical about work and co-workers. Such emotional vulnerability strains the relations within the team, eventually causing conflict and a decline in cooperation. If some employees demonstrate changes in their emotional response, the leaders should try to discover why this happens and offer ways to cope with such stressors.

Other symptoms of burnout include reduced performance. A burned-out person cannot focus on or complete their work properly and may need help with decision-making, forgetting some situations, or producing low-quality work. This decreased performance may be self-reinforcing since falling behind at work may persuade employees to work harder to compensate for perceived deficiencies, exacerbating their stress.

Other physical symptoms may include headaches, gastrointestinal problems, and disturbed sleep. Chronic stress may eventually wear down the body and lead to health problems. Employees may mention that they get sick, have tension headaches, or sleep poorly—all signs of burnout. Organizations should not ignore such physical symptoms, which may affect employees' overall health and productivity.

Other symptoms of burnout include a feeling of detachment or disengagement from work. Staff become increasingly disconnected from their jobs, and indifference toward their responsibilities sets in, with no excitement about their work contributions. This disengagement may be extremely significant as efficiency is at a private degree in groups, and the whole company's society is worried. For that reason, any leader should want to replace degrees of interaction and motivate free discussion of work concerns coupled with complete satisfaction.

Ultimately, a raised dependence on harmful dealing devices might indicate job tension. Employees might attempt to handle stress and anxiety via extremely high levels of caffeine intake, alcohol usage, or various other comparable actions. Identifying such actions is necessary to recognize what is producing stress. In this manner, companies can provide sources for healthier dealing approaches, like workshops on managing anxiety or access to psychological wellness experts.

Recognizing indications of task anxiety is valuable in advertising a healthy and balanced workplace and well-being among employees. Indicators such as persistent exhaustion, psychological instability, inadequate efficiency, physical signs and symptoms, detachment from the job, and unhealthful dealing systems need not be ignored. Great interaction and the construction of a society that appreciates psychological health assistance companies determine this very early and present methods to sustain staff members in restoring their equilibrium. Eventually, dealing with exhaustion boosts specific well-being and develops an extra involved, efficient, and resistant labor force.

6.4.2 Celebrating Perseverance and Determination

Perseverance and resolution comprise the fundamental high qualities that make it possible for the human spirit to triumph over all challenges and reach objectives regardless of obstacles. They have to do with identifying private ability and the society of durability, grit, and continual initiative within companies. By narrating determination, leaders can influence their groups, provide suggestions to the area, or remind them again that dedication is necessary for success. Resolution is the resolution to make every effort towards an objective regardless of troubles, troubles, or failings.

It is the spirit of not quitting even when the going gets difficult. Decision is enhanced by decision, a motivational sensation to press through obstacles. All this develops an atmosphere where one feels encouraged to take risks, gain from experiences, and expand. Narrating individuals or groups that have conquered major obstacles is among the best methods to commemorate perseverance and resolution. Success tales others share influence others to have such a way of thinking. These stories define the battles they run into, stress approaches, and sources they use to conquer them. Whether it be an individual account from a staff member functioning night and day to fulfill a target date or a task that asks for ingenious problem-solving to conquer unanticipated obstacles, these tales advise staff members that durability settles. Companies can additionally develop acknowledgment programs that recognize decisions and effort.

Acknowledgment can be made with honors, shout-outs throughout conferences, and inner interactions highlighting people and groups, including those top qualities. Companies strengthen effort and determination by openly recognizing their initiatives as worthwhile events. Acknowledgment will increase spirits and encourage others to design these qualities daily.

Produce chances to make team members associate with each other by informing and revealing their methods to dominate their troubles. Make normal discussion forums, workshops, or team-building tasks to advertise open conversations regarding problems and successes. Such an atmosphere enables one to gain from others and support a sensation of sociability in cumulative toughness. Sustaining the trips of staff members towards being equally encouraging develops a network of durability that progresses efficiency along with health in general.

Second, determination and decision-making can be instilled into the business society and objective. Leaders must express in their vision that determination and effort are part of success. By instilling determination into the business society, companies anticipate their participants will encounter problems with resolute decisions.

With official acknowledgment, there may be an excellent chance for casual events. Arranging group lunches, days of recognition, or health tasks fixated strength might aid in embracing and making it possible for the environment. In such events, groups would certainly cooperate in fellowship over commemorating their cumulative strength as a pressure within the company.

Casual events advise workers that their initiatives are enjoyed plus valued, producing a sensation of coming from and also commitment.

6.5 Implementing Regular Reflection Sessions

Routine representation sessions are an effective way of making certain developments, enhancing partnerships, and constantly enhancing groups with companies. These structured possibilities permit people and teams to go back and understand experiences together and pick up from them to assist in succeeding activities. By setting up normal representation in a company's society, groups can develop an understanding and a flexible mindset that, at some point, ensures efficiency and development. The significance of representation sessions is to generate time for thoughtful representation of previous experiences.

In such sessions, team members can review what went well, their obstacles, and the areas they can improve. This method allows team members to take ownership of their experiences and learn from successes and problems. Consequently, assessing activities and choices aids employees in developing patterns, acknowledging toughness, and determining areas for growth. Companies need to help with rhythms of normal representation, whichever helps their functional rhythm: once a week, bi-weekly, or even month-to-month. Uniformity assures that representation is an indispensable component of a group's operations. Holding such sessions when colleagues' other dedications are at their least expensive boosts involvement and interaction. A structured layout additionally boosts the performance of the representation sessions. Leaders can lead conversations with motivation and structures that assist groups in exercising vital reasoning.

For example, groups might wish to use the " Start, Stop, Continue" design, where staff members recognize methods that must be begun, stopped, or proceeded with. This intended method brings clarity and keeps conversations concentrated and efficient. Motivating visibility and sincerity is essential to allowing staff members to feel comfortable sharing their ideas and experiences without the anxiety of judgment or revenge. Standard practices include energetic listening, confidentiality of shared details, and regard for the points of view of others. These will certainly produce an encouraging setting that motivates open interaction. Leaders need to design these actions by being just as at risk and open when sharing their representations. Receptive sessions can additionally allow group characteristics, responsibility, and objective setup. Any group that assesses previous efficiency and discusses lessons learned will certainly establish workable objectives for the future. By doing this, assumptions are cleared up, and people are encouraged to take responsibility for their advancement. Certain and quantifiable purposes must be established throughout representation sessions to ensure that the understandings obtained convert into concrete activities.

Additionally, installing representation in job timelines brings about a much better understanding of outcomes. For example, providing a representation session at the end of a job or after a turning point can help the groups record understandings while experiences are fresh. This technique ensures that lessons learned are recorded and can be utilized for future jobs, avoiding repetition of errors while duplicating effective techniques. Finally, companies should commemorate understandings and enhancements from the representation sessions. This technique of valuing employees for important understandings throughout representation sessions while adjusting to comments becomes a constant understanding of society. By sharing success tales emerging from representations, a company enhances this method, producing even more need for consistent engagement.

Lastly, regular representation sessions will certainly assist in supporting a collective business that finds out about society and is continually looking for renovation. Organizations would certainly be much more reliable and resistant by allowing groups to understand their experiences and established objectives and commemorating development. Representation sessions offer people or groups possession of their knowing trip, resulting in technology and success in a developing landscape.

6.5.1 Encouraging Adaptability in Team Roles

Versatility is important to groups' success in today's fast-moving, transforming workplace. Versatility in group functions motivates private development and plants a society of versatility plus strength within companies. It assists them in producing nimble groups that can react quicker to brand-new difficulties together with chances by motivating a way of thinking that accepts adjustment and enabling a staff member to leave their common functions. One advantage of motivating adaptability in employees' duties is that analytic boosts.

If your team members have various functions and obligations, these numerous viewpoints cause varied abilities. A variety of ideas can lead to cutting-edge options and reliable choices. For example, when an advertising and marketing employee teams up with the sales group to recognize consumer responses, they can recognize voids in solution or item offerings, causing enhanced approaches. Encouraging cross-functional collaboration broadens individual skill sets and strengthens team cohesion.

Organizations should create a supportive environment that values continuous learning to adopt adaptability. This would be attained by training and career development, eventually making the members appreciate the need to acquire new knowledge and skills to perform their duties. Workshops, online courses, and mentorship programs will equip workers with the tools necessary to adapt to changed demands. In this manner, an organization communicates that it values growth and is committed to teams in navigating changes.

Second, leaders model adaptability. When leaders within an organization can show flexibility in their roles and acceptance of change, they are a strong example to other team members. In this respect, leaders must communicate openly about strategy or direction changes and engage team members in decision-making. It would help build confidence and provide them with the same approach. When employees see their leaders framing new challenges positively, they can feel empowered to do the same.

Cross-training and role rotation allow a team to be adaptable. Having members understand different roles will provide an organization with residents with deeper functional understanding and process knowledge. It helps employees develop new skills and encourages empathy and collaboration across the team. An example would be when a project manager is put in a technical role; the manager might understand challenges that come up for developers and, therefore, become a better planner and executor of projects.

Besides, acknowledgment and benefit systems can motivate participants to advocate flexibility even more. Acknowledging flexible individuals who approve brand-new duties will strengthen flexibility within the business society. Success from transformed habits is commemorated, urging others to do the same. Whether with even more official acknowledgment programs or basic appreciation, acknowledging the payments of flexible people to a group is one proven method to construct favorable settings where adjustment is considered a chance, not a hazard.

Ultimately, advertising the development state of mind urges adaptability in group functions. When personnel think their capabilities can be created via initiative and understanding, they are more likely to welcome brand-new obstacles. Organizations should support this by offering positive responses and motivating representation of previous experiences. By mounting obstacles as possibilities for development, leaders can aid staff members by watching versatility as an important possession in their expert toolkit.

6.6 Case Study: Navigating Challenges Together

Resilient management involves leading a company through negative problems in a stormy climate. A traditional instance is exactly how Johnson & Johnson managed the Tylenol situation in the 1980s by properly revealing that great management plus openness will certainly cruise with extreme examinations and preserve individuals' dependability and self-confidence. This occurrence shares a crucial lesson in durability: it is a cumulative act, a means for areas to find each other to conquer difficulty.

In September 1986, 7 individuals from the better Chicago location passed away instantly coupled with tragically after taking Tylenol pills tied with cyanide. The information drank the whole country, and the nation promptly doubted the item's safety and security. With lives and the business's credibility at risk, Johnson & & Johnson management had to make immediate choices in such a circumstance with its backup components.

First and foremost was the guarantee of consumer safety and open communication. Instead of minimizing the incident or trying to keep the public relations damage out of the spotlight, Johnson & Johnson immediately issued a nationwide recall of 31 million bottles of Tylenol, estimated at over $100 million. The bold move underlined its commitment to customer safety over profits, instilling trust in the consumers and stakeholders. By prioritizing transparency, the company spoke clearly and concisely about what was happening, answering questions and updating the public with new information.

Besides, the leaders at Johnson & Johnson energized their people around one single commitment: the safety and well-being of every one of their customers. They marshaled cross-functional marketing, publicity/PR, legal, and manufacturing teams to solve the crisis together. This helped in quick response and in realizing how effectively the challenges could be responded to with teamwork. The culture of collaboration within an organization was further instilled by emphasizing that challenges must be addressed end masse, bringing together diversified perspectives and skills to find an effective solution.

The company's resilience went a step further in proactively regaining consumer confidence. Following the crisis, Johnson & Johnson developed tamper-proof packaging and deployed an arduous quality control process. Such advancements boosted the security of the items and increased the market's bench regarding firms' duty for customer defense. Their readiness to purchase safety and security enhancements revealed that as difficulties occur, so do possibilities for development and renovation.

Besides modifications in procedures, Johnson & Johnson's monitoring also required restoring connections with clients and the public. They sought an all-encompassing market project to restore confidence in the Tylenol brand name with its brand-new security attributes and dedication to high quality.

This project was not just about recouping market share; it involved recovering trust funds and showing responsibility. This complies with the fact that this firm was much better able to utilize the dilemma as evidence of its strength and honest management by dealing with customers' stress and anxieties head-on. The Tylenol situation ultimately made Johnson & Johnson the shining example in dilemma administration, gaining customer regard and commitment. The reaction highlighted that durability is not simply an act but an energetic, relaxing approach to leading a company into the bedrock of security, openness, and neighborhood participation.

Final thought: The action taken regarding the Tylenol situation by Johnson & Johnson stands as a testimony to the durability of management at the workplace. They have revealed that durability includes recouping from difficulty and expanding more powerfully with a common initiative by focusing on customer safety and security, urging partnership, and introducing. This can function as an excellent instance where various other companies can find out important lessons plus recognize that encountering misfortunes with each other promotes depend on as well as produces a durable society that can hold up against misfortunes in the times ahead.

6.7 Key Point Donald Trump's potential re-election in 2024

> **Policy Stance:** Promoting a strong national defense and America-first foreign policy, appealing to voters concerned about international relations.

As Donald Trump prepares for his feasible reelection proposal in 2024, the complete series of diplomacy subjects will be at the forefront of his project method. With a focus on hardcore nationwide protection and an "America First" program, Trump has intended to reverberate with those worried about significantly intricate global relationships and nationwide protection. While doing so, this diplomacy structure does not represent him as resistant to defend the American rate of interests yet contrasts his political challengers. Among the cores of Trump's ideas is solid nationwide protection.

Trump claims a solid army deters risks and also maintains Americans secure. In his previous management, Trump promoted huge rises in protection investment in restoring what he claimed was a "diminished" army. He highlights that militaries must be focused on, underlining that a well-funded armed force can maintain America's management worldwide. At the same time, representing himself as a guard of nationwide protection, Trump initially attracts those who place security plus security, especially in a globe full of geopolitical competition versus expanding opponent powers like China and Russia.

The characteristic of Trump's diplomacy is "America First," indicating that American passions are initially placed before worldwide dedication. This specifically reverberates with the citizens who think that previous management has given up residential concerns for worldwide passions. He thinks worldwide contracts and partnerships ought to be renegotiated to profit the United States directly, sustained by plans initially setting apart American employees and sectors. This interest component of the citizens doubtful of globalization and anxious to shield American tasks from international competitors.

The second focus of Trump's diplomacy is readiness for a vibrant activity to secure the American interest rate. His management was noted by uncompromising resistance to any global companies coupled with arrangements viewed as in the displeasure of the U.S. He had taken out of the Paris Climate Agreement along with the Iran nuclear bargain.

Trump wants to interest those who like a durable leader who is vibrant and not scared to handle the facility. His method presumes unilateralism—American concerns preeminent in many intransigent terms. This interests those who think that a staunch, independent personality is required for success in the country.

> **Utilize Fear as a Tool**
> Present challenges as urgent threats that require decisive leadership.
>
> **Adapt Messaging**
> Be flexible in your messaging to respond to changing political climates.

In addition, numerous describe his presidency over Trump as one that has toughened up international relationships, making use of individual participation with North Korea as well as the normalization of relationships with Israel and also numerous Arab states. These successes are mounted as a component of a bigger approach to guarantee tranquility via stamina, which contrasts with conventional polite initiatives. By highlighting such successes, Trump wishes to guarantee citizens that his management design will properly browse global intricacies towards a progressively secure circumstance.

Trump also connects migration and boundary safety to nationwide protection in his international plan messaging. He claims that solid protection likewise implies solid security of the boundaries plus control of migration; he explains this as critical in safeguarding American sovereignty. This has interested the section of the populace that is interrupted by what they view to be the repercussions for residential protection and financial security.

As Donald Trump prepares for his feasible re-election in 2024, his international plan is determined on solid protection coupled with "America First" among his project's solid factors. He has highlighted dedication to the American rate of interest, safety, and security by appealing to the problems of all citizens in worldwide connections. This will certainly assist in concretizing his base and record undecided citizens who think toughness and decisiveness rate management are high qualities throughout unsteady times. As the political characteristics continue to move, Trump's diplomacy story will certainly contribute to forming the body politic's assumptions and options in this forthcoming political election.

Reference

1. Berge, J. (1990). *The Tylenol crisis: A case study in crisis communications*. Public Relations Review, 16(1), 3-12.

2. Broom, G. M. (1994). *Effective crisis communication: A guide for the public relations practitioner*. New York, NY: Longman.

3. Fink, S. (1986). *Crisis management: Planning for the inevitable*. New York, NY: American Management Association.

4. Coombs, W. T. (1995). Choosing the right words: The development of guidelines for selecting the appropriate crisis-response strategies. *Management Communication Quarterly*, 8(4), 447-476.

5. Kaplin, A. (1998). Media coverage of the Tylenol crisis: A retrospective analysis. *Journal of Business Ethics*, 18(1), 1-10.

6. Sheffi, Y. (2005). *The resilient enterprise: Overcoming vulnerability for competitive advantage*. Cambridge, MA: MIT Press.

7. Della Femina, J. (1982). Marketing insights during the Tylenol crisis. *Marketing Management*, 1(2), 34-39.

8. Johnson & Johnson. (1982). Corporate communications during the Tylenol crisis. Johnson & Johnson Archives.

9. McCarthy, J. (1990). The Tylenol crisis: A case study in corporate ethics. *Business Ethics Quarterly*, 1(1), 67-78.

10. McDonald, J. (1998). Crisis management: Lessons from the Tylenol case. *International Journal of Business Communication*, 35(3), 287-302.

11. Smith, D. (1990). The role of leadership in crisis management: The Tylenol case. *Journal of Leadership Studies*, 1(1), 45-54.

CHAPTER 7

The Heart of Collaboration: Building Stronger Bonds

Introduction

In today's connected world, collaboration is not just a positive attribute but an absolute necessity for success in every organization [1-4]. Chapter 7 studies the nature of collaborative relationships and their crucial importance in nurturing a high-performing workplace culture. Real collaboration does more than bring people together; it builds relationships in which people are meaningfully connected and enabled through sharing ideas, taking on challenges, and innovating [5-7]. It examines some basic principles and practices that will help adopt these close bonds among team members, which may improve productivity and satisfaction [8-10].

Trust is the basis of collaboration, a starting point for open communication and mutual respect [11-14]. Once team members have established trust, they are more likely to share their thinking and perspectives without fear of judgment. This chapter intends to adopt a safe space where people feel valued and heard [15]. Organizations can create an environment to support collaboration through active listening and transparent communication; the chapter covers diversity in collaboration [16]. A diverse team has a rich collection of viewpoints, experiences, and expertise that add significant value to collaborative efforts. A company can harness every staff member's capacity by embracing a comprehensive society sustaining varied voices and one-of-a-kind toughness, making results much more cutting-edge and reliable. The chapter supplies useful understandings on producing and keeping varied groups, highlighting the worth of partnership in taking advantage of this variety.

In addition," The Heart of Collaboration" specifies the role of psychological knowledge in forming joint strong partnerships. Leaders with compassion and understanding can exercise their methods more fluently in group characteristics and solve problems or obstacles with empathy. This chapter goes over exactly how leaders need to create psychological knowledge in their groups to make sure that they might get in touch with a much deeper degree. Focusing one's concerns on psychological recognition and partnerships with other companies can make it possible for society to grow on partnership.

Chapter 7 summarizes how to recognize and execute the actual heart of partnership within companies. It has been highlighted that collaboration is not a procedure; however, it is an essential part of any effective business society that enables far better interaction, imagination, and general efficiency. At the heart of the partnership is the opportunity for groups to get incredible outcomes when everyone functions sympathetically with common purposes and appreciates each other.

7.1 Understanding the Value of Collaboration

The partnership is a crucial component in any company's success because it surpasses a single person's capacities by simultaneously combining the cumulative stamina of a group. It uses an atmosphere where numerous histories combine, providing imaginative options for issues with far better addressing. When staff members team up, they share expertise, abilities, and experiences that improve decision-making and embrace a feeling of possession and duty among individuals. This can bring about greater efficiency because several angles of strategy toward jobs lead to even more comprehensive and imaginative results. The value of collaboration suggests that the whole is greater than its parts, and the essence of working together can drive organizations to pursue their goals.

Table 7.1 The importance of collaboration within an organization.

Technique	Description	Benefits
Team Workshops	Conduct workshops on collaborative skills.	It enhances teamwork and builds trust.
Cross-Functional Projects	Involve teams from different departments in joint projects.	Promotes diverse perspectives and innovation.
Peer Feedback Sessions	Hold sessions for team members to provide feedback on collaboration.	Encourages accountability and improvement.
Collaboration Tools Training	Hold sessions post-project to discuss collaboration outcomes.	Increase efficiency and communication.
Reflection and Debriefing	Share successful collaborative projects to inspire others.	Highlights benefits and encourages participation.
Mentorship Programs	Pair experienced employees with newer ones to model collaboration.	Build skills and adopt a collaborative culture.
Interdepartmental Meetings	Schedule regular meetings between departments to align goals.	Strengthen relationships and collaboration.

Furthermore, it enhances interpersonal relationships and develops a sense of community at work. While working together, a sense of bond and trust develops among them that helps establish an excellent organizational culture. Such relationships facilitate accessible communication for the members to share their ideas and views without hesitation. It would develop risk-taking behavior and innovative ideas without fear of criticism. This supportive climate contributes to employee satisfaction, affecting retention and engagement. Most of all, the worth of partnership consists of recognizing its existence in constructing an appropriate office atmosphere where individuals feel encouraged to add, introduce, and grow with each other.

7.2 Facilitating Effective Team Meetings

Effective group conferences involve cooperation, interaction improvement, and driving business performance. To have reliable conferences, one should think about a schedule that details the goals coupled with subjects one will certainly go over. This will certainly aid individuals in getting ready ahead of time and keep the emphasis on the conference, maintaining it on course. By sending out the schedule well in advance, employees can come ready with appropriate details plus understanding that will make conversations efficient and not taxing.

The schedule imitates a guide to direct the conversations, so there is minimal opportunity for digression. A 2nd essential success element is the energetic engagement of all conference guests. An in-person conference is an area where each voice ought to be listened to and valued. The facilitators attain this by utilizing round-robin sharing strategies or escaping into smaller teams to go over a factor before resuming as an entire. This would mean creating an environment that adopts open dialogue and psychological safety. Individuals share suggestions and ideas when they feel comfortable sharing themselves without judgment. Promoters can urge energetic involvement by recognizing all individuals and ensuring cooperation supplies an abundant exchange of numerous perspectives.

Finally, effective meetings culminate in clear action items and follow-up plans. At the closing of each meeting, it is necessary to summarize the key points discussed and state particular tasks assigned to individuals or teams, with deadlines included. The clarity ascertains accountability and sustains momentum even after the meeting has closed. The advantages are that follow-through on action items at future meetings or through digital communication reiterates commitments and allows progress to be tracked. By implementing these practices, organizations can turn meetings from a ho-hum duty into dynamic sessions that assure engagement, advance collaboration, and improve outcomes.

7.2.1 Encouraging Cross-Departmental Collaboration

Interdepartmental collaboration stimulates creativity and influences the overall performance of the organization. Working in teams within departments brings together diverse perspectives, skills, and expertise that approach problems from every angle. Organizations can stimulate this by developing formal opportunities for interaction through joint projects, workshops, and brainstorming sessions. These efforts not only facilitate knowledge sharing but also help break down silos, which usually exist across departments, and encourage a culture of teamwork and problem-solving together.

Table 7.2 The success of cross-departmental collaboration initiatives.

Step	Measurement Method	Metrics/Indicators
Kickoff Meeting Effectiveness	Surveys/Feedback Forms	• Understanding of collaboration • Initial concerns/suggestions • Engagement levels (attendance and participation)
Cross-Functional Teams	Project Outcomes	• Number of projects completed on time • Quality of work (customer satisfaction ratings) • Revenue generated from new initiatives
Regular Check-Ins	Meeting Attendance and Participation	• Attendance rates at check-ins • Engagement in discussions • Action item completion rates
Workshops and Training	Employee Surveys and Recognition Metrics	• Improvement in skills (pre- and post-assessment) • Value ratings from participants
Feedback and Recognition	Customer Feedback and Sales Metrics	• Perceptions of collaboration (survey results) • Frequency of recognition for collaborative efforts
Overall Performance Indicators	Customer Feedback and Sales Metrics	• Customer satisfaction scores (NPS) - Sales data and revenue from collaborative projects - Employee retention rates

One effective way to attain cross-functional cooperation is by setting clear objectives requiring various departments' input and collaboration. Organizing departments around shared objectives will help organizations motivate people to appreciate the result of working together. Also, cross-functional teams for projects should provide elaborative interaction amongst people from different departments, using each one's strengths and expertise. This approach improves project outcomes and relations among team members by enhancing the understanding of each department's role and challenges. Employees will be willing to work together when they realize their contributions are interconnected.

Also, leadership may play a significant role in encouraging collaboration across different departments. Leaders must establish an instance and prompt their groups to engage as long as feasible with various other divisions. They could additionally supply particular rewards that impose such teamwork, like acknowledgment programs or efficiency assessments, including some team effort metrics. In this open atmosphere, which is risk-free for remarks or comments, depending would certainly be embraced, and individuals would certainly team up instead of acting in seclusion. Companies can improve their analytic abilities by supporting interdepartmental participation and producing an extra natural and ingenious work environment.

7.2.2 Using Collaborative Tools and Technologies

Today's business teaming and interaction in an electronic atmosphere have to be based upon collective devices plus innovations. Instances include job monitoring software applications, video clip conferencing, and real-time file partnership. A seamless interaction among team members occurs within the same building or across different parts of the world. This technology helps streamline the workflow for greater efficiency by offering a single place for sharing information, assigning tasks, and tracking progress. For instance, Slack or Microsoft Teams offer space for instant messaging and file sharing, thus giving teams real-time collaboration and ongoing dialogue that keeps people informed and engaged.

Moreover, collaboration technologies encourage diversity within teams and enhance participation. Virtual meeting tools like Zoom or Google Meet allow face-to-face interaction even when a group is separated by distance.

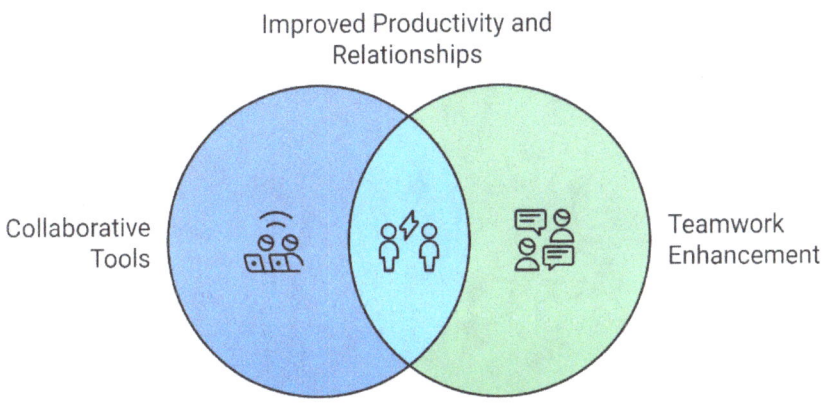

Figure 7.1 Using collaborative tools and technologies.

Such accessibility is essential for organizations operating under fully remote or hybrid models, as it will ensure equity of voice and productive collaboration. Screen sharing, breakout rooms, and collaborative whiteboards help participants brainstorm ideas and contribute to discussions more easily. Companies embracing such collaboration tools will become dynamic and better workplaces, allowing employees to cooperate fruitfully to innovate and meet shared objectives.

7.3 Building Trust Through Shared Experiences

Gaining trust in teams is crucial for adopting collaboration toward organizational success, and shared experiences are paramount to the process. When team members participate in activities together through team-building exercises, collaborative projects, or social events, they build relationships that advance knowledge of each other on a deeper level. Interacting with others apart from their professional roles allows them to show empathy and friendship. In trust, team members overcome challenges and celebrate success, developing a sense of belonging and mutual respect.

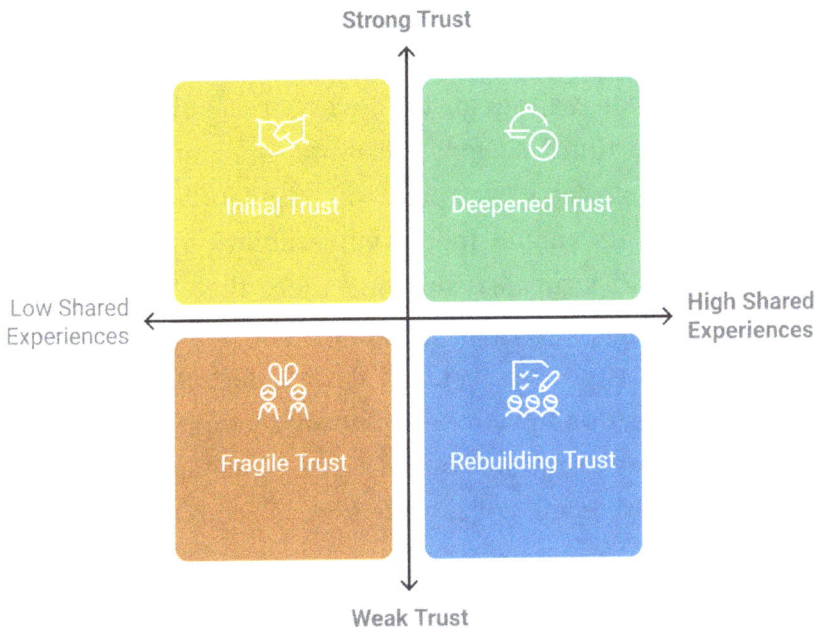

Figure 7.2 Building trust within teams is essential for adopting collaboration and achieving organizational success.

Shared experiences also create an avenue for the free flow of communication and feedback, thus cementing trust among members. Individuals working closely on a project or participating in group activities will likely be more open toward sharing their thoughts and feelings. This openness creates a platform where team members feel safe expressing themselves and their views without being judged. With increased trust, the team members will depend on each other, consult for help, and work well together. This develops individual relationships and cements team cohesion, improving performance and productivity.

Besides, leaders play a significant role in facilitating shared experiences that help build team trust. Leaders can promote interactions that will help to create trust by intentionally creating opportunities for collaboration, such as cross-departmental projects, retreats, or regular team meetings. Moreover, leaders should model vulnerability by sharing their experiences and struggles, showing them that trust goes two ways. In shared experiences, when the leaders themselves actively take part, the teams know trust is part and parcel of life in the organization. Eventually, through emphasizing shared experiences, organizations build a trust-based culture where teams can innovate and collaborate to reach common goals more effectively.

7.3.1 Establishing Clear Roles in Collaborative Efforts

Well-defined roles within team collaborations are very vital in any team project accomplishment. If the team members know exactly what they are to do and how it contributes to the whole project, accountability and efficiency will arise. Clearly defined roles evade overlaps and misunderstandings that may create confusion and frustration. This way, by determining who is responsible for what, teams can ensure that their processes are correct, timely, and of high standard. It will also enhance the performance of the individual and the general effectiveness of teams.

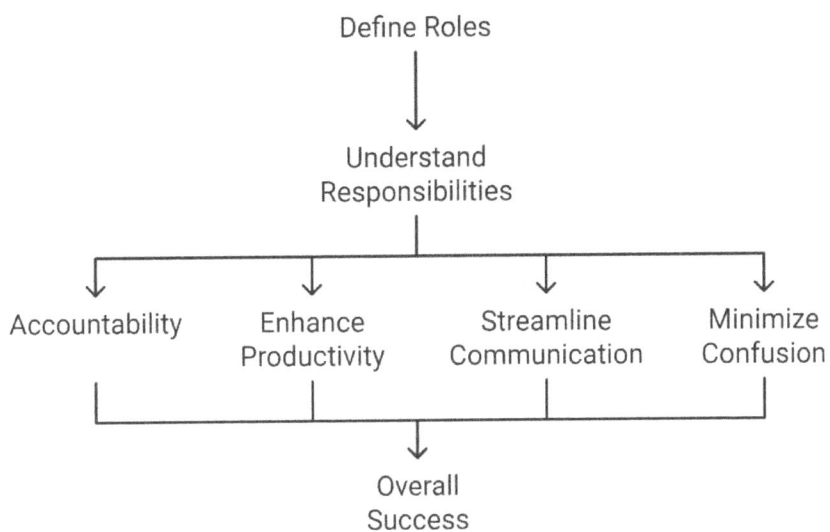

Figure 7.3 Establishing clear roles in collaborative efforts is crucial for the success of any team project.

Besides, clarity of roles leads to effective communication within the group. People know their responsibilities and, therefore, will interact better with others whose tasks involve or complement theirs. The team players are more likely to request input or comments from each other to ensure better project quality. For example, a marketing campaign needs to spell out the specific roles a content creator, designer, and analyst has to undertake so that people are ready and working toward the same goals. The more effective communication between team members, the quicker they can get through setbacks and adapt to changed circumstances, and the better their collaborative effort.

Finally, well-defined roles have a positive influence on morale and team motivation. People with a particular sense of responsibility who can see how their contribution fits into the team's success will be proud to work and contribute to ownership. Such ownership could increase engagement and lead to a more significant commitment toward realizing the team's objectives. Besides, acknowledging individual contributions increases the importance of each team member, thus creating a nurturing environment in which everyone is valued. Organizations that concentrate on developing clear duties develop a joint society where groups can increase with each other and introduce a lot more.

7.3.2 Encouraging Diverse Perspectives

Variety in a group's beliefs motivates imagination as well as technology. Individuals from various histories, experiences, and viewpoints bring several concepts and understandings that can be integrated to produce even more options—varying points of view test traditional reasoning and influence employees to consider choices they might never have considered. Organizations should proactively choose and be worth these varied viewpoints to prosper, enabling creative thinking to prosper, resolving troubles better, and making far better choices.

Useful motivation of varied viewpoints calls for leaders to develop an inclusive society where distinctions are valued and appreciated. This consists of establishing open discussion techniques, such as constant conceptualizing sessions and comments in online forums, throughout which all participants feel comfortable sharing their ideas. Leaders have to likewise design inclusiveness habits by proactively getting to quieter staff members and acknowledging the payments of people from numerous histories. Motivating an environment of regard and visibility can lead workers to share varying viewpoints. This will enrich the conversations and enhance the ingenious outcomes. Ultimately, variety reinforces group connections that assist companies in flourishing in today's complicated and extremely affordable setup.

7.4 Recognizing and Valuing Contributions

Recognizing and valuing payments is core to producing a favorable business society and enhancing staff member involvement. A staff member is probably encouraged in their work when their initiatives are viewed to be identified. Acknowledgment can take several forms, from spoken appreciation at conferences to official honors and rewards. Arranging events for specific and group efficiencies gives workers a feeling of belonging and recognition, hence boosting morale and increasing performance. Performance recognition reinforces desired behaviors and inspires others to achieve excellence.

Table 7.3 The strategies for recognizing and valuing contributions within a team.

Strategy	Description	Implementation Methods	Expected Outcomes	Metrics for Success
Public Recognition	Acknowledge achievements in meetings and newsletters.	Weekly shout-outs and monthly highlights.	Increased morale and team cohesion.	Employee engagement survey results, recognition frequency.
Peer-to-Peer Recognition	Encourage team members to	Use recognition platforms and peer programs.	Strengthened relationships and	Several peer recognitions and feedback

	recognize each other.		collaboration.	on the program.
Personalized Thank-You Notes	Send personalized notes of appreciation.	Managers and team members write notes.	Enhanced sense of value and job satisfaction.	Survey on feelings of appreciation, number of notes sent.
Incentives and Rewards	Provide tangible rewards for performance.	Develop a reward system (bonuses, gift cards).	Boosted motivation and performance levels.	Performance metrics and participation rates in reward programs.
Celebration Events	Host events to celebrate achievements.	Organize quarterly parties and celebrate milestones.	Strengthening team spirit and morale.	Event attendance and post-event satisfaction surveys.

Beyond that, valuing contributions means involving employees in decision-making processes and project planning. When people on the team notice that their ideas and inputs are considered seriously, that gives them additional confirmation that they are needed inside the organization. Involvement might ultimately construct empowerment and a feeling of possession in their job outcomes. In developing chances for partnership and looking for comments, the company proves that each voice matters, allowing innovation in an absolutely comprehensive atmosphere.

Offering value and acknowledging initiatives can assist group characteristics and enhance specific inspiration. When staff members commemorate a group's successes, sociability coupled with dependability are established as important active ingredients of partnership. Acknowledgement of payments can likewise display varied stamina inside a group where staff members learn to value each other's varied abilities and points of view. This common regard, therefore, boosts interaction and partnership to boost group efficiency. Organizations focusing on acknowledgment and worthwhile payments develop an extra-involved workforce and drive cumulative success.

7.4.1 Creating Team Rituals and Traditions

This will certainly assist in establishing group rituals and customs to improve the bonds between employees and the feeling of coming from. Group rituals and customs differ from regular group conferences, brainstorming sessions, and events for achieving task landmarks or individual success. In developing constant techniques that staff members can anticipate, companies produce a common experience that enhances sociability and reinforces group identification. Rituals give a foreseeable framework that can assist groups in browsing their job's ins and outs while supplying minutes of link and interaction.

Group rituals can additionally be an effective way of sharing business worth with society. For example, a once-a-week "shout-out" session in which employees recognize others' payments aids in constructing a society of gratitude plus assistance. Considerate rituals-such as post-project evaluations or conversations of " lessons found out"- are reliable in advertising recurring enhancement and understanding. By incorporating these rights into the group's regular, companies can assist in infusing their core worths as a component of everyday actions and maintain the staff member lined up with their goal and objectives.

Rituals and customs can additionally reinforce durability in times of difficulty. Predefined routines can provide security and convenience to groups when points are challenging or when stress is high. An example could be something as easy as a group coffee break or some enjoyable team-building workout that advises every staff member concerning the power of cumulative assistance. Such minutes alleviate stress and inform the staff members that they're all in something with each other, developing a feeling of area plus participation.

Lastly, by developing coupled embracing group routines along with routines, companies would certainly have the ability to construct an encouraging and joined ambiance where individuals would feel favorable and add to the typical success.

7.4.2 Facilitating Team Retreats and Workshops

Group hideaways and workshops also help with cooperation, depending on the imagination of participants. These immersive experiences allow one to leave ordinary issues and participate in tasks that catalyze even more significant partnerships among associates. Several hideaways combine team wellness with method preparation sessions, permitting individuals to contemplate objectives while bonding with associates to a much deeper degree. It can allow groups to connect openly, learn about the disturbances of the basic office, conceptualize originalities, and check out ingenious collaboration methods.

Workshops can, nevertheless, be personalized to deal with details, obstacles, or ability shortages in a group. A company might additionally arrange interactive sessions for knowing and advancement by looking for the solutions of outside facilitators or using inside readily available abilities. As an example, an interaction abilities workshop will certainly allow the employee to improve their connections with each other, for this reason, making certain excellent partnerships. Problem-solving or imaginative reasoning workshops offer just as much help in preparing the group for bigger jobs. Via assisted knowing procedures, specific capacities are established, and a group society is produced.

Through this, resorts and workshops benefit from establishing the usual objectives and visions all share. On such occasions, groups can have tactical conversations where their tasks straighten with the company's objectives. By having top priorities established jointly coupled with functions specified, staff member understands exactly where their payments drop within the better goal. This alignment bolsters accountability and motivation because the working professionals witness firsthand the impact of their efforts on team success. Finally, team retreats and workshops gather several people to adopt collaboration and skill-building and reinforce a common sense of purpose and commitment among the members.

7.5 Setting Collaborative Goals

Determining collaborative goals is one important step in teamwork that ensures people have something in common to work towards. When teams set an objective, they create a clear roadmap guiding their actions and adopting ownership among the team members. Teams should strive to make collaborative objectives SMART- that is, specific, measurable, attainable, relevant, and time-bound- to enable members to track progress and celebrate success. Your organization should involve the team members in setting goals to tap different perspectives and make all committed to their realization. This inclusivity aspect heightens motivation and encourages accountability since the team members recognize their contributions to collective success.

Second, going through and adjusting collaborative goals regularly provides the momentum for change in variable circumstances. A team working towards achieving set objectives should periodically check performance and see where further hindrances might come from. In such a way, teams can keep themselves agile and responsive to ensure the goals remain relevant and aligned with the organization's overall strategy. By embracing open interaction networks for renovation, companies enable groups to create objectives and techniques jointly. This establishes the tone for the last act: revisiting and establishing collective objectives solidifies synergy and improves efficiency, driving success for usual results.

7.5.1 Measuring Collaborative Success

Determining collective success will certainly assist in identifying exactly how well the group functions or where it requires renovation. Quantifiable and qualitative metrics can be used to figure out group partnerships. Quantifiable procedures might entail keeping an eye on the task conclusion price, time frame, and attaining collection objectives. These metrics give concrete information regarding the group's efficiency coupled with effectiveness. Organizations can likewise measure performance by the variety of jobs finished or results created from collective initiatives to examine how well a group interacts as a natural device.

On the other hand, qualitative procedures provide certain information on group characteristics and basic wellness in partnership. Studies and comment sessions might be utilized to obtain assumptions from the team regarding their experiences when collaborating regarding interaction, depend on, and problem resolution. It may suggest efficient performance with participants of the group, high qualities of communication, and obstacles happening amongst the employees.

Besides, normal representation conferences permit groups to freely discuss collective procedures to develop a society of constant renovation. Quantitative coupled with qualitative analyses integrate into supply a company with an extensive understanding of the success of participation. The understandings from gauging joint success likewise feed right into future methods and campaigns. When companies recognize where their toughness and weak points in joint working lie, they can establish targeted training or growth programs to handle the voids.

For instance, if the responses recommend an interaction issue, workshops on interacting successfully can be started. Acknowledging and commemorating great cooperation strengthens favorable actions and can inspire groups to succeed.

Consequently, the dimension of collective success ought to be focused on to guarantee that companies enhance team effort to accomplish purposeful and impactful end results.

7.6 Case Study: Building Stronger Bonds

Advancement functions best with partnerships, as shown at the center between NASA and personal firms like SpaceX. Such cooperation personifies exactly how the summoning of teamwork on enthusiastic objectives improves the future of room expedition. Such collaborations incorporate know-how from federal government companies with the talent and the advancement of exclusive ventures to develop a one-of-a-kind setting where groundbreaking suggestions can thrive. This aids additionally technical developments by harmony as well as creates closer connections amongst individuals as well as companies concentrated on something acquainted.

Amazing occasions have actually taken place in a partnership between NASA and SpaceX, with the Crew Dragon releasing astronauts to the ISS. For the very first time since 2011, when the Space Shuttle program finished, American astronauts have actually been released from American dirt. It's an exceptional instance of what can be achieved as a result of partnership. NASA's substantial experience in area goals, combined with SpaceX's sophisticated innovation and business spirit, is a winning formula.

This collaboration materializes just how varied toughness can be utilized to deal with intricate obstacles, showing that companies can accomplish amazing outcomes when they combine their abilities. Nonetheless, a common collection of objectives, in addition to common regard and depend on that expands between groups, develops the heart of this cooperation. Excellent interaction plus a dedication to openness maintains the functioning of the connection. Also, NASA and SpaceX can figure out issues with each other coupled with changes to conditions as they transform. As staff members of both companies continue to interact, partnerships grow, and a society of development is taken on.

This participating perspective exceeds technological success; it produces a vision for the future of room expeditions, motivating a brand-new generation of researchers, designers, and travelers. Ultimately, NASA and SpaceX's collaboration serves as a powerful testament to the strength of teamwork in achieving ambitious goals, underlining that the heart of cooperation is indeed building stronger bonds that propel us toward a shared vision.

7.7 Key Point Donald Trump's potential re-election in 2024

> **Republican Party Unity:** Gaining support from key Republican figures and aligning with party leadership to strengthen his candidacy.

Any candidate desiring a party nomination and intending to win the general election does so in a dynamic environment in which party unity is one of the variables. However, the support of important Republicans and political alignment with party leadership can substantially enhance the credibility and appeal of a candidate. This strategic positioning consolidates resources and networks and signals a cohesive vision concerning the party's future to the electorate. With the ever-changing political climate, candidates who can focus on unity within the party present themselves as a unifying force to bridge the gap and garner wide-ranging support across the spectrum of Republican constituents.

One of the best ways this can be encouraged is through endorsements by high-ranking members of the Republican Party. Such endorsements are some of the strongest validators, showing the electorate that the candidate has the qualifications and vision necessary to lead. For instance, the support of former presidents, governors, or any other influential member of Congress will raise one's prominence and credibility. These endorsements can also mobilize grassroots supporters and attract crucial campaign funding- a snowball effect of increased visibility and outreach for the candidate. Candidates will, therefore, seek to make a strong coalition by seeking key endorsements from respected party figures to make them even stronger and more united in candidacy.

> **Engage with Media**
> Use media appearances to shape narratives in your favor.
>
> **Cultivate Loyalty**
> Promote loyalty among your supporters through consistent engagement.

Equally important is the question of alignment with party leadership and a clear commitment to the party principles and priorities. This can take several forms, which include attendance at party meetings, engagement in policy debates, and responsiveness to the concerns of various party factions. The more candidates are involved with party leaders, the better their chances of having their platforms exemplify the party's core values while attempting to address the concerns of diverse Republican constituencies. This builds goodwill among party members and reduces potential divisions that would weaken his chances for primary and general elections. Emphasis on unity, gaining support from influential Republican figures, and moving toward party leadership becomes crucial in a candidate attempting to lead the Republican Party and maneuver through the complications of the electoral process.

Reference

1. Ancona, D. G., & Caldwell, D. F. (1992). Bridging the boundary: External activity and performance in organizational teams. *Administrative Science Quarterly*, 37(4), 634-665.

2. Barlow, J., & Kearney, R. (2020). *Building collaborative teams: A guide to successful partnerships*. New York, NY: Routledge.

3. Brown, J. S., & Duguid, P. (2001). Knowledge and organization: A social-practice perspective. *Organization Science*, 12(2), 198-213.

4. Catmull, E., & Wallace, A. (2014). *Creativity, Inc.: Overcoming the unseen forces that stand in the way of true inspiration.* New York, NY: Random House.

5. Cohen, S. G., & Bailey, D. E. (1997). What makes teams work: Group effectiveness research from the shop floor to the executive suite. *Journal of Management, 23*(3), 239-290.

6. Dyer, J. H., & Nobeoka, K. (2000). Creating and managing a high-performance knowledge-sharing network: The Toyota case. *Strategic Management Journal, 21*(3), 345-367.

7. Edmonson, A. C. (2012). *Teaming: How organizations learn, innovate, and compete in the knowledge economy.* San Francisco, CA: Jossey-Bass.

8. Hargreaves, A., & Fullan, M. (2012). *Professional capital: Transforming teaching in every school.* New York, NY: Teachers College Press.

9. Katzenbach, J. R., & Smith, D. K. (1993). *The wisdom of teams: Creating the high-performance organization.* New York, NY: HarperBusiness.

10. Lencioni, P. (2002). *The five dysfunctions of a team: A leadership fable.* San Francisco, CA: Jossey-Bass.

11. Morgeson, F. P., & Humphrey, S. E. (2006). The Work Design Questionnaire (WDQ): Developing and validating a comprehensive measure for defining work design dimensions. *Journal of Applied Psychology, 91*(6), 1321-1339.

12. O'Leary, M. B., & Mortensen, M. (2010). Go (team) science! *Science, 330*(6000), 319.

13. Schein, E. H. (2010). *Organizational culture and leadership.* San Francisco, CA: Jossey-Bass.

14. Smith, J., & Berg, D. N. (1987). *Paradoxes of group life: Understanding conflict in groups.* San Francisco, CA: Jossey-Bass.

15. Tuckman, B. W. (1965). Developmental sequence in small groups. *Psychological Bulletin,* 63(6), 384-399.

16. West, M. A., & Lyubovnikova, J. (2013). Illusions of team working in health care. *Journal of Health Organization and Management,* 27(1), 134-142.

CHAPTER 8

Empowering the Pack Delegation and Trust

Introduction

Within effective leadership, a delicate dance exists between two crucial elements: delegation and trust. Empowering the Pack Delegation and Trust discusses how leaders can establish an enabling culture that allows for the free flow of delegation while instilling deep trust among team members. Empower teams to own their work, from productivity and creativity to morale. When leaders delegate effectively, they demonstrate to the members of their teams that they can trust them and successfully hand over key responsibilities. This empowerment is not only about workload division but also about building a strong, involved workgroup of valued and motivated people who are set to achieve goals put forth by the organization [1].

Many leaders consider delegation a challenge since one is supposed to give up some control of tasks and decisions [2]. However, this chapter develops the understanding that effective delegation is a crucial enabling skill that encourages efficiency and innovation [3]. According to this approach, a leader assigns responsibilities to team members about their strengths and interests, allowing them to carry out orders and initiate problem-solving and decision-making activities [4]. Consequently, this approach encourages professional development and enables team members to learn new skills, initiate new things, and participate more in decision-making [5]. The chapter identifies some practical ways to achieve effective delegation, including clearly spelling out expectations, ensuring the availability of resources, and maintaining open lines of communication, which are important to make teams thrive [6].

Trust is the base on which effective delegation has to be built; for lack of trust, there could be micromanaging and disengagement, which leads to defeating the whole purpose of empowerment [6]. Chapter 8 discusses building trust through transparency, consistency, and support: leaders showing vulnerability and authenticity create a safe place where team members can take risks and openly share their ideas. Trust earned can have the leader build an environment that adopts collaboration, innovation, and resilience [7]. This, in turn, is a chapter that takes the leader through how to empower his teams through effective delegation of duties and instilling trust: where leaders invest in their people, they develop the full potential of the pack; therefore, individual and organizational success is achieved.

8.1 Understanding the Importance of Delegation

Delegation is the fundamental leading skill that enhances organizational effectiveness by enhancing team productivity. Realizing the importance of this tool initially has to do with leaders being incapable of doing everything themselves; they need to transfer a portion of the responsibility to their team so the work gets managed and the set goals are accomplished. Through effective delegation, leaders relieve their time for strategic planning and decision-making to ensure better management of resources [8]. This will lessen the burden on the leaders to manage the projects, and projects will be right on schedule without delays, making the organization effective [9].

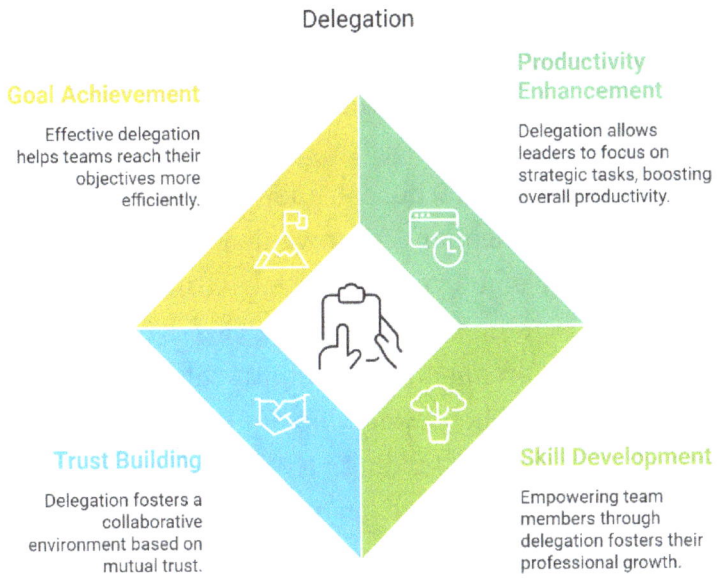

Figure 8.1 Delegation is a fundamental leadership skill that enhances organizational effectiveness and team productivity.

Besides, delegation empowers team members and develops them professionally. When leaders delegate responsibilities to their employees, this indicates to them that they believe in their capabilities, thus boosting morale and motivation noticeably [10]. With such empowerment, the team members learn new skills, take responsibility for their work, and contribute more practically towards the team's goals [11]. In meeting new challenges, individuals derive irreplaceable experience and insight that enhance job satisfaction and belonging to their group. Growth and development naturally trickle down in benefits to the individual and make the team much more capable and resilient in a changing environment.

Finally, effective delegation further spawns a culture of collaboration and mutual trust in a team. Leaders believe in the team's collective ability when they delegate tasks, encouraging openness and teamwork. In such collaboration environments, diverse perspectives may be considered for more innovative solutions with a consequent improvement in problem-solving. Additionally, when employees are involved in decision-making through their assignments, they take a closer interest in their work results, reinforcing their commitment to team success. This will be possible when leadership embraces delegation as an indispensable tool in building a workplace environment supported by cooperation, further individual development, and higher levels of collective performance.

8.2 Identifying Tasks to Delegate

The art of leadership is identifying the tasks that need to be delegated. It helps managers manage their time, team efficiency, and people development. The steps of delegation involve analyzing responsibilities and determining the role that can be passed on yet still allow the attainment of organizational goals. Leaders can work on priority activities that call for exclusive expertise by tactically passing on responsibilities down the line, allowing members to grow and develop.

Figure 8.2 Identifying tasks to delegate.

Delegation requires leaders to carefully assess their workload and determine what essential functions they can perform for others. In one helpful sense, it may go through the categorization into complexity and urgency. This will help identify routine tasks that either take much time or do not demand special skills of the leader - functions that may well be delegated. These could be administrative duties, data recording, or even preliminary research- a division that could free leaders to give time to higher-order thinking, strategy, or decision-making. In identifying those opportunities, the leaders unload their tasks and, at the same time, open valuable learning for the team members.

Table 8.1 Example to identify tasks to delegate.

Task Description	Complexity Level	Suitable Team Member(s)	Rationale for Delegation
Data entry for project reports	Low	Ahmed (detail-oriented)	Ahmed excels in attention to detail and can complete this efficiently.
Preparing marketing materials	Moderate	Ali (creative skills)	Ali has a strong background in design and can bring fresh ideas to the project.
Conducting client follow-ups	Moderate	Khalid (good communicator)	Khalid has excellent interpersonal skills and can build rapport with clients effectively.
Financial analysis for budgeting	High	Maria (analytical skills)	Maria has a strong analytical background and can provide insights that enhance decision-making.
Social media management	Low to Moderate	Majed (social media savvy)	Majed is experienced with social media platforms and can engage audiences effectively.
Organizing team meetings	Low	Talal (organizational skills)	Talal has a knack for logistics and can ensure meetings run smoothly.
Researching industry trends	Moderate	Kalood (research-oriented)	Kalood enjoys research and can gather valuable insights to inform strategy.
Updating the company website	Moderate to High	Nouaf (tech-savvy)	Nouaf's technical skills make him ideal for managing website updates efficiently.

Another important aspect is considering team members' strengths and development needs when selecting tasks to delegate. Leaders should assess individual skills, interests, and career goals to ensure the delegated tasks align with the team members' capabilities and aspirations. This alignment increases the likelihood of successful task completion and enhances employee engagement and motivation. Giving project management work to a team member interested in developing leadership skills is just one example that may adopt a sense of ownership and responsibility. Additionally, it's about supporting and providing resources while giving tasks to a team member; a leader should guide and give feedback to make them feel confident to take up new responsibilities. Leaders can provide a more effective, enabled, and team-oriented environment by giving much-needed thought to determining which tasks to delegate.

8.2.1 Selecting the Right Team Members for Tasks

The success or overall effectiveness of any project in an organization relies on choosing the right members for delegated tasks. This process should begin with clearly understanding the task's complexity, the required skills, and expected outcomes. Leaders must assess task demands to determine which team members possess the necessary expertise and capability. This is where a job that needs hefty evaluation would certainly be ideal for a staff member with fairly some experience in information evaluation. In the same breath, an imaginative advertising project would certainly suit a staff member with a style for style and efficient interaction. This placement will ensure that the job is done both effectively and qualitatively.

Besides technological abilities, leaders need to consider individual features and function designs for the participants in their groups. Efficient delegation implies comprehending each person's toughness, weak points, and choices. For example, some might succeed under stress and appreciate doing intricate jobs, while others desire points to be extra systematized. These leaders enhance team characteristics by matching jobs with individualities to ensure that each specific remains encouraged and participative. Such judicious selection increases the probability of successful completion of tasks. It leads to a conducive working environment where the team members feel their importance and are understood.

Other key determinants of the right team members include the current workload and ability to handle tasks. Assigning tasks to individuals with quite a lot on their hands may lead to burnout and low productivity. Leaders should regularly check their capacity and willingness to undertake team tasks. This consideration will ensure that the delegation process will not negatively impact team performance or morale. Aware of each team member's current commitments, leaders can make informed decisions to balance the workload and make their work more satisfying.

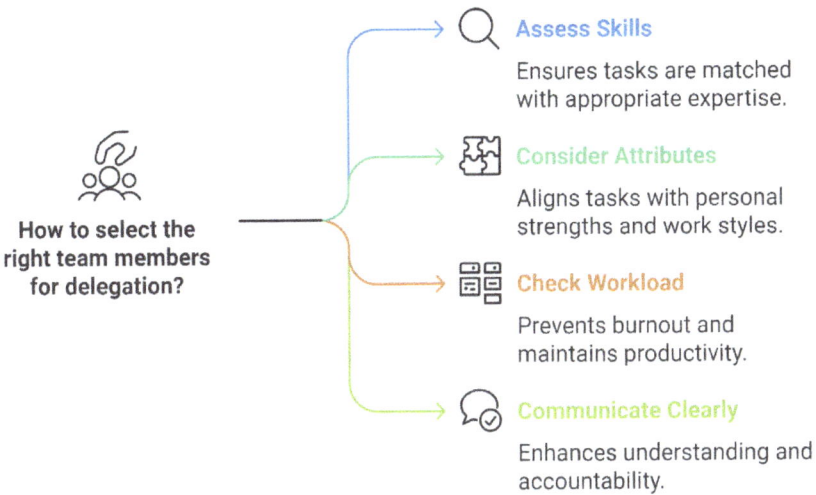

Figure 8.3 Selecting the right team members for delegated tasks.

Finally, there is a need for clarity in the provision of responsibilities by leaders for proper understanding by team members. It can enhance commitment and responsibility by considering the task, why it is important, and how it will help achieve results for the team. Additionally, leaders should allow dialogue where team members are at will to ask questions or raise concerns regarding their assignments. This approach advances a collaborative atmosphere where team members feel empowered to share their insights and take ownership of their work. But perhaps most importantly, we should have leaders who ensure that that team is productive, engages, solves challenges, and succeeds through effective communication and selection.

8.2.2 Providing Clear Instructions and Expectations

Clear instructions concerning what is gotten out of the person is a crucial element of efficient allowance and also considerably affects the outcome specified or task. In the allowance procedure, leaders should describe certain goals, the results they want, and any appropriate due dates for the job. By providing these elements upfront, team members will understand better what is required, reducing confusion and laying the groundwork for accountability. Clarity of instructions will ensure that all are on the same page regarding their goals and working toward them without ambiguity, raising productivity and efficiency.

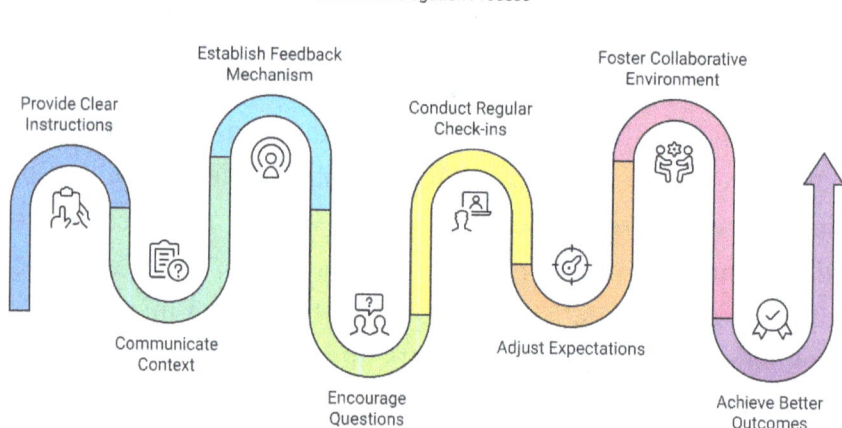

Figure 8.4 Providing clear instructions and expectations.

In addition, leaders should also provide the context and meaning of the task about the overall organizational setup. Explaining how the delegated task relates to the team's goals and the organization's mission motivates the team members by reinforcing the importance of their work. Showing them the big picture allows people to experience a sense of purpose and ownership of the work. When team members understand what they are to do and why it matters, they are far more likely to engage with the task at a deeper level and pursue the highest level of execution.

Moreover, leaders should institute mechanisms for feedback regarding continuous communication throughout the delegation process. In essence, the team members will be allowed to ask questions or make clarifications to reinforce the understanding that the leader is approachable and concerned about their performance. In other words, periodic checks can be an opportunity to discuss progress, describe setbacks, and, when necessary, reset expectations. This is two-way communication, building a team environment in which one feels supported and empowered, and, hence, better outcomes; thus, a more dynamic and cohesive team. Providing clear instructions and maintaining open lines of communication can significantly enhance the leader's ability to delegate effectively.

8.3 Encouraging Autonomy and Ownership

Choosing proper staff members for the jobs handed over is important in constructing a society of freedom and possession within groups. In designating jobs for individuals, considering their stamina, passions, and knowledge, leaders guarantee that staff members take complete responsibility for the jobs designated. This is greater than matching abilities with features, recognizing their inspirations and functioning techniques. Leaders straighten the features with individuals who can do the job and enjoy it. By doing so, satisfaction and responsibility emerge, and each participant will certainly do his work with excitement.

Specifically, in today's busy job setting where the requirement for freedom amongst staff members ends up being progressively noticeable, the management needs to sustain and motivate this requirement. This is where leaders can grant freedom to decide and lead within the assignment's parameters when delegating to the right people. That would give them the autonomy to explore creative solutions and implement their ideas for innovative outcomes. For instance, if he thinks out of steps to reach a solution instead of trying various approaches, putting together a marketing strategy may be less attractive to the group members. This will lead to great job satisfaction and drive performance and engagement.

Another important ingredient that effective delegation brings on board is ownership. A team that owns a task will likely be proud of it and strive for perfection. The feeling of ownership can be adopted by bringing the team members, right from the beginning of the decision-making process, their input and preferences regarding how they think the task should be approached. When people feel that their ideas matter, they take the most initiative and turn out a quality job. Also, the leaders can strengthen the ownership mentality by rewarding and celebrating success, continuing to breed the self-rewarding cycle that keeps team members striving even harder.

Worker Empowerment and Involvement. Better selection of team members concerning tasks while allowing autonomy and ownership gives birth to the workforce. It builds better performance individually and with enhanced teams to adopt and collaborate properly. A leader learning to adopt this trust builds on a culture of accountability and innovation. This will drive improved performance and position the organization to adapt and prosper within an ever-changing environment enabled by its employees, who are key to long-term success.

8.3.1 Building Trust Through Empowerment

Empowerment is important in gaining trust in a team and ensuring successful cooperation and achievement of goals in the organization. If the management makes people responsible for tasks and gives them substantial decision-making powers, it means that they believe in the strengths of their team members. Empowerment will enhance an individual's self-confidence and strengthen the confidence between the leader and the team. When employees feel that their leaders are willing to hand them meaningful tasks, they are more likely to show loyalty and commitment, which forms a positive feedback loop in the dynamic strengthening of the whole team.

Empowerment also invites open communication, probably the bedrock of trust. Being empowered, team players become less hesitant to share their ideas, concerns, and feedback for fear of repercussions. This openness means embracing diverse perspectives, ensuring richer discussions and innovative solutions. Those leaders who invite input and make space for dialogue show respect for the insight of their team, further cementing their trust. As a result, whereas team members discuss it openly, they develop much better relationships, which in turn makes it easier to work through difficulties together and be more productive.

Table 8.2 The strategies for building trust through empowerment in a team setting.

Strategy	Description	Expected Outcomes	Examples of Implementation
Encourage Autonomy	Allow team members to make decisions within their roles.	Increased confidence and ownership.	Assign projects where individuals set their own goals.
Provide Resources	Ensure team members have the tools and information they need.	Enhanced performance and reduced frustration.	Offer training sessions and access to necessary software.
Open Communication	Create an environment where team members feel safe sharing ideas and concerns.	Strengthened relationships and collaboration.	Hold regular team meetings and feedback sessions.
Recognize Achievements	Acknowledge individual and team contributions publicly.	Boosted morale and motivation.	Celebrate successes in team meetings or through company newsletters.
Support and Guidance	Be available to assist when needed without micromanaging.	Increased trust and reduced anxiety.	Schedule regular one-on-one check-ins to discuss progress.
Set Clear Expectations	Communicate goals and performance standards.	Improved clarity and focus in tasks.	Provide written guidelines and ensure everyone understands their

			roles.
Encourage Skill Development	Support team members in pursuing professional growth opportunities.	Enhanced capabilities and job satisfaction.	Offer training programs or support for attending workshops.
Solicit Feedback	Regularly ask for input on processes and decision-making.	Increased engagement and a sense of ownership.	Conduct anonymous surveys or suggestion boxes for team input.

Moreover, empowering employees can eventually lead to much accountability. Once people are granted the power to decide where their work is concerned, they tend to own the results. In the sense of ownership, accountability ensures that each team member strives to their highest standards, hence a culture of excellence. At this point, the leader can make follow-ups by providing resources and support and holding the team members responsible for performance. As the employees realize that their contributions make all the difference in team success, trust in the leaders and their peers deepens, creating a more cohesive and motivated team environment.

Eventually, building trust through empowerment will result in high-performance teams and a positive workplace culture. Engaged, satisfied employees are trusting, empowered employees. Perhaps this leads to reduced turnover rates and a greater commitment to the organization's mission. In addition, with increased trust, the team will be resilient regarding adversity. Empowerment in a team can help teams better adapt, innovate, and collaborate, hence driving success for the person and organization in this increasingly complex and dynamic landscape.

8.3.2 Creating a Feedback Loop for Delegated Tasks

A feedback loop of activities delegated is important in gauging whether leaders and members can address one another during the process. In a well-constituted feedback loop, the leader can follow progress, challenges, and guidance, while team members can always share their observations and views. Such constant interaction can reproduce partnership and also assistance, for this reason enhancing the possibilities of reliable job conclusion. Normal check-ins and progression updates allow leaders to understand whether the passed-on jobs are on the program, make modifications, and step in if required. Comments loopholes likewise make individuals liable and also devoted to their jobs. When they understand that every item of the job will certainly be talked about, they tend to take their task seriously and do their best.

Leaders better highlight this responsibility when discussing success, give positive comments, and recommend enhancements. Such communications will certainly aid employee in brightening their abilities together revealing their payments are valued, therefore encouraging them to be deeply involved in their jobs. Crucial producing a comments loophole allows continual renovation to penetrate the group society. By urging employees to assess their experiences and share their points of view on the delegation procedure, a leader can discover much regarding what functions well and what can be boosted. This will help build better delegation strategies in the future since the leaders will know how to align tasks according to the strengths and preferences of individuals. A strong feedback mechanism enhances the performance of delegated activities and adds to overall development, such as the growth of a cohesive and high-performing team.

8.4 Celebrating Successful Delegation

Success with delegation is a cause for celebration; it recognizes individual and team achievements, reinforces a culture of empowerment, and further advances collaboration within an organization. Of course, there is every reason to value the contribution of team members where leaders take time to recognize and celebrate that tasks have been well handled. This can be through public recognition in team meetings, personally written thank-you notes, or small rewards. Recognition of such achievements will surely uplift morale and motivate the leaders towards high performance.

More so, celebrations of successful delegations have the merit of bringing a sense of ownership and pride among the members. Once people see their efforts appreciated, they are most likely willing to invest more in their jobs and take the initiative to handle duties in the future. A feeling of ownership could consequently drive better engagement and even a desire to handle new challenges. For instance, recognizing a team member who led a project successfully can motivate others to step up and take on leadership roles in their assignments. In turn, this influences a ripple effect where the capability of the entire team is enhanced because other members are more prepared to take risks and contribute creatively.

A successful celebration is also important because it helps solidify the experience learned from the delegation process. It provides an excellent opportunity for leaders to reflect on what went right and discuss how the delegation process is improved. Shared experience from successful projects can help teams note the best practices for future tasks. This reflective practice will improve individual and team performance and contribute to a culture of continuous improvement where learning from experience is valued and encouraged.

Finally, celebrating successful delegation strengthens team cohesion and the general workplace culture. When teams celebrate together, they develop camaraderie and reinforce their identity together. This way, a shared experience will forge deeper relationships among team members and make collaboration conducive to easy flow. Greater trust and rapport in the team mean that individuals are better prepared to support one another, share ideas, and work together effectively. Hence, celebrating successful delegation acknowledges individual effort and amplifies the team's collective strength toward the continuous success of the organization.

8.4.1 Overcoming Barriers to Delegation

Overcoming the barriers to delegation is essential to good leadership and excellent team performance. Many reasons lead leaders to seek help on delegation, including lack of confidence in one's team, desire not to lose control, and poor quality of work done by others. A leader can only address these barriers by acknowledging his perceptions and beliefs about delegation. Recognizing that it is not a sign of weakness but one of the most strategic approaches to increase productivity and develop teams will create a different mindset for leaders. Such a shift in perspective will help team members feel empowered and form a culture where delegation is viewed as added value.

Overcoming Barriers to Delegation

Supportive Culture
Fostering an environment that values collaboration and growth.

Trust in Team
Building confidence in team members' abilities to handle tasks.

Empowerment
Encouraging team members to take ownership and develop skills.

Clear Communication
Ensuring expectations and guidelines are understood by all.

Figure 8.5 Overcoming barriers to delegation.

One of the most general obstacles to delegation is the fear that tasks will not be done to standard. Leaders must communicate expectations and provide the resources and support to defeat this. Clear parameters and defined desired results address concerns about quality. Secondly, the leader can establish a feedback loop in which frequent check-in and update points are scheduled. This approach ensures that tasks stay on track and enables team members to ask questions and seek clarification, adopting a collaborative spirit. As leaders learn to trust their team members' capabilities, they will become more comfortable delegating responsibilities.

Another big obstacle to overcome is misunderstanding, which adds to the leader's workload. A common fear among many leaders is that one will have to spend extra time overseeing and managing the operating tasks, increasing stress. However, effective delegation should result in a net decrease in workload over time. Likewise, leaders ensure the team's development of a sense of ownership regarding tasks through proper selection and allowing team members autonomy. This relieves the workload on the leader and also contributes to the betterment of the skills and capabilities of team members, which they will eventually apply to the betterment of the team.

Overcoming the barriers to delegation requires, on the one hand, an enabling organizational culture that will support cooperation and empowerment. This can be enabled through active advocacy of the benefits by the leaders through sharing stories related to successful delegation within an organization. Training and resources can help them overcome their fears and misconceptions about effective delegation practices. Leaders can adopt an environment that encourages delegation of authority, allowing team members to engage in risk-taking, building new competencies, and delivering results against important organizational goals. Leaders can overcome the delegation obstacles and lead a more empowered, engaged, and high-performing team.

8.4.2 Training Team Members for Success

Training team members for success is a high-yield investment that pays off in long-term individual and organizational divi-dends. More importantly, training prepares the employees with the necessary skills and knowledge to confidently assume new responsibilities and build on prior knowledge. This training may be completed through formal workshops, a mentor system, or on-the-job training. This automatically ensures that team members will be more open to being delegated, which means the work gets done in a shorter time and is better quality-wise. A well-trained team is more competent and motivated since people see themselves growing professionally.

Training allows continuous learning to flourish and increases improvement within a company. When leaders stress the need for skill development, leaders are telling the teams that the growth of skills matters. Leaders motivate employees to pursue other opportunities, which is key to continued innovation. As team members feel supported, they are more likely to experiment with newer ideas and methods. The leaders can facilitate training sessions in various skills, such as technical and soft skills like communication, teamwork, and problem-solving, to bring a rounded workforce to tackle the challenges. Working collaboratively in a collective environment will go a long way in individual performance and team dynamics.

Finally, proper training should include feedback and evaluation so that team members can successfully apply their skills. Constant analyses and follow-ups allow the management to understand exactly how well the training functions or if any other locations require even more focus. A comments loophole enables the leader to urge staff members' experiences and understand right into their understanding trip. Identifying accomplishment as well as progression can encourage staff members with training. Ultimately, companies can be ensured of a qualified, certain, and encouraged company to handle a continually altering service setting via financial investment in training and growth.

8.5 Recognizing Individual Strengths in Delegation

Entrusting each individual's stamina is among the vital parts of management choices that establish efficiency and spirit amongst the functioning groups. Each includes abilities, experience, and understanding of offices that might aid their leaders in advancing one of the most matched works according to everyone. By doing this, leaders can pass on far better by evaluating and valuing what each staff member is proficient at, making sure features are matched to the right people. This will certainly increase the opportunities for success and encourage the employee because they will feel valued due to their payment.

Likewise, with strengths-based delegation for the leaders, possession plus inspiration rise among participants. One will certainly be extra thinking about working with jobs mirroring toughness coupled with passions. For example, one with exceptional logical abilities might wish to service information evaluation while an additional proficient at interaction might want to manage or discuss with customers. This positioning guarantees far better distribution, boosts self-confidence, and raises complete employee work satisfaction, creating a favorable and effective job setting.

Identifying toughness can embrace private efficiency and promote a society of group cooperation. When staff members understand each other's stamina, they can collaborate more properly, using the toughness of others to match their very own. The leader can embrace this collective mindset by giving staff members ways to share abilities and understanding. People are valued for their stamina and equipped to sustain their coworkers. It also boosts analytics and advancement by unifying varied viewpoints when approaching difficulty. 3rd, as well as last, leaders have to go back to specific stamina sometimes since group characteristics and duties alter. Constant comments and open interaction are crucial in recognizing how staff members' abilities might be created with time and even in feedback to brand-new difficulties. By preserving versatility in strategies for delegation, leaders can readjust job projects towards the most effective fit of the present stamina of their staff members. This proceeding procedure of acknowledgment and adjustment improves the efficiency of delegation, enhances a society of development and growth, and makes people really feel sustained in their expert trips, inspiring them to contribute to group success.

8.5.1 Evaluating Delegation Outcomes

Analysis of the results of delegation assists a leader in recognizing the factors in which the methods are functioning and where improvement might be required. Analysis of the delegation results entails inspecting the last results of jobs passed on and the effects on team characteristics, private efficiency, and business goals. In this context, organized results evaluation might offer leaders a thorough insight into exactly how well delegation techniques work and assist them in making educated choices on future delegation initiatives. This reflective technique develops the basis for continual renovation coupled with societal responsibility.

Figure 8.6 Cycle of Delegation Evaluation.

Among the most crucial points to consider when evaluating the end results of delegation is the success of the finished jobs. When a job is being passed on, leaders are meant to develop detailed standards for success, consisting of objectives, target dates, and high-quality criteria at the start. Upon the job's conclusion, leaders evaluate these requirements to see whether the results satisfy assumptions. Both measurable information, such as conclusion prices, efficiency metrics, and qualitative comments from employees, might enable a complete sight of the efficiency of the delegation.

This double method allows leaders to analyze completion items, procedures, and the teamwork associated with attaining the outcomes. In addition to whether the job available achieves success, various other factors should be considered in analyzing the result of delegation, including group spirit and specific growth. The employees must be asked about their points of view concerning their experiences when taking care of passed-on jobs. Discover exactly how these obligations have influenced their involvement and also complete satisfaction.

How delegation influences the group's characteristics and the growth of the specific can be located when leaders recognize the finest methods and locations that may require modifications. For example, mean comments reveal that the employee felt overloaded or unassisted on their job. In that case, leaders might improve their delegation method so that the assignments will more clearly match up with the strengths of the individuals and the resources available next time.

Finally, regularly assessing delegation outcomes creates a transparent culture between members. The leaders shall share such assessment results and discuss lessons that might have been learned therein. This encourages further collaboration among team members by providing feedback and sharing views. This openness will bring trust among leaders and their teams and jointly inspire ownership in the delegation process. By evaluating the outcomes of delegation, an organization can fine-tune its methods constantly and is likely to achieve better performance, improved relations, and empowered people to face any challenges in the future.

8.6 Case Study: Delegation and Trust

In today's fast-moving service globe, supervisors ought to understand how to equip their workers with technology and high business efficiency via efficient delegation. A fine example of this method is Zappos, an on-the-internet footwear coupled with an apparel store renowned for terrific customer care. Zappos deals with a version of delegation where staff members with degrees are encouraged to choose, directly influencing consumer contentment. Zappos equips the front lines to have problems and execute options, taking consumer experience to the next degree while developing count on and responsibility in their labor force.

At Zappos, permission remains in the firm's DNA: customer support. Workers are encouraged to take possession of concerns and make choices without supervisory authorization, considerably minimizing feedback time and enabling tailored consumer communications. As an example, when a client contacts a problem, staff members can use it for reimbursement, exchange, or added rewards without forwarding the issue to a manager. This degree of permission results in quicker resolutions and brings certain possession within workers, as they feel valued for their judgments and experience. The elimination of administrative difficulties releases an active labor force in Zappos that can be fast and effective in its client actions.

In the Zappos required version, trust funds are vital to recognizing its success. The leaders provide their staff members with considerable training and a society where open interaction encourages them. This suggestion is based on the belief that the workers can make suitable choices where the business has actually established core values and objectives. Zappos encourages dedication and solid commitment, creating an atmosphere of assistance in which staff members feel relied on. Staff members are most likely to go above and beyond for consumers when they can see that their payments matter and are equipped to act in the best interests of the consumer and the firm.

Ultimately, with Zappos, it becomes clear that customer service and organizational culture do great things if employees can be trusted to do the job. By putting responsibility upon employees to take matters into their own hands about their jobs and make decisions, customer satisfaction is gained, and a motivated, participative workforce is built up. This model shows that leaders who work to empower and create trust produce an environment where employees are wanted and desire to participate in organizational success. With the world moving into an environment where customer service will differentiate a person from another, Zappos presents an exemplary scenario on the issue of packing through effective delegation and establishing trust.

8.7 Key Point Donald Trump's potential re-election in 2024

> **Media Strategy:** Using social media and alternative news outlets to communicate directly with supporters and counter mainstream media narratives.

As Donald Trump approaches the 2024 re-election, everything will fall into place based on how he engineers his media strategy to achieve victory. His strategy will involve appealing directly to his base through social media and alternative news. Trump promised to bypass mainstream news, as he usually accuses them of biased and misrepresentative coverage, through such media outlets. This direct communication strategy will enable him to establish his faithful base, speak his messages without filters, and contrast with mainstream media-driven narratives.

Social media platforms like Twitter and Facebook have significantly influenced Trump's political communication since the 2016 campaign. He can address his audience directly in real-time updates, mobilize support, and fight opponents. This immediacy forms a bond with his followers; their network is huge. Besides, going viral and using trending topics are ways he will always be relevant in a fast-changing environment. Such support for fans to share his messages produces them as yard ambassadors, prolonging the past to his adherence.

> **Focus on Economic Messaging**
> Center your platform around job creation and economic growth.
>
> **Promote Nationalism**
> Appeal to national pride and identity in your rhetoric.

Additionally, the participation with different information media understanding of Trump's political views. This partnership supplies electrical outlets where his plans and activities can be checked out in a favorable light. At the same time, it talks to those who feel marginalized by the mainstream media. By acting as a champ for freedom of speech plus an adversary of what he explains as "incorrect information," Trump galvanizes his base while encouraging them of his story. This two-pronged technique of social media site usage, together with alternate information, permits him to create a natural media setting that would certainly promote his project by reducing the results of damaging protection from standard resources.

Eventually, Trump's media strategy for the 2024 political election highlights how straight calls and different stories are vital in creating public understanding. Utilizing social media sites and also alternative information, he has a hard time equipping his advocates while attempting to regulate the story together with responding to mainstream media uncertainty. This strategy shows an understanding of the nature of the modern media landscape and how it changes according to transforming interaction characteristics. Through this strategy, he will certainly be able to mobilize his base on political election day and make certain of a 2nd term in the workplace for himself.

Reference

1. Zappos. (n.d.). *Customer service philosophy*. Retrieved from https://www.zappos.com/c/return-trans-options

2. Blanchard, K., & Johnson, S. (2013). *The new one minute manager*. HarperCollins.

3. Covey, S. R. (2004). *The 7 habits of highly effective people: Powerful lessons in personal change*. Free Press.

4. Goleman, D. (2000). *Leadership that gets results*. Harvard Business Review, 78(2), 78-90.

5. Hackman, J. R., & Oldham, G. R. (1976). Motivation through the design of work: Test of a theory. *Organizational Behavior and Human Performance, 16*(2), 250-279.

6. Hargrove, R. (2007). *Mastering the art of delegation*. Leadership and Management in Engineering, 7(1), 1-9.

7. Lencioni, P. (2002). *The five dysfunctions of a team: A leadership fable*. Jossey-Bass.

8. Mintzberg, H. (2009). *Managing*. Berrett-Koehler Publishers.

9. Senge, P. M. (2006). *The fifth discipline: The art and practice of the learning organization*. Crown Business.

10. Ulrich, D., & Brockbank, W. (2005). *The HR value proposition*. Harvard Business Review Press.

11. Yukl, G. A. (2013). *Leadership in organizations* (8th ed.). Pearson.

CHAPTER 9

Celebrating Wins: The Importance of Recognition

Introduction

Acknowledgments and events of success have become the recognition secrets for staff members' interaction and complete satisfaction in today's business society. This chapter explores the extensive effect acknowledgment can carry on people and groups. Alarifi claims recognizing success can establish a favorable workplace, raise inspiration, and develop more powerful groups. This chapter shows that acknowledgment is not a procedure but an intense method causing continuous business success.

The chapter starts by laying out the mental structures of acknowledgment, using a study highlighting exactly how recommendation can satisfy integral human requirements for gratitude and also coming from. Alarifi provides proof recommending that staff members who feel identified are more likely to be involved, efficient, and dedicated to their companies. Real-life instances plus studies of how various companies have applied acknowledgment programs to take their work environment society to the following degree show how acknowledgment and staff member spirits are attached [1-4].

Besides, Alarifi asserts the timeliness coupled with the importance of acknowledgment. Commending victories purposefully reinforces preferable actions plus developments and continual enhancement in society. In this chapter, he has recommended different efficient methods leaders can use to recognize successful individualized acknowledgments, public events, or peer-to-peer acknowledgment campaigns. In so doing, Alarifi outfits the leader with the needed devices to install acknowledgment right into the core material of the company.

9.1 Understanding the Psychology of Recognition

Workplace recognition is critical to employee behavior, motivation, and overall job satisfaction. Understanding the psychology of recognition helps an organization realize how it deeply impacts its employees' psyche. Recognition satisfies basic psychological needs, especially appreciation, belonging, and being needed [5]. When employees feel their contribution to the company is valued and recognized, they have a sense of purpose and commitment to their jobs [6].

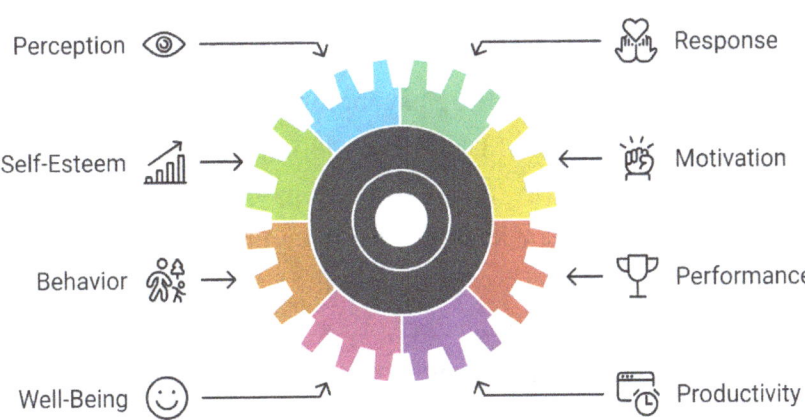

Figure 9.1 Recognition in the workplace plays a crucial role in shaping employee behavior.

Research in psychology underlines that recognition activates the reward centers in the brain, releasing neurotransmitters such as dopamine. This neurochemical response reinforces feelings of happiness and strengthens the repetition of behaviors that result in recognition [7]. When employees are recognized for their efforts, they are likely to repeat those behaviors, thus increasing productivity and engagement. This becomes a reinforcing circle important in developing a motivated workforce [8].

Moreover, recognition is one sort of social signal that breeds a sense of belongingness within teams and organizations. Humans are social animals, and the workplace is no exception. Recognition given to an individual raises their self-esteem and aligns them with colleagues. This may lead to better interpersonal relationships, good teamwork, and a collaborative attitude. Conversely, a lack of recognition leads to isolation and disengagement, adversely affecting morale and productivity.

Additionally, there is the psychology of acknowledgment: timeliness and importance. Acknowledgment should specify a specific success to be better. Common appreciation tends to appear insincere and will likely not accomplish business needs. For example, when the staff member makes an ingenious concept in a group conference, that acknowledgment allows others to recognize their suggestions can be approved, opening up an opportunity for freedom of ideas and advancement.

Acknowledgment of staff members directly connects with companies experiencing far better retention and commitment. Valued workers continue to be with their companies, thus decreasing turnover-related expenses while producing security within the offered job atmosphere. On the various other hand, leaders' capacity to understand some emotional concepts underlying numerous acknowledgment techniques commemorates their payments towards companies at big.

9.2 Creating a Recognition Program

Developing an acknowledgment program is vital for establishing a favorable job society and raising worker interaction. An acknowledgment program recognizes private and group payments while enhancing wanted actions and the worth of a company. In producing a structured technique to acknowledge, firms can make terrific strides in improving spirits, boosting retention prices, and guaranteeing general efficiency. This procedure must begin with specifying clear goals lined up with the company's objectives and the labor force requirements.

Table 9.1 The comprehensive guide for organizations looking to create an effective recognition program

Component	Description	Examples	Implementation Strategies	Evaluation Metrics
Program Objectives	Define the goals of the recognition program.	• Increase employee engagement • Improve retention • Adopt teamwork	• Conduct surveys to understand employee needs • Align objectives with organizational values • Set clear, measurable goals	• Employee engagement scores • Retention rates
Types of Recognition	Identify the different forms of recognition that	• Peer recognition • Managerial recognition	• Develop categories for recognition	• Number of recognitions given

	will be offered.	celebrations	• Create guidelines for nominations • Encourage spontaneity in recognition	• Types of recognition utilized
Recognition Frequency	Determine how often recognition will occur.	• Weekly shout-outs • Monthly awards • Annual ceremonies	• Schedule regular recognition opportunities • Incorporate recognition into team meetings • Plan annual celebration events	• Frequency of recognition events • Participation rates
Recognition Format	Decide on the recognition format (e.g., verbal, written, awards).	• Certificates • Plaques • Social media posts	• Design visually appealing certificates • Create a social media strategy for recognition • Develop a recognition platform (e.g., an app or internal website)	• Employee feedback on formats • Engagement on social media posts
Communication Plan	Outline how the program will be communicated to employees.	• Email announcements • Intranet updates • Team meetings	• Develop a comprehensive launch plan. • Use multiple channels for communication • Create engaging content to explain the program	• Employee awareness levels • Participation in launch events
Training and Support	Provide training for managers and employees on how to give adequate recognition.	• Workshops Online modules • Resource guides	• Schedule regular training sessions • Create easily accessible online resources • Encourage managers to model recognition behaviors	• Training Attendance • Post-training feedback

Feedback Mechanism	Establish a way for employees to provide feedback on the recognition program.	• Surveys • Suggestion boxes • Focus groups	• Conduct regular surveys to gather insights • Hold focus groups to discuss program effectiveness • Encourage open dialogue about recognition experiences	• Feedback response rates • Changes made based on feedback
Celebration Events	Plan events to celebrate achievements and recognize employees publicly.	• Annual awards ceremony • Team-building events • Holiday parties	• Schedule events well in advance • Involve employees in event planning • Promote events through various channels	• Attendance rates • Employee satisfaction scores
Continuous Improvement	Create a process for regularly reviewing and improving the recognition program.	• Annual reviews • KPI tracking • Benchmarking	• Set up a committee to oversee the program • Regularly analyzed data collected from evaluations • Stay informed about best practices in employee recognition	• Progress towards objectives • Adaptations made based on evaluation

The first step in establishing a successful recognition program is to define its goals. Companies need to consider what they wish to attain: raising spirits, enhancing group communication, or motivating advancement. With certain objectives in mind, management can tailor the program to satisfy the particular demands of their labor force. For instance, if staff member retention is of the utmost significance, the program would certainly target long-lasting payments as well as success-causing commitment.

The program's success depends heavily on staff member participation in its advancement. Encouraging your workers with studies or emphasis teams can give leaders useful insight into what sorts of acknowledgment mean a great deal to their groups. Such actions might assist in molding the program for approval because various individuals have various choices. While some workers like public acknowledgment at conferences, others might enjoy individual acknowledgments from their supervisors. Recognizing these choices boosts the program's efficiency and guarantees that acknowledgment feels authentic.

As soon as the goals and workers' choices are understood, companies can quickly figure out what kind of acknowledgment best fits. A well-implemented program should contain some formal and informal strategies. Peer-to-peer recognition may further inspire teamwork and friendliness among colleagues, and the leaders must recognize their reporting personnel. Formal awards like the "Employee of the Month" and milestone events celebrating greater successes may also be influential. This would certainly boost uniformity and openness, structuring the acknowledgment procedure with clear standards and timelines.

Lastly, leveraging innovation can improve the acknowledgment procedure and drive engagement. Many companies use online recognition platforms where employees can give and receive recognition in less than a minute. It can also track recognition activity, providing much-needed data to measure the program's effectiveness over time. Besides, the program should be communicated regularly and promoted. Awareness and participation are raised through different channels, such as emails and team meetings. By sharing success stories and communicating positive outcomes, organizations reinforce recognition as an important part of the workplace culture.

In other words, it is a strategic step to change organizational culture and employee engagement. Such a culture can be developed in an organization where employees' contributions are valued and celebrated by clearly defining objectives, involving employees, selecting appropriate methods, and leveraging technology. An extensively carried out worker acknowledgment program boosts spirits coupled with inspiration to drive far better efficiency, raising commitment and performance.

9.2.1 Celebrating Small and Big Wins

Commending tiny plus huge success is critical in developing a favorable office society, plus keeping high worker spirits. Tiny success, such as finishing a tough job or getting to a turning point in a task, offers prompt possibilities for acknowledgment and inspiration. Such recommendations go a lengthy method producing a feeling of development plus inspiration amongst staff members. Whenever the staff members experience that their initiative is very much valued on pointless tasks, it supports their promises and dedication in the direction of the job.

Events of little triumphs brighten energy as groups with self-confidence tackle larger obstacles in a perky way. On the other hand, large successes are crucial in joining the labor force by developing satisfaction in common successes; these could vary from company-wide occasions and honors events to a shout-out at a conference. In such instances, highlighting significant successes improves spirits and enhances the value of cooperation and partnership in achieving business objectives. It aids the company in recognizing the society of recognition: each tiny and huge victory urges staff members to keep far better group characteristics with successive victories.

9.2.2 Utilizing Peer-to-Peer Recognition

Peer-to-peer acknowledgment urges a favorable office society and also raises staff member involvement. Unlike conventional methods of acknowledgment, where supervisors or managers are meant to identify success, peer-to-peer acknowledgment equips staff members to value others and commemorate their payments. It enhances employee connections and produces an incorporated setting where everybody feels vital. A company can use its labor force's cumulative stamina by executing an energetic peer-to-peer acknowledgment program, causing much better spirits, partnership, and general efficiency.

One of the most crucial benefits of peer-to-peer acknowledgment is that it infuses a society of recognition and assistance within the groups. When staff members reveal gratitude for their coworkers' initiatives, it aids in developing sociability and trust amongst individuals, therefore creating far better social partnerships. This is specifically so in varied work environments where cooperation throughout various functions and histories is crucial. This breakthrough is a feeling of coming, so companies might concentrate much more on complete work satisfaction and reduction of estrangement by developing settings that permit the employees to affix their worth to each other's ideas.

An efficient peer-to-peer acknowledgment program entails some actions. Initially, companies must make clear exactly how to provide acknowledgment and for what actions. This might specify specific requirements, like team effort, advancement, or anything extraordinary regarding client service. The second is to provide a place for acknowledgment. An online device and even easy devices such as a notice board together with time exploded of a conference for shout-outs supply the networks for making acknowledgments readily available and simple for all to join.

Furthermore, the society of peer-to-peer acknowledgment ought to be grown through business interactions and training. The need to recognize peers should be an ongoing discussion in the organization. Training can help employees understand the value of recognition and how to give feedback. This enhances recognition quality and makes employees comfortable participating in the program. Celebrations of the power of peer recognition, such as telling success stories or highlighting frequent contributors, may also be used to stir participation and enthusiasm.

The positive effects of peer-to-peer recognition extend beyond individual morale; they can lead to tangible benefits for the organization. Teams that engage in regular recognition are often more collaborative, innovative, and productive. When employees feel appreciated by their peers, they are expected to go above and beyond in their work, contributing to higher overall performance and achieving organizational goals. In addition, organizations can develop it to increase retention rates since individuals will be retained more in an environment where their contributions are recognized and valued.

9.3 Incorporating Celebrations into Team Culture

Celebrations are among the most effective ways to engender employee engagement, enhance camaraderie, and create a positive work atmosphere. Celebration or small- gives reason for teams of individuals to come together to reflect on their achievements and cement their bonding. By engraining celebration into the fabric of team culture, an organization creates an atmosphere that exudes success and motivates employees to achieve excellence.

Another successful approach toward celebrations is to acknowledge certain achievements of individuals and teams frequently; it can be work anniversaries, finished projects, or resolved challenges. Celebrations can include team lunches, casual gatherings, or recognition ceremonies. Feeling valued for their hard work, morale is boosted, and commitment toward the team and its goals will be strong. A well-structured calendar of celebrations means no single achievement goes unnoticed, and recognition becomes part of the team's routine.

Besides being able to recognize achievements, celebrations also tend to help bring members of the team closer together. Social events, like team-builders or theme parties, let workers interact with one another in an atmosphere of ease, improving relationships aside from the conventional work environment. These will tear down the barriers and build cooperation, including a sense of belonging within the team. Feeling connected with colleagues means employees will be communicative and work as a unit more effectively, enhancing productivity and building creativity.

In addition, team culture celebrations will help reinforce an organization's values and mission. Celebrating behaviors aligned with company goals, such as teamwork, innovation, and customer service, can lead an organization to effectively communicate what is valued in the workplace. For example, highlighting a team doing a great job collaborating on a project honors the effort and models the correct behavior for others. Such alignment through celebrations with organizational values creates harmony in the culture, where the employees understand the values and try to replicate them.

Involving employees in the planning process ensures that celebrations are meaningful and inclusive. Soliciting input on how to celebrate achievements and what types of events resonate with the team can lead to a more tailored approach. This involvement adopts ownership and enthusiasm for the celebrations, making them more impactful. Additionally, being mindful of diverse backgrounds and preferences will help create inclusive celebrations that resonate with all team members.

9.3.1 Highlighting Success Stories Publicly

Publicly highlighting success stories is among the best ways to build recognition and motivate organizational culture. When revealed, success stories not only applaud private and group efficiencies but might likewise serve as a motivational pressure to increase efficiencies throughout the workforce. By making such tales noticeable, companies construct a favorable story that strengthens values, motivates the finest techniques, and establishes worker satisfaction.

Among the significant positives to shared success stories is acknowledgment of individuals or groups included coupled with verification of their effort and commitment. This increases spirits together and motivates others to pursue such quality criteria. When staff members see their peers commemorating their job initiatives, they are motivated to provide their finest payments, understanding they could be identified. This produces a favorable circle of acknowledgment, where gratitude boosts dedication and performance.

Success stories can be efficiently used to share understanding within the company. These tales can supply valuable understanding and lessons by defining exactly how particular difficulties have been predominated or how cutting-edge solutions were carried out. For example, a group that released a brand-new item can connect the approaches they used, problems they encountered, and the group partnership that made them effective. This highlights their success and supplies a structure for others to reproduce in their tasks, boosting general business performance.

One more crucial factor of sharing success tales is that the company can link them with core values and goals. When companies have success that shows assisting concepts, they enhance what is very important to society. For instance, if the company has synergy coupled with technology, tales of joint initiative and imaginative options can motivate others to imitate. This straightens the work environment society with a much better quality of what the company anticipates or desires. The company can display success tales with different networks. Sharing can be done inside with e-newsletters, company-wide conferences, and social media sites. An area on the firm intranet or website can be produced as a database for success tales that are easily available to all workers. Visual elements, such as videos or infographics, can enhance the impact of these stories even more, making them more engaging and shareable.

9.3.2 Personalizing Recognition Efforts

Personalization in recognition efforts is an essential engagement of employees to build up a positive workplace culture. At a time when workers are looking for meaningful connections and appreciation, a well-thought-out recognition initiative might bring a significant change in morale, motivation, and overall job satisfaction. As personalized recognition resonates with them much more powerfully, valued, and understood, it will create a sense of loyalty and commitment towards the organization.

Personalization is all about understanding your employees' preferences and motivational aspects. Not everyone responds to recognition in the same manner. Some employees like public recognition, but others will appreciate private, genuine acknowledgment from the manager. Organizations take time to understand every employee's preference through informal conversations, surveys, or feedback and adapt the recognition activities to fit their needs. This would personalize the recognition, making it far more effective and showing the individuals that the organization cares about their experience.

Specificity in recognition efforts further enhances its power. Recognizing the context of the employee's achievement-such as challenges they had to overcome or innovative ideas they contributed-adds depth to the acknowledgment. Instead of just the general "great job," a manager could say, "Your creative approach to solving the client's issue not only saved us time but also impressed the client immensely." This particularity ensures the employee that the manager is aware of his contribution, hence adopting worth and importance.

In addition, personalization can extend to recognition: the way organizations offer celebrations, handwritten notes, gift vouchers, or personalized awards. If the recognition relates to an employee's interests or preferences, the emotional attachment to the recognition is further felt. For example, a staff member interested in professional growth may appreciate a training course voucher as a recognition of their effort, whereas for another, it could be a team outing.

Additionally, when workers join the acknowledgment procedure, acknowledgment can be much more individualized. A company can offer a range of opportunities whereby workers can self-nominate or be chosen for acknowledgment by others, therefore enabling the complete expression of private recognition. Customized acknowledgments plus a thankful society wash through a company where workers witness one worker commemorating others. In this scene, excellent actions encourage constant acknowledgment amongst all degrees.

9.4 Measuring the Impact of Recognition

Determining the effect of acknowledgment at the workplace is critical to examining its efficiency and ensuring that acknowledgment programs include staff member involvement and business success. By using a structured technique to examine the effect of acknowledgment on staff member habits, spirits, and performance, companies can additionally create and enhance their programs and obtain an extra encouraged labor force. Companies can utilize a series of crucial techniques and metrics to determine the effect of their acknowledgment initiatives.

Possibly one of the most straightforward methods of determining acknowledgment results is with staff member studies. Interaction studies or normal comments that a company runs provide sufficient chances to catch firsthand exactly how staff members feel concerning acknowledgment methods. The concerns might vary from the regularity with the kind of acknowledgment to how that specific acknowledgment forms work contentment and inspiration. Evaluating study outcomes determines the stamina and chances for enhancement to develop a precise image of how acknowledgment influences staff members' spirits. One more crucial statistic is the retention price.

A company must understand the turnover prices before and after any acknowledgment program to establish whether a relationship can be attracted between the acknowledgment initiative and staff member commitment. High retention prices might suggest that workers feel valued plus are dedicated, while enhancing turnover might show prospective concerns concerning acknowledgment techniques. Furthermore, companies can keep track of the actions from leave meetings to determine whether a failure to acknowledge belonged to the factor for worker turnover. Performance metrics likewise function as a substantial indication of acknowledgment's influence.

Companies can determine vital efficiency signs associated with worker outcomes, such as sales numbers, job conclusion prices, or client contentment ratings before and after presenting acknowledgment campaigns—enhanced metrics signal acknowledgment, producing an inspired and effective labor force. More vital, they contrasted groups or divisions that proactively participate in acknowledgment with groups that do not, giving ideas concerning how such campaigns function.

However, qualitative details play a crucial duty in gauging influence, including worker statements coupled with tales concerning their understanding of exactly how acknowledgment has actually shaped them at the workplace. This consists of a study managing certain circumstances where enhanced team effort, development, and analytical skills were accomplished by identifying great. This type of study highlights the measurable information from even more concrete locations of an individual's life, assisting in offering a much better understanding with corresponding measurable comments.

Ultimately, it is necessary to regularly analyze and change the acknowledgment programs based on the built-up information. Organizations ought to consistently examine their acknowledgment approaches in light of worker choices and business purposes. Companies can make smart modifications in their acknowledgment ventures to keep them present and legitimate by evaluating the trends in staff member comments, retention, performance, and measurable understandings.

9.4.1 Encouraging Gratitude Among Team Members

Admiration among employees assists in constructing thankfulness, raising spirits and cooperation among team participants. There are sentiments of thankfulness amongst employee support partnerships while embracing complete satisfaction and efficiency in work. Additionally, appreciation in the office could be summoned via various possibilities, such as techniques that even more substantially supply admiration and recognition- a method that comes naturally in the direction of an involved labor force. One efficient way to urge appreciation is to develop normal techniques to motivate employees to share recognition.

This can be done by including thankfulness right into group conferences, where participants take a couple of minutes to recognize and thank their peers for their certain payments. For example, this can be accomplished at the beginning of conferences by having a "thankfulness round" where workers share their recognition for others, establishing a tone of positivity right from the start. This develops a society of gratefulness and visibility in interaction and reinforces teamwork bonds. Companies can develop a formalized system for identifying appreciation habits and acts of recognition amongst employee gamers.

They can likewise produce systems where staff members can refer among their peers for revealing thankful acts, either with encouraging acts, team-oriented tasks, or mentoring suggestions, to raise the significance of recognition in the business setup. Acknowledging individuals presenting thankfulness assists in strengthening actions and establishes a requirement for others. Highlighting such activities with e-newsletters, notice boards, or company-wide news can produce appreciation within the company. Various other reliable approaches include training and sourcing financial investment in the values of gratitude at the workplace. Workshops or workshops on the benefits of recognition, such as psychological wellness and collaboration together with durability, aid in furnishing personnel with expertise and methods of valuing each other in their everyday tasks. By advertising the method of thankfulness in both individual and expert contexts, employees embrace a mindset that values acknowledgment and is encouraging. Producing chances for outdoor social communications jobs can also progress staff members' thankfulness. Arranging team-building tasks, get-togethers, or casual celebrations permits workers to attach directly, making sharing recognition for every other simpler.

When staff members have partnerships that extend beyond their specialist duties, they are more likely to feel comfortable sharing gratitude and recognizing each other's contributions. This social link can function as a structure for a society of gratitude that penetrates daily communications. Management also designs and influences the spirit of gratefulness within a group. When company leaders freely reveal appreciation to staff members, such habits might establish an example for others to follow.

Leaders who constantly value workers' payments permit the sensation of gratefulness to take hold, not just to be valued but to be anticipated. A business society might, therefore, develop gratefulness right into its group's communications by exercising this from management downwards.

9.4.2 Recognizing Effort as Well as Results

Effort and results are important in today's dynamic work environment to nurture a culture of engagement and motivation. Although achieving tangible results is, no doubt, important, equally important is the hard work, dedication, and perseverance that precede those results. Organizations could create a more inclusive and encouraging atmosphere by valuing effort and achievement that promotes employee growth and improvement.

Recognizing effort helps an organization adopt a growth mindset. When staff see that hard work and effort will be recognized, they are confident to make attempts and face any challenge since their contribution, whatever the result, counts. In this way, the organization adopts innovation and develops the resilience of team members in the workplace. When employees feel their efforts are valued, they are more likely to see setbacks as opportunities to learn and grow. After that, a society of trial and error as well as imagination is supported.

Additionally, recognizing initiative can improve group characteristics and partnership. When companies commemorate the procedure, staff members are more likely to sustain each other and work collectively toward typical objectives. Acknowledging the effort of people promotes a feeling of sociability and shared regard as staff members comprehend that every person's payments, despite their straight influence on results, are crucial to cumulative success. This collective setting can boost interaction, increase count, and enhance coworker partnerships.

Effective recognition of effort may take place, for instance, through several strategies at an organizational level, further emphasizing the journey beside the destination. An example will be how managers can combine in regular check-ins about projects' results, challenges that were taken up, or how hard a team works. Celebrating milestones, such as reaching the end of a challenging project phase, allows time to reflect and appreciate all the hard work that brought them to this moment. It reinforces the habit of not giving up and instills camaraderie.

Also, by making employees appreciation agents apart from formal recognition programs, any culture of appreciation can be elicited from an organization. Performing peer recognition initiatives where one member of a team identifies the hard work of his teammate builds a supportive environment that esteems collaboration and respect for one another. This could result from maximizing the impact of recognition events in place and establishing ownership and accountability among wage earners as they are driven to appreciate their colleagues for their respective contributions.

What's more, the leaders themselves should model recognizing effort. Wherever the manager consistently recognizes effort among his teams, it sets a higher bar for the rest of the organization. The leaders should highlight the particular acts and behaviors that brought success and reinforce the view that effort is just as significant as the result. By doing so, the organizations will be able to build a culture where every employee, irrespective of the outcome, is valued.

9.5 Using Technology for Celebrations

Of course, one of the most striking ways technology has been applied to celebrations involves virtual events. Companies use video conferencing platforms like Zoom, Microsoft Teams, or Google Meet to conduct live celebrations that employees can join to share appreciation of achievements, successes, and milestones. Besides, it is possible to perform several fun activities during these virtual gatherings: quizzes, games, themed parties, etc., that involve people in interaction and engagement. In fact, by making the celebrations accessible to remote and hybrid workers, organizations ensure that all feel included and valued, irrespective of the environment in which they work. Other than virtual events, an organization can use social media and an internal communication platform to extend celebratory messages and messages of achievement. A space for appreciation, telling stories of success, and celebrating each other's contributions could be Slack, Microsoft Teams, or an intranet site. By creating channels for recognition, team members are allowed to post shout-outs and share positive feedback, adopting a culture of appreciation. Additionally, leveraging social media platforms to recognize achievements publicly can help amplify the celebrations and show the organization's commitment to valuing employee contributions to a broader audience.

Various other functional methods to apply events consist of acknowledgment software application that assists in continuous events and recognitions. Several companies currently use electronic acknowledgment systems, such as Bonusly or Kudos, permitting staff members to provide and obtain acknowledgment in real-time. These systems frequently include a game-like acknowledgment procedure with factor systems, badges, plus leaderboards. With modern technology incorporated into the acknowledgment procedure, a company can develop a vibrant atmosphere where staff members are constantly commemorated in their initiatives to enhance total spirit and involvement. Furthermore, modern technology will certainly make parties a lot more individualized. Automated systems can send individualized congratulatory messages or suggestions regarding a staff member's job, wedding anniversary, or birthday celebration. All that mindfulness does marvels for staff members' sensation valued plus valued. To make workers feel unique on vital days, occasions can be individualized with tailored electronic cards, video clip messages from management, and even digital present shipments.

Lastly, information analytics devices can be utilized to gauge the efficiency of the celebration campaigns. Simply put, companies can track the degree of involvement, online occasion engagement prices, and acknowledgment regularity to identify their initiatives' performance. From there, companies can additionally readjust event techniques to reverberate with workers and favorably add to the work environment. Understanding what kind of event plus acknowledgment most reverberates with the workers will certainly be a lengthy process in educating them on additional enhancements towards lining up their choices.

Innovation made use of to commemorate turning points will certainly enhance involvement and engender an excellent society in the work environment. This shall be possible through virtual events, social media, recognition software, personal messaging, and data analytics to ensure that such celebrations are inclusive and memorable to recognize achievement and contributions. Embracing technology helps bring employees together and adopts a culture of appreciation and support, igniting motivation and commitment to employees. Celebrating success with technology is advantageous and needed to help create a great culture in an organization where day-to-day life has to be digital.

9.5.1 Creating a Yearly Celebration Event

Holding an annual celebration of success is a guaranteed way to appreciate success, engender team spirit, and push the organizational culture. Events like this allow the employees to come together and reflect on the past year, celebrating success individually and as a group. If done well, a well-planned annual celebration provides an enjoyable and memorable experience that improves morale and cements camaraderie among all levels of staff.

Setting clear objectives is always the first step in developing a successful annual celebration event. Organizations need to determine what they want to achieve through the event, whether recognizing outstanding performances, team bonding, or even increasing employee morale. Stated objectives will, therefore, provide guidelines on how the activities would be designed to achieve the set goals. For example, if the aim is to recognize achievements, then award ceremonies for the top performers and teams may feature.

Second, the date and format are significant when choosing. The event date should be selected when most employees can attend, such as at the end of the fiscal year or during the holiday season. The format may also vary depending on organizational culture and resources. Options include formal gatherings, casual parties, outdoor picnics, or virtual celebrations, especially for hybrid or remote teams. Each format has its benefits, but the most important thing is to select one that will make people participate and reflect the values and culture of the organization.

Second, the date and format are the important aspects of planning the event details: venue, catering, and entertainment. An in-person event requires the selection of a venue that accommodates the size of the team and makes them feel welcome. Using engaging virtual event platforms is important for allowing interaction and participation. Besides, introducing some entertaining elements, such as guest speakers, live performances, or team-building activities, will enhance the experience and keep the participants engaged with the event.

Recognition should be one of the focal points in the yearly celebration. Celebration of Individual and team performance can raise the bar of the occasion. In order to do so, awards and certificates would not be necessary; even mentioning a person for a particular thing will keep the employees motivated. Success stories through presentations, videos, or employee testimonials could be reflected upon with satisfaction. Ensuring success recognition represents various organizational levels and areas is a key challenge.

Finally, it is essential to have feedback after the event to make further improvements. The organization should seek input from the employees regarding their experiences and any suggestions for future events. This might offer a concept of what went right and what did not, enhancing future events. Additionally, sharing some minutes of the occasion might be pictures, video clips, or crucial takeaways that maintain the event's spirit long after the occasion has finished.

9.6 Case Study: The Importance of Recognition

Success in acknowledgment creates the core of a favorable office society and boosts staff member involvement. Acknowledgment compensates for crucial success by people and groups while enhancing a company's worth with teamwork, inspiration, and gratitude. In this respect, Salesforce has been an outstanding instance. The "Cheers for Peers" program motivates staff members to acknowledge each other. This reveals how essential peer-to-peer acknowledgment is and how it alters work environment characteristics.

Salesforce's Cheers for Peers" enables staff members to acknowledge peers for their initiatives in real-time. This effort allows staff members to openly recognize their peers for details, whether finishing an effective job, ingenious concept, or outstanding team effort. This sort of peer acknowledgment develops a comprehensive setting where staff members really feel valued and sustained by their colleagues. By proactively participating in the acknowledgment procedure, staff members construct more powerful partnerships and boost group cohesion, creating an extra collective and encouraged workforce.

The advantages of identifying victories via programs like "Cheers for Peers" exceed private recommendations. When workers really feel valued, it enhances their spirits and task contentment, boosting general performance. Acknowledgment can substantially influence worker inspiration, enhancing interaction and retention rates. Commemorating success enhances the habits preferred by companies while advertising responsibility and dedication, which are important components of job society. This results in favorable comments; workers are urged to do their best, recognizing their initiatives will certainly not go undetected or unappreciated.

Additionally, peer acknowledgment programs pass on to the office coming from. They acknowledge specific initiatives in varied groups towards one typical objective, each bringing various points of view and payments. Acknowledgment programs such as "Cheers for Peers" urge staff members to value colleagues' varied abilities and viewpoints together while embracing shared regard and understanding. This sensation is considerable for the welfare of the workers. It might also lead to greater degrees of technology as staff members feel even more comfortable sharing concepts and taking threats. To effectively use an acknowledgment program like "Cheers for Peers," an organization ought to ensure that the effort sustains the core worth of society. A user-friendly system to identify an application, intranet, or social media site network can help with engagement and smooth the procedure. Besides, leaders must role-model the acknowledgment actions by recognizing staff members' payments frequently, and establish a pattern for others to comply with. Educating sessions on why acknowledgment is crucial can encourage staff members to do the same, ensuring that commemorating success enters the business society.

Recognizing wins is a way to celebrate and build a positive and productive work environment. Initiatives such as Salesforce's "Cheers for Peers" epitome the magic of peer-to-peer recognition in driving employee engagement, morale, and teamwork. Where organizations nurture a culture of valuing and celebrating their people's contributions, it naturally inspires them to be better and work toward a shared feeling of belonging that propels success. Recognizing big and small wins strengthens the fabric of an organization, leading to a more motivated, innovative, and committed workforce.

9.7 Key Point Donald Trump's potential re-election in 2024

> **Critique of Opponents:** Effectively framing opponents, particularly within the Democratic Party, as out of touch with average Americans.

The 2024 presidential election, therefore, becomes one of strategic positioning on the part of any re-election campaign by Donald Trump and framing his opponents, notably those within the Democratic Party, as out of touch with the average American. This strategy has been one of the strong points in Trump's total political technique today, reaching a substantial part of those who feel disenfranchised or forgotten by even more conventional political elites. By adequately assessing his challengers, Trump looks to galvanize his base while trying to cut right into the undecided ballot through credibility and relatability.

> **Simplify Complex Issues**
> Break down complicated topics into easily digestible messages.
>
> **Utilize Surrogates**
> Leverage trusted allies to spread your message and defend your positions.

Among Trump's most considerable stamina in mounting his challengers is his capacity to brighten regarded detachments between Democratic plans plus the day-to-day truths of the American people. In a genuine feeling, the rising cost of living, climbing gas costs, plus financial unpredictability have gone to the center of the general public frame of mind. Trump and also his allies suggest that a lot of Democratic leaders are so inside their political bubble that they do not comprehend the difficulties encountering middle-class households. It places Trump as a champ for the typical American who recognizes their battles and agrees to combat for them.

Furthermore, Trump's objections frequently concentrate on particular Democratic plans that he suggests run out of touch with traditional worths. For example, the focus on dynamic schedules, such as comprehensive environment policies or well-being programs, is a concern for taxpayers and small companies. By saying that such plans focus on ideological objectives over functional remedies, Trump looks to repaint his challengers as elitists who focus on their schedules over the demands of daily people. This is a highly efficient story, in turn, in states and locations where financial concerns go to the forefront of Trump's mind; it enables Trump to use his company history as a comparison to political leaders who might lose touch with their components' financial truth.

In addition, Trump's interaction design dramatically allows him to mount his challengers. His use of social media sites and straight messaging enables him to bypass conventional media filters, placing him directly with the selection—such immediacy breakthroughs affection. In mounting challengers with those callous, remarkable words, Trump enhances his picture as a genuine, no-rubbish leader who globalizes for the voices of common Americans, except for political accuracy or the problems of any elite.

Nonetheless, the strategy constantly brings dangers. Movie critics claim it additionally takes the chance to streamline substantial intricate problems and the department of individuals. Yet to those citizens, it talks with a very receptive target market; to numerous other individuals, it shows up as dissentious and dismissive of even more nuanced plan argumentation. As we closer to this political election, challengers will certainly increase initiatives to counterbalance Mr. Trump's story, highlighting plans and options that can have added to economic battles or social chaos on his watch.

In the end, much of Donald Trump's potential 2024 re-election campaign depends on his ability to criticize his opponents within the Democratic Party effectively. So, he positions his opponents as out of touch with ordinary Americans to solidify his base and appeal to undecided voters who feel ignored by the political establishment. Therefore, based on this, his direct-communication strategy is oriented to current and relatable issues, underlining his approach to mobilizing support to return to the White House. This will be tested during the election, based on an evolving political landscape and responses from his opponents.

Reference

1. Gallup. (2021). *State of the global workplace: 2021 report.* Gallup. https://www.gallup.com/cliftonstrengths/en/253868/popular-cliftonstrengths-assessment-products.aspx

2. Salesforce. (2024). *Cheers for peers: A guide to peer recognition programs.* Salesforce. https://www.salesforce.com/communications/

3. Society for Human Resource Management. (2016). *The importance of employee recognition.* https://www.shrm.org/resourcesandtools/hr-topics/employee-relations/pages/employee-recognition.aspx

4. Towers Watson. (2012). *The power of recognition: How to engage employees with recognition programs.*

https://www.wtwco.com/en-US/Solutions/employee-engagement

5. Harvard Business Review. (2019). *The feedback fallacy.* https://hbr.org/magazine

6. Carnegie, D. (1936). *How to win friends and influence people.* Simon & Schuster.

7. O.C. Tanner Institute. (2019). *How employee recognition impacts retention and engagement.* https://www.octanner.com/resources

8. Workhuman. (2020). *The impact of employee recognition on retention.* https://www.workhuman.com/company/our-story/

CHAPTER 10

Continuous Growth: Cultivating a Learning Environment

Introduction

In today's fast-moving and constantly changing work environment, continuous employee development can be best achieved by developing a learning atmosphere. A learning culture helps individuals develop their skills and knowledge, which, in turn, helps drive organizational innovation and adaptability. Investment in a learning-atmosphere culture empowers an organization's workforce, improves employee engagement, and leads to long-term success. A learning environment is based on the belief that growth is not a one-time event but a continuous process. Organizations must instill in employees a culture that learning is not something added to the work-life but rather interwoven into it. It creates a growth mindset in which employees believe their abilities and intelligence develop through hard work and commitment. Leaders become key players. They model that mind themselves and are openly willing to share with others how those experiences with failures and successes have shaped their lives. If employees find their leaders take growth seriously, their attitudes will also change. Diverse learning opportunities must be presented to adopt an appropriate learning environment. The organization should make different formal and informal learning options available: workshops, seminars, online courses, and mentorship programs. E-learning platforms with resources may have an added advantage since one learns independently according to one's time. Another aspect that could help improve the learning culture is encouraging peer-to-peer learning through collaboration and knowledge sharing [1-3]. Building opportunities for employees to present their expertise or share insights develops a sense of community and reinforces the notion that all have something of value to contribute [4].

Feedback is another important constituent of the learning environment. Constructive feedback helps employees recognize further areas for improvement and encourages them to take responsibility for their development [5, 6]. Organizations should provide opportunities for regular feedback through processes like performance reviews and individual check-ins. Feedback should be supportive, focusing on growth more than criticism. When comfortable sharing their challenges and triumphs, employees are more likely to seek opportunities to learn and invest in themselves.

Equality is the recognition of efforts towards learning and development. Recognizing employee achievements through a formal recognition program or informal acknowledgments helps solidify the value of continuous learning in employees' minds. Employees, after all, are likely to participate in further learning if they see how much growth efforts are valued. Internal communication can highlight success stories, such as employees who have pursued professional development and the positive outcomes that have impacted their work.

Moreover, psychological safety will enable learning culture. Individuals should not hesitate to take risks and make blunders without worrying about charges. The company will motivate open conversations with varied viewpoints and proactively sustain workers' discovery initiatives. When workers feel secure sharing their suggestions and difficulties, they are more likely to participate in conversations that bring about advancement and renovation.

10.1 Promoting a Culture of Lifelong Learning

Supporting a society of continual enhancement is crucial in a quickly transforming and progressively complicated globe. Continual education and learning and the advancement of brand-new abilities equip individuals to adjust to developing needs while allowing business advancement and durability. Installing long-lasting discoveries in the office makes possible an atmosphere where workers feel inspired and can expand the team and add to their complete capacity. Nonetheless, the core of a long-lasting understanding of society is that understanding never quits.

As a result, organizations should support a perspective that infuses workers with an inquisitiveness for even more expertise than what is needed by their work obligations. This can begin with leaders modeling a dedication to learning via additional education and learning, going to market meetings, and sharing current analyses. When leaders prioritize understanding, it establishes the tone for workers to do the same, producing a causal sequence throughout the company. Organizations can supply various understanding opportunities that fit various preferences and designs for long-lasting understanding: official training, online programs, workshops, and accessibility to academic sources.

Enhancing these official approaches, a company might arrange lunch-and-learn or mentorship programs in which workers can learn from other staff members. It might also offer various discovering systems where everybody has an area that functions best for them to discover and expand. Besides expertise sharing, urging partnership will certainly be one more crucial inspiring variable for producing a society of long-lasting discovery. When urged, workers will certainly gain from each other's experiences and also their particular expectations on points. Cross-functional groups for tasks drive development, aid staff members in developing brand-new abilities, and develop links throughout the company. Examples include collective or administration systems, where important understanding and the finest techniques can be recorded and shared.

Recognition will significantly help motivate employees to engage in lifelong learning. Organizations need to recognize and celebrate the employees who take courses for professional development, obtain certification, or share knowledge with others. Recognition could come in the form of appreciation in meetings or even formal awards for learning achievements. In this way, an organization communicates that continuous learning is valued and is a plus for career advancement.

Furthermore, lifelong learning needs an environment of psychological safety. People must be comfortable with risks, questions, and mistakes without consequences. The organization can inspire psychological safety through open dialogue, active listening to feedback, and space for experimentation. If employees feel that it is safe to explore ideas and question the status quo, they will engage more in the opportunities provided for learning, thus building an innovative culture.

Therefore, organizations need to continuously analyze and change their learning undertakings to remain fresh and relevant. They should also listen to their employees' views and experiences while learning to improve further. By continuously evolving their approach to learning, organizations can be in a better position to answer the workforce's needs and the industry's evolution.

10.2 Identifying Learning Opportunities

In today's fast-moving workplace, scoping learning opportunities becomes significant for employee growth and enhancing organizational performance. By proactively determining locations for growth, a company will certainly develop a society of continual enhancement that equips staff members to increase their abilities and adjust to transforming needs. The procedure includes a couple of crucial approaches that aid companies in recognizing beneficial opportunities for their labor force. A reputable method for determining the understanding requirement is the abilities gap evaluation. This strategy considers present staff members' expertise with those required for attaining business goals.

The private capability examinations are combined to provide the big picture of the groups' capacities. For example, if a company is most likely to embrace brand-new innovation, workers might be required to learn additional facets of using the system properly. Normal analysis of proficiencies helps ensure that learning opportunities align with specific desires and business concerns. Staff member responses are another important foundation in recognizing and discovering demands. To comprehend the workers' viewed demands plus passions, studies, meetings, or emphasis teams can be performed. By opening lines of interaction, companies allow workers to reveal their favored methods of discovering and obtain knowledge in areas where staff members think they can gain from more advancement. This participatory technique enhances a feeling of ownership in individual development and enhances involvement in offered learning programs.

In addition, there is much to be learned from checking any type of market's patterns and improvements. Every company ought to remain up-to-date with the adjustments within its market about brand-new innovations, techniques, and ideal methods. Leaders can recognize the chances that are most pertinent to preserving labor force competition by participating in sector meetings, webinars, and specialist networks. The companies will certainly make certain workers are ready for success in an incessantly altering atmosphere by straightening training campaigns with market growth. Peer understanding and mentoring programs are one more reliable method of determining and establishing learning opportunities. A company accomplishes this by matching knowledgeable staff members with others who intend to discover new abilities and constructing a durable expertise transfer setting. The coaches might suggest particular abilities or occupation growth courses, while the mentees might bring originalities on arising fads. The communication of finding out additional expands the specific to concrete communication and partnership in groups.

Companies can additionally make use of efficiency evaluations as possibilities to find out requirements. Continuous efficiency testimonials might explain workers' stamina and weak points; conversations of professional wishes coupled with advancement prepared in such evaluations can assist companies in developing targeted knowing paths that fulfill private plus business objectives. The knowing chances relate together with customized to the staff members' requirements.

Lastly, curiosity and expedition society will certainly aid in recognizing continual knowing chances. Companies ought to develop an atmosphere where workers feel secure enough to ask inquiries, look for new obstacles, and seek expert advancement. Involvement in workshops, on-the-internet programs, and cross-departmental tasks can be boosted to elevate passion in knowing and also discover covert development chances. Through motivated interests in exploring new knowledge, an employee will have better possibilities of identifying opportunities for himself or herself and contributing to a continuous improvement culture.

10.2.1 Implementing Training and Development Programs

Training and development are very important to any organization that seeks to improve employees' skills, engagement, and overall performance. A well-structured training program equips your staff with the right tools to perform better while embedding a learning and professional development culture. Therefore, the organization should take great care in the planning, execution, and assessment of its training programs.

The first step in undertaking training and development programs involves the needs assessment process that ascertains specific skills and competence for different organizational roles. Employees, managers, and other stakeholders involved might prove very informative in identifying current and future needs regarding such training. Understanding an organization's strategic direction and goals implies that leaders could connect training initiatives with broader business objectives; in other words, it makes appropriate resource allocations relevant to real issues.

Organizations should formulate such programs based on an identified need for training, focusing on different learning styles and preferences. A blended learning approach, which integrates traditional classroom training with online modules, workshops, and on-the-job training, would be particularly appropriate. This allows the employees the flexibility to learn independently, while reinforcement is achieved by learning in multiple ways. These can be interactive with group discussions, case studies, or simulations to facilitate greater interaction and retention.

Another ingredient that composes an efficient training program is skilled trainers and facilitators. The organization shall select people with expertise on the subject matter who can engage and motivate participants in the training. Trainers need appropriate resources and support, whether with updated materials or technology, to provide quality training. In addition to this, the trainers also share experiences and insights where there will be more interactivity in learning and finding relevancy to the lives of the working employees.

Communication is very important during the implementation of training and development programs. Organizations should communicate the training initiatives' purpose, benefits, and expectations to all employees through internal newsletters, meetings, and digital platforms. By building a positive narrative around training, organizations will create a culture that embraces learning and encourages participation in training programs. Sharing success stories from past training initiatives will go a long way in motivating the employees to embrace new programs.

Organizations are supposed to create a solid evaluation mechanism for ascertaining the effectiveness of the training and development programs. The organizations need to evaluate both the immediate outcomes of the training and the effectiveness of the training over time. This can be done using participant feedback, before-and-after training testing, and performance metrics. Such frequent reviews and analyses of this data enable an organization to make required changes in the training initiatives that are relevant and useful.

Besides, it is important to create an enabling atmosphere that allows continuous growth and development to sustain the benefits gained from the training programs. To complement this, an organization may allow for other means, such as online classes, seminars within the same industry, or professional advancement. Encouraging personal development goals among employees and furthering their education may help to maintain momentum and interest in learning.

10.2.2 Encouraging Knowledge Sharing Among Team Members

A high degree of knowledge sharing among team members is necessary for collaboration, innovation, and continuous improvement. Indeed, while information abounds and keeps growing at unimaginable speeds, creating the right enabling environment that encourages the flow of knowledge can boost problem-solving capacity and efficiency to bring along a wider sense of community among staff. In light of this, every organization should set mechanisms to adopt communication and ensure shared expertise is valued in its knowledge sharing.

Setting up an open culture that allows collaboration is one of the bases for knowledge sharing. Leaders have to set a good example; it should come from them as a commitment to knowledge sharing. When leaders are committed to sharing their ideas and experiences, it sets the ball rolling for team members to follow suit. Encouraging informal interactions, such as team lunches or brainstorming sessions, would also be a promising avenue where employees can connect and share ideas in an informal setting. Such informal engagement helps break down barriers and builds comradeship, making sharing their knowledge easier.

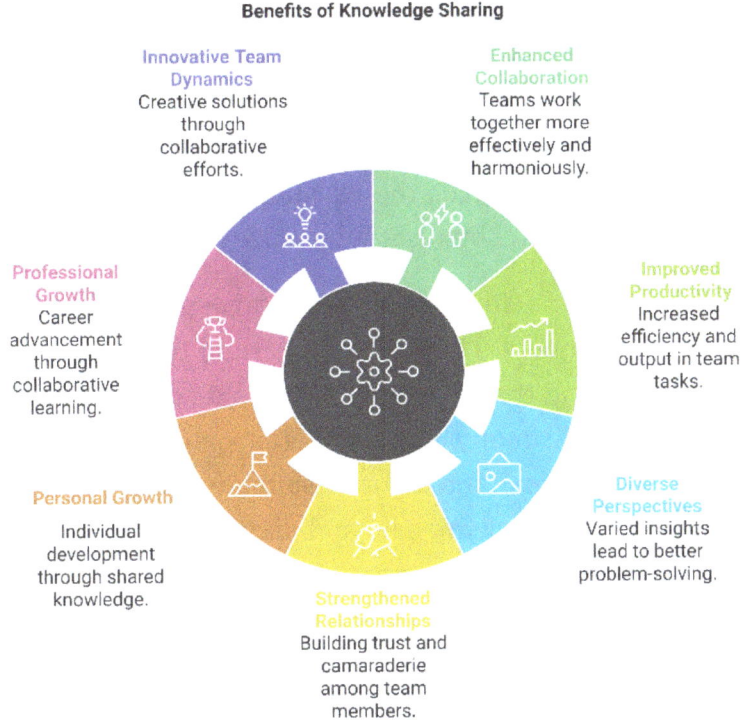

Figure 10.1 Encouraging knowledge sharing among team members.

Creating structured platforms for knowledge sharing would be crucial. Organizations should provide collaboration tools, intranets, wikis, or knowledge management systems in which employees can document and share expertise. Such knowledge platforms provide a single place where team members can access useful resources, best practices, and lessons learned from previous projects. In addition, regular meetings or workshops regarding knowledge sharing will encourage employees to share their knowledge in the form of presentations on specific topics.

The second viable way of realizing this sharing of knowledge is through mentorship programs. Mentorship would match experienced workers with less experienced workers or those seeking development in certain areas to realize direct knowledge transfer. Such guidance, industry insight, and support through mentors and challenges can be realized in mentoring. This relationship reinforces the learning process, improves the dynamics of teams, and builds a supportive culture.

Trust is the major component of encouraging expertise-sharing among team members. They must be certain their concepts are taken seriously and that sharing them would not hinder them. It helps when there is motivation to interact, pay attention to staff members' statements, and offer a suitable sector for sharing such suggestions if they are safe and secure and have high self-worth concerning competence. Acknowledgment plus the incentive of knowledge-sharing initiatives will certainly increase the staff members' interest rate in the technique. A company can establish acknowledgment programs to recognize people or groups that proactively add to the company's knowledge-sharing efforts.

It might consist of highlighting employees in business e-newsletters, rewarding participation in mentoring programs, or commemorating effective joint jobs. By valuing such payments, companies enhance the value of expertise sharing and urge others to do the same.

Last, continual enhancement ought to be among the assisting concepts of knowledge-sharing efforts. The company ought to regularly examine its knowledge-sharing methods' efficiency and look for staff member comments. This could be done through studies, focus groups, or casual conversations to comprehend what works well and what might be enhanced. Organizations can develop an extra reliable and interesting knowledge-sharing society by reacting to staff member demands and adjusting methods as necessary.

10.3 Setting Learning Goals

Establishing and discovering objectives is vital for staff members and the company to expand and create constantly. Discovering objectives supplies instructions, motivation, and a clear structure for getting brand-new abilities plus understanding. Establishing certain quantifiable, possible, pertinent, and time-bound objectives will certainly boost the discovering experience and bring about much better efficiency that adds to the success of people and groups coupled with the company.

The primary step toward establishing efficient knowing objectives is self-assessment. This will involve reflection on current skills and knowledge and areas for improvement. Employees should also reflect on their career aspirations and what specific learning goals could help them accomplish them. For instance, a worker aspiring to become a leader may realize that he needs to develop either team management or strategic thinking skills. This self-awareness enables individuals to set relevant and meaningful goals that align with personal and professional objectives.

Figure 10.2 Setting learning goals is vital for employees and organizations aiming for continuous growth and development.

Once the growth areas have been identified, specific learning goals should be formulated. Goals must be specific. Instead of a general goal like "improve my skills," it is better to set a specific goal: "I want to finish the project management certification by the end of the year." This clarity lets them know precisely what they need to focus on and helps them stay motivated and track their progress.

Measurable goals allow one to gauge progress made in achieving success. One needs to set ways of measuring success, such as by the number of training sessions one has completed, feedback from peers or mentors, and how well the new skill was applied in a project. For instance, an employee might set a goal to attend three workshops on effective communication and then apply those skills in team meetings. Measurable elements help individuals celebrate the milestones they achieve while trying to motivate themselves throughout the process.

Another important characteristic of a good goal is achievability. While challenging oneself is good, unrealistic goals only create frustration and disengagement. One should consider one's current responsibilities and resources and ensure one's goals are achievable in a certain time. For example, a busy employee could commit to taking an appropriate online course over six months instead of one month. In that way, commitment to learning is balanced by the level of existing responsibility.

Relevance ensures that learning objectives align with individual aspirations and organizational objectives. Workers need to assess exactly how their objectives contribute to their job development and their company's general objectives. For example, if a company is undertaking electronic improvement, a staff member might wish to discover brand-new electronic advertising approaches. This, subsequently, will certainly improve individual growth and position them to contribute purposefully to the success of their company.

Ultimately, developing a duration for accomplishing learning goals develops a feeling of seriousness coupled with liability. Target dates make certain that people remain concentrated and focus on their knowledge. For example, a worker might intend to finish a management training program within 3 months. This maintains the energy and reveals a clear endpoint to reassess progression.

10.3.1 Providing Resources for Professional Development

In an affordable labor market, these companies have an advantage over various other companies in terms of winning the interest and commitment of top-quality staff members. Organizations using numerous advancement sources assist in improving staff members' abilities and expertise while motivating a society of constant knowledge and interaction. Certainly, expert growth is an important device that makes it possible for a company to purchase its biggest possessions, offer it the skills to do well, adjust, and introduce feedback to moving sector needs.

These will certainly become the most effective methods of offering specialist growth sources: organized training programs, workshops, and online training courses targeted to worker requirements. For example, a company can set up programs on management, job administration, or technological abilities from instructional organizations or training suppliers. By doing this, companies can guarantee significance to staff members' functions and job desires for optimum involvement and influence. Companies can likewise develop opportunities for accessibility to digital training websites that offer a wide range of training courses and sources. Better, LinkedIn Discovering Coursera, and also Udemy offer workers the possibility to learn self-paced topics that intrigue them. Whether these programs can be funded or paid will suggest that their intent and dedication to staff member advancement in continual discovery are real and appropriate.

Accessibility to varied subjects, from soft abilities to technological experience, ensures that workers can customize their growth to individual and business objectives. Advisors, as well as training programs, likewise supply possibilities for specialist advancement. Coupling staff members with less experience with seasoned experts opens up chances for expertise transfer, advancement, and networking. The coach overviews and shares understandings concerning the sector to help the mentees in their professional courses. A structured mentorship program with objectives and regular check-ins can additionally improve understanding and develop high-quality expert partnerships within the firm.

Various other sources include opportunities to attend market meetings, workshops, and networking occasions. Such discussion forums enable personnel to learn from sector specialists, stay updated on the most recent trends, and network with other experts. Companies can urge specialist advancement by funding workers' participation at pertinent occasions, preparing in-house meetings, and welcoming outside audio speakers.

This assists in updating workers' understanding base yet also helps in embracing a feeling of neighborhood and partnership within the company. Producing a society of expertise sharing is another component of expert advancement sources. Organizations can establish systems through which staff members share experiences, best techniques, plus lessons found; this can be done utilizing interior e-newsletters, partnership devices, or routine group conferences on understanding sharing. It's an atmosphere where workers are valued for payment towards a common understanding and renovation.

Comments and routine efficiency evaluations are necessary to highlight specialist advancement initiatives. Every company needs to create treatments for useful comments and help staff members recognize their locations for development and possibilities for advancement. Through efficiency testimonials, staff members can be motivated to establish individual growth objectives, dressmaker specialist advancement, and even more significant experiences.

10.3.2 Utilizing Mentorship and Coaching

Mentorship and coaching are powerful tools for professional development, making a big difference in employees' performance, engagement, and jobs. An organization can unite experienced and growing professionals by creating an enabling environment that encourages constant learning and enhances working skills. With their effective utilization, mentorship and coaching would benefit individual employees, strengthen teams, and enable overall organizational success.

Mentorship encompasses a relationship in which the more experienced mentor leads, supports, and advises a less experienced mentee. The relationship is priceless to employees trying to navigate their career paths, develop specific skills, and gain insights into practices in their respective industries. Mentors often share their experiences, provide feedback, and help the mentee set and achieve professional goals.

Figure 10.3 Mentorship and coaching are powerful tools for professional development.

While initiating a mentorship program, an organization should specify its objectives. These could range from increasing employee retention to developing future leaders to enhancing specific competencies among the participants. Once objectives have been set, matching may be done based on the similar interests, goals, and expertise of mentors and mentees. Training mentors about effective coaching and communication techniques can enhance the quality of mentoring experiences.

Conversely, coaches usually perform a more formal process for enhancing certain skills or specific performance outcomes. They work with individuals or teams to identify areas for improvement, set achievable goals, and develop actionable plans to reach those goals. Unlike coaching, which typically highlights individual growth and occupation, navigating training concentrates much more on boosting work efficiency and accomplishing particular outcomes. Organizations can properly utilize training by integrating it into efficiency monitoring procedures. For example, supervisors can recognize workers requiring training during efficiency testimonials and refer them to interior or outside training. By doing this, routine mentoring sessions will help staff members acquire brand-new abilities and overcome difficulties, plus enhance their performance in their particular functions.

A training or mentoring society needs companies to concentrate on continual knowing together with development ideology. The advantages of training or mentoring have to be interacted with within the company; individuals need to be motivated to look for mentoring possibilities, plus companies need to offer sources to help them. These mentoring tales and training success stories can be showcased and shared with the company to highlight functions. Examining the efficiency of mentoring coupled with training programs is crucial for continual enhancement.

Organizations need to develop metrics to assess the effect of these campaigns on worker efficiency, interaction, and retention. Studies, response sessions, and efficiency analyses can give insight into the efficiency of mentor and mentoring partnerships. By evaluating this information, organizations can make educated changes to boost program layout and execution. Done well, mentorship plus training can profit staff members and companies considerably. By developing healthy and balanced partnerships between advisors and mentees and normally arranged mentoring, a company encourages its individuals to boost their abilities, recognize their objectives, and usually enhance their efficiency. Dedication to mentorship and training produces specific development, strengthens team effort, and ensures business success. These advancement techniques will certainly develop the proficiencies, dedication, and inspiration required in a regularly transforming company atmosphere.

10.4 Creating a Safe Environment for Experimentation

Today, when the business world encounters strong competitors and also transforms characteristics practically daily, a society that makes it possible for testing is essential to development and growth. A safe-to-fail setting for testing can assist workers in discovering originalities and taking computed threats without worry of failing. This will certainly urge even more creative thinking, drive technology, and boost business efficiency. Safety and security to try out ways mental security.

Amy Edmondson, an educator at Harvard Business School, specifies this term as the " environment in which individuals can promote without anxiety of effects or judgment. "When individuals in companies feel their contributions will certainly be valued and they can chat openly about failure and success, they're most likely to think innovatively and experiment. Leaders should design open interaction along with susceptibility to develop mental security. Therefore, leaders must be open to their experiences of failing and what they picked up from them.

In doing so, leaders can assist staff members in redefining difficulties as chances for development instead of hazards to task safety. Another way to create a safe environment for experimentation is to encourage calculated risk-taking. The organization needs to signal that not every experiment will work, and that's okay. Guidelines on what type of experiments are reasonable could help employees determine what constitutes an acceptable risk. For instance, teams may be empowered to set small, attainable experimental goals to test ideas without placing significant resources at risk.

Besides, the organization can provide resources and facilitation for trying out experiments. For example, training, available tools, and technology that may facilitate testing an idea can be provided. The organization removes obstacles and supports employees in developing and testing ideas.

A culture of experimentation means that it's important to learn from failure. An organization should be interested in teams revisiting the results of successful or unsuccessful experiments. Regular review processes, whereby employees present their experiments and discuss what worked, what didn't, and why, adopt much-needed learning. Reflective practice builds individual capacity and contributes to the organization's knowledge base.

Celebration of success and failure is also necessary. Recognition of teams or individuals that take the initiative and try, regardless of the outcome, helps to reinforce that experimentation will be rewarded. Organizations could recognize innovation programs to indicate innovation done and inspire others to follow in those footsteps.

Effective communication channels are needed to provide a safe environment for experimentation. Every organization should design channels through which employees can share ideas, receive feedback, and work on projects together. This could include weekly brainstorming sessions, innovation workshops, or ideas-sharing forums. When employees feel they have a voice and their ideas are considered, they will experiment more.

Creating an environment where experimentation is safely made is critical in driving innovation and ensuring organizational success. By cultivating psychological safety, encouraging calculated risk, learning from failures, and allowing open communications, organizations could empower their employees to try new things and take risks. In so doing, organizations build their capacity to innovate while nurturing an involved, motivated, and prepared workforce to take on the challenges of a changing business landscape. Here, experimentation becomes ingrained into the fabric of organizational culture for continued growth and betterment.

10.4.1 Evaluating Learning Outcomes

Assessment of learning results is a very important component in any educational or training program, as it enables an organization to evaluate the effectiveness of its learning processes and their impact on employee performance. Systematic measurement of learning outcomes serves organizations by assuring proper training orientation toward business objectives, determining the areas of improvement, and justifying investments made toward employee development.

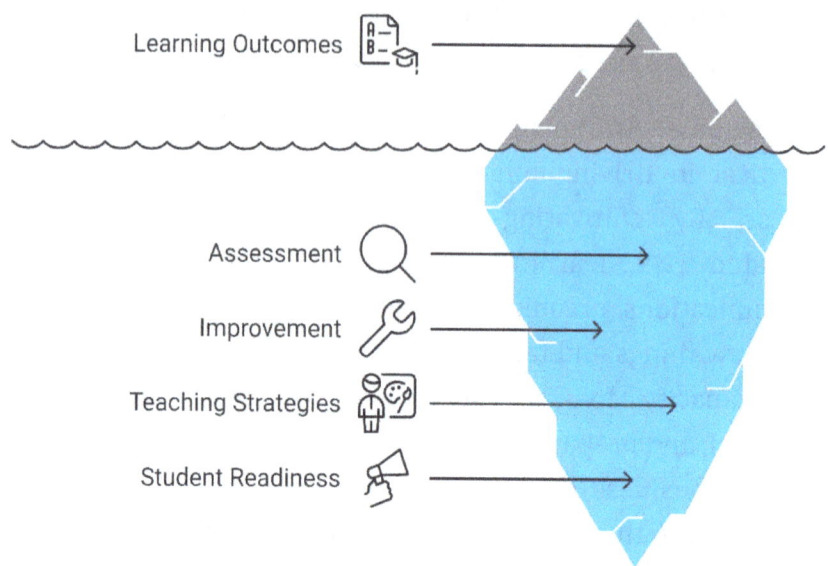

Figure 10.4 Evaluating learning outcomes is critical to any educational or training program.

The main purpose of learning outcome evaluation is to establish whether the objectives of the training or education program have been achieved. It will provide insights into the effectiveness of the content, the delivery methods, and the overall learning experience. Understanding how well employees have absorbed knowledge and developed skills ensures that training programs contribute to individual and organizational success.

Additionally, measuring learning results enables an organization to account for training investments. By showing measurable changes in their employees' performance, productivity, and engagement, an organization has a much better case to request continued or additional funding for learning. Accountability is also very important in today's competitive business environment, with organizations striving to optimize resources while maximizing return on investment.

Several frameworks can guide an organization in assessing learning outcomes. One of the most utilized models is Kirkpatrick's Four-Level Training Evaluation Model, which evaluates the effectiveness of training at four levels:

1. This level measures participants' immediate response to the training. Surveys and feedback forms can measure feelings about the training's content, delivery, and relevance.

2. This level assesses how participants have acquired the intended knowledge and skills. Pre- and post-training assessments, quizzes, and practical demonstrations can offer quantitative data on learning outcomes.

3. This level examines how well participants apply what they learn at work. Observations, self-assessments, and supervisor feedback can determine the change in behavior and performance over time.

4. The final level examines the overall impact of the training on organizational goals. These might be measured by key performance indicators, such as productivity measures, employee retention rates, or customer satisfaction scores, which show whether the training is serving to meet business objectives.

Organizations should use various methods to collect data to analyze learning outcomes efficiently. Surveys and questionnaires could be considered for immediate feedback from learners regarding reactions and satisfaction levels. Quizzes and skill tests for assessment would show the amount of knowledge retention and acquisition. Performance reviews and 360-degree feedback are also bound to provide views about behavioral changes and applications of acquired skills at work.

Certified techniques of meetings and emphasis teams might add more depth to this examination research study. This technique allows for a much deeper exploration of individuals' experiences, problems, and recommended renovation locations, therefore enhancing an extensive view of the training's influence. Examination of knowing outcomes must not be a single procedure but a continual procedure. A company must consistently research and examine the information accumulated to determine fads, successes, and locations for renovation.

This comments loophole permits companies to improve their training programs, making sure they continue to be pertinent and efficient in dealing with the developing labor force requirements. Additionally, sharing the analysis results advertises openness and participation with all stakeholders, such as workers, monitoring and educating carriers. Including the stakeholders in the procedure may produce even more concentrated enhancements and higher approval for future training.

Knowing examination is crucial to attaining the maximum feasible worth of training and growth programs. By executing organized assessment structures, using several information collection techniques, and maintaining a continual renovation society, a company might ensure that the discoveries provided in numerous campaigns will certainly recognize substantial company advantages. This dedication will increase staff members' abilities and efficiency and add to general business success in a significantly affordable atmosphere.

10.4.2 Incorporating Feedback into Learning Plans

Comments are incorporated into finding strategies to constantly boost a company's staff members. This gives an effective understanding of each person's efficiency, determines locations for development, and aids in determining purposes with business objectives. This will certainly assist companies in methodically installing comments into discovering strategies to develop a more vivid coupled with receptive specialist growth strategy.

Feedback can also take various forms: formal appraisals, informal conversations, peer review, and self-analysis. Each level of feedback offers essential information to the instructor for use in planning for learning and to the employee as a means of understanding strengths and weaknesses. Employees who have received constructive feedback understand where their performance stands concerning expectations and in which areas they need to concentrate their efforts to become more skilled.

Embedding feedback into learning plans helps employees set realistic and relevant goals. It builds a culture of openness, communication, and continuous learning. If feedback is valued and acted upon, employees feel more motivated to pursue their development goals. This engagement is critical in creating a workforce committed to personal growth and organizational success.

The organization must establish structured feedback mechanisms to effectively embed feedback in learning plans. Ongoing insights can be provided to the employee through regular performance reviews, check-ins, and feedback sessions. Discussion must, therefore, be constructive and focus on the details of behaviors and outcomes instead of generalities. Rather than telling a person, "You need to improve your communication skills," an effective feedback comment might sound like this: "I noticed during our team meeting that your explanations were unclear. Let's brainstorm some strategies together to make your points clearer.

It would also be helpful if the organizations encouraged peer feedback about learning. In the end, it has to be said that those collaborative environments where every worker might receive or give feedback will make up a community for themselves by holding shared responsibility toward the learning process. For 360-degree feedback, input on performance and growth from supervisors, peers, and subordinates, as well as comprehensive assessments, becomes entirely possible.

The feedback collection must then be followed by including such information in a structured Individual Learning Plan. The workers must reflect upon feedback, identify learning objectives per the development requirements, and implement them accordingly. For example, an employee might understand through feedback that project management is required; such a person can go for relevant training courses or request mentoring from a more experienced worker.

Organizations should also provide resources to enable employees to act on feedback. This could mean anything from training programs or workshops to coaching opportunities on identified competency gaps. By connecting discovering goals to workable responses, companies ensure that growth is deliberate and also impactful. Comments from a finding-out strategy ought to be identified as a component of the constant renovation cycle. Carry out adjustments based upon this input; after that, they are additionally required to reconsider even more regarding their progression occasionally by collecting even more input. That consistent adjustment and improvement supply chances for proceeded enhancement of finding out strategies in communication with private and specialist functions along with business assumptions.

Just as crucial, companies must additionally permit events of development and success arising from incorporating responses. Identifying staff members for seeking and executing feedback enhances the society of continual knowing and also urges others to seek comments. Comments incorporated into discovering strategies support a society of continual enhancement plus specialist growth. A company can establish structured devices for responses, web link responses to discover purposes, and develop a continual renovation cycle that boosts staff member interaction and efficiency. Eventually, it profits the specific staff member and includes worth to the company in search of total success and flexibility in a constantly transforming service setting. Highlighting the value of comments aids in growing a positive, resistant labor force devoted to long-lasting understanding.

10.5 Celebrating Learning Milestones

Turning point events involve constructing and making it possible for society to develop and advance continually in the company. Identifying these turning points will inspire staff members, enhancing the idea that discovery belongs to expert and individual growth. Acknowledging and commemorating the turning points can boost staff member interaction and morale, along with a feeling of the area to advertise constant knowing. Acknowledging discovering turning points offers several vital features.

Initially, it provides a reputation for workers' initiative and time in attaining their growth objectives. Whether completing a training program, attaining a certification, or mastering a new skill, recognition makes employees feel appreciated and valued. This, in turn, can contribute a lot to job satisfaction and a positive workplace culture.

Second, it helps encourage a growth mindset within the organization. If an employee sees others recognized for achievements, it simply supports that learning and development are part of the culture and that each can grow. This encourages the employees to participate in their learning because they know their efforts are well-recognized. When employees can acknowledge others' cultural learning, this promotes initiative and allows them to take on new challenges in a warranted manner.

Organizations can celebrate learning milestones with activities that best fit their culture and employees' preferences. Strategies include ▪▪ Formal recognition programs, which indicate employee achievement. These may include "Employee of the Month" based on learning accomplishments or special recognition at company meetings or in newsletters.

- Occasions, like lunch-and-learns or group events, are arranged to commemorate the turning point. Staff members can additionally share their experiences and understandings from their learning trips during such occasions. This will certainly again assist in a breakthrough partnership and sharing of understanding.

- Digital badges or certifications for finishing programs or attaining a landmark might be offered.

- These would certainly work as concrete suggestions of what has been attained. They can, after that, be displayed on expert accounts or perhaps over social networks, providing various other workers an instance of exactly how to function towards comparable success.

- Personal time required to acknowledge a worker's success does a lot. A transcribed note by the supervisor or a shout-out throughout the group conference better strengthens private turning points with even more genuineness and recognition.

- Celebrating learning turning points properly calls for the supportive setting of a company that embraces continual growth. This requires offering resources and possibilities for staff members to seek their discovering objectives while corresponding success honestly.

It is additionally essential to include comments in the event procedure. Staff members must be permitted to review their learning experiences and share what they found useful. This boosts the event and also supplies insights that can assist in enhancing future learning campaigns. Honoring finding out turning points has to do with producing and allowing society of constant business renovation and interaction.

Arranging acknowledgment for staff member accomplishments can inspire individuals to develop and grow. Official acknowledgment, event occasions, individual acknowledgment, and electronic badges can enable the structure of an atmosphere that would certainly care for and sustain knowing. Ultimately, it may boost a person's inspiration for their great success and the company's durability in the vibrant globe. Highlighting the significance of discovering coupled with growth will produce a much more energetic labor force that is aggressive and devoted to long-lasting discoveries.

10.5.1 Adopting Innovation Through Learning

In today's busy service globe with hefty competitors, the capability to influence advancement becomes critical for companies to remain in advance. An ingenious society can best be raised with continual understanding. Giving precedence to learning and development will create an environment where creativity is adopted, new ideas are welcomed, and people are empowered to explore new grounds. This linkage of learning to innovation is what assures sustainable growth and adaptability.

Learning and innovation go hand in hand. Employees' Continuous learning results in acquiring new knowledge, skills, and perceptions that can spark innovative thinking. Exposure to diverse ideas and concepts develops an individual's ability to connect dots from apparently unrelated areas, which can trigger an act of creativity and inspiration for finding new solutions to existing problems. Organizations practicing a learning culture allow their people to think critically, challenge the status quo, generate fresh ideas, and be innovative.

Instead, organizations should create a supportive learning culture, enabling efficient learning and innovation. This requires a setting where one feels comfortable sharing concepts, attempting brand-new techniques, or picking up from failings. Leaders play a vital role in modeling individuals' development attitudes and revealing enthusiasm for their discoveries. In each discovering job, leaders need to add seriously by accepting trial and error, given that this can reveal groups' most effective instances by taking the chance and seeking cutting-edge options. This can be promoted by executing organized methods and developing a knowing society.

Organizations should supply training programs, workshops, and internet training courses that give their labor force cutting-edge abilities. Expertise sharing could be taken on with normal group conferences plus inner discussion forums; this can activate a rise in collective reasoning, enabling staff members to gain from each other. Additionally, creating a safeguarded room for attempting brand-new points in cutting-edge research laboratories or pilot jobs will allow staff members to check their suggestions without the anxiety of failing. It develops an environment of exploration coupled with creative imagination.

Lastly, suffering in a society of technology with knowledge calls for acknowledgment and benefits for cutting-edge initiatives. Commemorating landmarks via official acknowledgment programs or laid-back recognitions enhances the worth put on imagination and testing. Companies can influence others to work together by informing success tales and highlighting cutting-edge options. The strengthening favorable circle developed below better gas technology makes finding out together with creative thinking stay at the heart of the company's objective. Ultimately, innovation with knowledge is necessary for the success of any company in a frequently transforming organizational atmosphere.

10.6 Case Study: Cultivating a Learning Environment

Producing a continual enhancement society implies constructing an organization that will certainly flourish in continuous adjustment. Developing a knowing atmosphere that motivates individuals to welcome obstacles, take dangers, and consider failings as chances for growth is concerning. A wonderful example is Amazon.com, which is based on the understanding of the ingenious society at Amazon.com, which has permitted it to grow throughout numerous organizations. This allows for better staff member involvement, greater flexibility, and total efficiency, making it possible for continual development. Amazon.com discovered that society is underpinned by the approach that technology originates from trial and error.

Workers are motivated to take calculated risks and seek originalities even if those suggestions do not always result in urgent success. This method is encapsulated in Amazon.com's "stop working quickly" approach, which advertises quick prototyping and screening of brand-new principles. It considers failure not a loss but a procedure that furnishes it with essential experience, permitting Amazon.com to discover the virgin region and increase the perspective of what is possible. The firm's dedication to comments and representation is at the heart of Amazon.com's finding out the atmosphere.

Routine efficiency evaluations and group instructions permit staff members to review what functioned, what did not, and why. This method progresses a society of responsibility and also motivates staff members to gain from each other's experiences. Groups can boost and introduce themselves jointly by sharing understandings and approaches, developing a vibrant cycle of constant development. Additionally, Amazon.com purchases expert growth sources.

Workers can access different training programs, workshops, and mentorship to increase their abilities and understanding. Additionally, proof of this dedication to finding out is the "Career Choice" program, which supplies financing for workers' outdoor education and learning and training in high-demand areas. By concentrating on staff member development, Amazon.com is much better placed to develop a gifted and inspired labor force to aid the business in expansion.

Finally, management is a prominent aspect of the learning setting at Amazon.com. Leaders must design a development mindset by demonstrating how much they discover and expand. Leaders need to develop a setting that's secure for trial and error, with open conversations, assistance for ingenious concepts, and acknowledgment of staff members for attempting, regardless of their results. This would certainly assist in developing worker self-confidence, enabling individuals to take campaigns toward continual development.

Eventually, it appears that producing a knowing society is vital for continued development in companies. Amazon.com shows how a risk-embracing society that sustains comments purchases growth constructs excellent leaders and advances technology and worker interaction. By welcoming comparable worths, companies can develop a society of continual discovery commemorated for continual success and versatility within an ever-evolving market.

10.7 Key Point Donald Trump's potential re-election in 2024

> **Focus on Law and Order:** Advocating for law enforcement and public safety, which resonates in areas concerned with crime rates.

With the 2024 presidential election fast approaching, Donald Trump's probable re-election campaign will be anchored by a "law and order" platform that will appeal strongly to voters concerned with rising crime rates in many urban areas of the United States. This stress on public safety and the support of law enforcement is one of the cornerstones of Trump's appeal, framing him as a candidate for the security and stability of American communities.

One of the few things that Trump has been consistent with in his political career is his support for law enforcement. He has made himself appear a solid ally to police and other first responders, claiming that only a strong police presence and well-resourced police will keep people safe. During his past administration, Trump spearheaded programs to strengthen law enforcement agencies, such as increased funding for police departments and expanding programs designed to fight violent crime. With the surge in crime rates in some regions of the country during and after the COVID-19 pandemic, this approach will likely favor those voters for whom safety and security are a top concern.

> **Target Key Demographics**
> Identify and cater to specific voter demographics that align with your vision.
>
> **Stay on Offense**
> Maintain a proactive stance rather than a defensive one in political battles.

Concerns about crime-especially violent crime-have increasingly become salient in American political discourse. With many cities trying to grapple with growing gun violence, theft, and other criminal activities, many voters are looking for candidates who will take such issues seriously. This focus by Trump on law and order permits him to tap into constituent anxiety about safety in their communities. As mentioned, it also allows him to be a strong leader in voters' minds, promising a safer community through law enforcement that will work efficiently.

The messaging of Trump's campaign probably includes the following: he is the candidate who will "restore law and order" and "back the blue," which may resonate with voters who believe that current leadership has failed to support law enforcement. This narrative can be particularly effective in suburban and rural areas, where concerns about crime are often more pronounced. By highlighting specific crime cases and offering solutions that involve increasing police resources and engaging communities, Trump attempts to provide a sense of urgency around his platform.

Trump might also connect his law and order message to broader national security and border control themes. In so doing, he links domestic safety to national policies on immigration and crime prevention—a key selling point for voters who view the issues as interrelated. This comprehensive approach reinforces his image as a tough-on-crime candidate who gives paramount importance to the safety of American citizens, both at home and at the borders.

All in all, the 2024 re-election bid of Donald Trump is set to be anchored on a very strong law and order campaign, which is very appealing to the psyche of those concerned about rising crime rates in the country. Trump is advocating for law enforcement, rising crime, and national security to make him appear a strong leader who takes the security of the American communities seriously. Closer to the election, this focus on law and order is expected to take center stage in his campaign strategy, shaping not just the narrative of his candidacy but perhaps even voter sentiment.

Reference

1. National Association for the Education of Young Children. (2022). *A new vision for high-quality preschool curriculum.* Retrieved from https://www.naeyc.org/accreditation

2. National Academies of Sciences, Engineering, and Medicine. (2015). *Transforming the workforce for children birth through age 8: A unifying foundation.* The National Academies Press. https://doi.org/10.17226/19401

3. U.S. Department of Education. (2019). *Creating safe, equitable, engaging schools: A comprehensive framework for school improvement.* Retrieved from https://www.ed.gov/grants-and-programs/money-college

4. Hattie, J., & Timperley, H. (2007). The power of feedback. *Review of Educational Research*, 77(1), 81-112.

5. Darling-Hammond, L., Hyler, M. E., & Gardner, M. (2017). *Effective teacher professional development.* Palo Alto, CA: Learning Policy Institute. Retrieved from https://learningpolicyinstitute.org

6. Gay, G. (2018). *Culturally responsive teaching: Theory, research, and practice* (3rd ed.). New York, NY: Teachers College Press.

CHAPTER 11

Adapt and Overcome: Embracing Change with Confidence

Introduction

In a world becoming more dynamic daily, adapting and overcoming obstacles has become central for individuals and institutions. Technological advancement, fluctuating market demands, and shifting societal norms drive change in one form or another. Those who can confidently face change are resilient and better prepared for new opportunities and uncertainties. Adaptability is key to innovation, enhanced problem-solving skills, and personal and professional development.

It means that accepting change needs to be part of a person's mentality so that he views challenges as opportunities for growth and learning [1]. Persons with this mindset will likely approach change with curiosity and openness, explore new possibilities, and discover strategies [2]. This re-framing will turn fear and resistance into motivation and action [3]. It's an important way of being proactive in today's fast-moving environment, where being able to pivot and adjust can be the difference between success and stagnation [4].

Organizations are also supposed to adopt a culture of flexibility. Leaders should model behaviors that promote team flexibility and resilience [5]. When an organization advances to an environment where experimentation is welcomed and failures are considered opportunities for learning, employees can be empowered to change confidently [6]. This will bring about better team cohesion and innovation since people with different ideas can put forward their points of view [7].

Besides, change often demands the development of new competencies and skills. In this respect, continuous learning is crucial, whereby individuals and organizations seek to remain relevant in the dynamic environment. Investment in training and development can grant employees the confidence to approach new challenges head-on. This further cements individual performance and helps the organization with its overall capability.

The ability to adapt and overcome is important in a constantly changing world. With confidence in change, individuals and organizations can work successfully through uncertainties, create innovation, and support ongoing growth. This introduction sets the stage for exploring strategies and mindsets necessary for thriving in a landscape where change is the only constant, underlining the importance of resilience, learning, and a positive approach to transformation.

11.1 Understanding the Nature of Change

Modification is an indispensable component in life, influencing every aspect of our individual and professional lives. People and companies desirous of successfully solving their puzzles must recognize its nature. Change can be of many types—planned versus unplanned, incremental versus transformational—and such a distinction forms the basis for devising strategies appropriate for managing it.

Planned change is a willful and systematic attempt at changing organizations, processes, structures, or behaviors. Such organizational change usually comes with stated and explicit objectives, be it improving efficiency, raising productivity, or responding to market dynamics. As an example, a business might wish to start the application of a brand-new innovation system that would certainly assist in enhancing its procedures. On the other hand, unanticipated adjustment unravels all of a sudden with little time for representation. Examples include natural disasters, sudden market fluctuations, or unexpected events like the COVID-19 pandemic. Appreciation of these differences aids an organization in its preparation and response to differing situations.

Change can be either incremental or transformational. Incremental change consists of small steps of adjustment that refine existing processes or practices. This type of change is often manageable and less intrusive; therefore, the organization can evolve without significant disruption. For example, a firm may add new features to the existing product based on customer suggestions. On the other hand, transformational change is essentially the alteration in the organization's structure, culture, or strategy. It is the kind of change that is usually more challenging to enact and may call for entirely new systems and practices. Understanding if the change is incremental or transformational allows leaders to craft an appropriate strategy to ensure they are providing the right resources and support. Understanding the emotional aspects of change is equally important. Change usually involves feelings, including fear, anxiety, and resistance. Some may be unsure about their role or what the future direction might be for their organization. The leader needs to acknowledge the employees' feelings and support them through the transition. Communication is the key;

clear, regular messaging can help eradicate fears and instill trust. The more organizations can make individuals feel that their opinions and ideas are valued and heard, the less resistance to change there will be and the more positive the response will be.

Change management deals with adaptability. People and organizations that learn to adopt a flexible mindset are much more open to new situations and challenges. It's embracing change and being watchful for opportunities to grow and improve. The organization should have a culture of continuous learning to drive adaptability: employees would have a greater sense of empowerment by enhancing their skills and embracing new solutions. Not less important are training and development, which are individuals with the necessary tools to succeed in a changing world.

The nature of change is important in negotiating the maze of personal and organizational change. By understanding the types of change, emotional responses to change, and the development of adaptability, individuals and organizations are better positioned for success. Approaching change as an opportunity rather than a threat may provide innovative solutions and enhanced resilience in uncertainty. As change remains the only constant, a thorough grasp of its nature would better prepare man to adjust to and flourish in a world of continuous change.

11.2 Identifying Sources of Change in the Workplace

Workplace changes are inevitable and will continually evolve from many sources. Understanding the source of its origin will help an organization and employees foresee, adapt, or change to new challenges in readiness. The source for initiating change enables organizations to devise a proactive culture by building the ability to be resilient and innovative, thereby positioned towards thriving in turbulent turbulence.

A major source of change comes from the organization itself. Internal factors include leadership change, organizational structure, and company policy. When a new CEO or manager takes over, for instance, they often bring new vision and priorities, changing company culture and expectations of employees. Similarly, restructurings, mergers, or departmental changes affect the style of working and team dynamics since employees may become part of other teams. Identifying these internal sources will facilitate organizations in moving their workforce into transition and aligning corporate strategies accordingly.

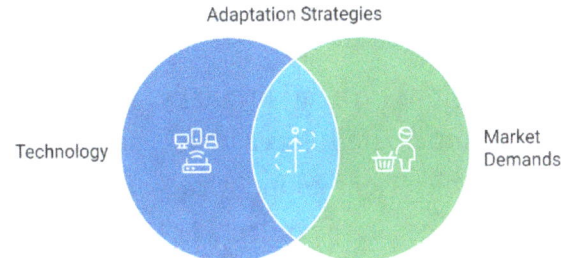

Figure 11.1 Change in the workplace is inevitable and can arise from various sources.

Other internal sources of change that are considered critical deal with technological advancement. Rapidly changing technology can sometimes drastically alter the way things are done. For example, new software or an automation tool may increase the efficiency of operations but sometimes require employees to learn a new skill and adapt to different processes. Organizations that foresee such technological changes can train and invest in resources to equip their employees to adapt to this change with less productivity disruption.

Besides inner variables, office adjustments can also be driven by different outside resources. Market characteristics, law adjustments, and public fads have effective impacts that companies must deal with. As an example, transforming customer actions or financial variations might compel companies to alter their means of operating. Similarly, adjustments in regulation or the promulgation of brand-new policies might ask for modifications in just how points run and, as a result, plans together with conformity techniques of companies. By identifying these external resources for adjustment, companies can stay active and receptive to the advancing landscape.

International occasions are additionally solid stimulants for modification. Unanticipated occasions, such as all-natural calamities, pandemics, or geopolitical changes, can create substantial disturbances in the office. For example, the COVID-19 pandemic required many organizations to change their function from residence and quickly reconsider their functional designs. These international occasions make getting ready for unanticipated adjustments essential, as well as constructing backup strategies that allow fast adjustment to any situation.

Recognizing the resources of adjustment in the office is essential for any effort to develop a flexible and resistant society.

Recognizing inner and external pressures for adjustment enables companies to prepare for future obstacles and possibilities. It makes a company much more receptive and also better promotes a positive advancement strategy. In this changing workplace, recognizing and adapting to the sources of change will significantly determine long-term success.

11.2.1 Developing Change Management Strategies

Change is inevitable in an organization. Market dynamics change, technologies shift, and customer needs fluctuate. However, the success of managing that change is different. In this respect, effective change management strategies can be developed whereby leaders smoothly navigate their teams through transitions while at the same time ensuring a lesser level of resistance and a higher level of engagement. A structured approach to managing change will lead to smoother transitions, thus empowering employees to create a culture of adaptability and resilience.

Figure 11.2 Developing change management strategies.

Defining the change is the first step in developing change management strategies. The leaders should elaborate on the change's reason, objectives, and expected outcomes. This clarity provides a framework for understanding the need for change, enabling employees to view it not as a disruption but as an opportunity for growth. The leaders should communicate openly about the change and address concerns or uncertainties from team members. By giving a clear overview, the leader can reduce anxiety and advance trust in the team.

After defining the change, it is very important to involve employees in it. Such involvement in the early stages with team members creates a feeling of ownership and buy-in. Workshops, response sessions, plus collective preparation will certainly aid the leaders in getting this participation. Via their input, the staff member's leader can analyze possible mistakes or obtain additional details to assist in executing the adjustment. This comprehensive strategy encourages workers and aids in exposing cutting-edge options to feasible barriers in advertising a society of partnership. Training and assistance are two other vital parts of taking care of modification.

Resources coupled with training ought to be readily available for the workers to adjust to brand-new procedures, modern technologies, or frameworks when modifying. Their leaders should create a group training program to ensure that every staff member has the needed abilities and understanding to undergo the shift duration without trouble. The mentorship and coaching provided by follow-through support could help employees find competence and confidence within themselves while doing their jobs. Also, regular check-ins will enable adjustment and reinforce feelings of community during change through feedback loops.

Lastly, measuring the impact of the change and celebrating successes along the way is crucial to sustaining momentum. Leaders should establish metrics to evaluate the effectiveness of the change management strategies and collect feedback from employees about their experiences. Celebration of small wins raises morale and reinforces the plus side of the change, encouraging continued adaptation and growth. By recognizing and rewarding individual and team input, leaders can nurture a culture that embraces the dynamics of change as quite natural and, therefore, useful for organizational life. In other words, change management strategies should be underpinned by an enabling approach through which organizations could thrive with continuously changing scenarios.

11.2.2 Communicating Change Effectively

Communication effectively acts as the cornerstone for effective change management. When organizational changes in structure, technologies, or strategies occur, how leaders communicate these changes will greatly influence employee acceptance and general morale. Clear, transparent, and consistent communication soothes uncertainty, builds trust, and empowers employees to look forward to the change in prospects.

First, effective communication of change must be presented in an articulated rationale. This includes leaders taking a storytelling approach to explain why the need for the change exists and what this will achieve. The benefit to the organization and the impact on individual levels must be spelled out. Helping team members understand the "why" of the change allows leaders to build a sense of purpose and urgency that encourages individuals to approach the process positively.

Second, communicate through various channels: Do not rely on one communication channel, such as email or corporate announcements; this may lead to misunderstanding and disengagement. The leaders should, therefore, use different communication formats, like town hall meetings, workshops, newsletters, and one-on-one discussions. This multi-faceted method ensures the message gets to all staff members regardless of their favored interaction design. In addition, discussion possibilities give a method for inquiries to be asked, issues to be increased, and sights to be revealed by staff members, which aids in installing a society of visibility. The 2nd vital element of reliable modification in interaction is uniformity.

As adjustments are made, management should ensure the messaging is lined up throughout the process.

Confusion and counting on might create resistance amongst staff members when regular details are reproduced. To be constant, leaders should establish an interaction strategy consisting of crucial messages, timelines, and duties. Routine updates will likewise be needed to allow staff members to recognize exactly how the adjustment is unraveling and if there are any modifications. This recurring interaction would certainly assist the company in enhancing its openness approach and maintaining staff members' passion throughout this change.

Lastly, the worker's sensations must be identified and replied to during the interaction procedure. Modification can be a psychological procedure that can range from exhilaration to stress and anxiety. Leaders must be sensitive to others' feelings. This might suggest offering networks where feelings or sights can be broadcast, such as comment sessions or confidential studies.

Recognizing sensations and providing assistance via therapy or peer assistance teams can supply a more understanding method. By confirming staff member experiences and guaranteeing leaders construct strength and urge a favorable function to alter. Interaction throughout adjustment lays the bedrock for a favorable business society. Leaders can effectively lead their groups through changes by plainly verbalizing the factors for adjustment, utilizing numerous interaction networks, and dealing with worker feelings. This aggressive method improves worker involvement and reinforces the general performance of adjustment campaigns, therefore positioning the company for long-lasting success.

11.3 Encouraging Flexibility Among Team Members

Today, companies are transforming quickly. Enhancing unpredictability and intricacy has resulted in group versatility being crucial to success. Urging adaptability amongst employees has several extra results for the private and company: being extra resistant, imaginative, and collected. As organizations face ongoing, evolving challenges, new technology, and shifting market development, a culture of flexibility is crucial to long-term performance and innovation.

Promoting flexibility requires the lead in adaptable behaviors from the very leader. This means being open to change, embracing new ideas, and being willing to change strategies if necessary. When team members see their leaders handle uncertainty with poise and agility, they will likely adopt similar attitudes. Leaders can share experiences about overcoming challenges in the past and how responsiveness and agility are important in doing so. Transparency provides that the nature of change is viewed as normal work and will help team members adopt flexibility as one of the core values.

This involves developing an environment that can support flexible working habits. Leaders must consider remote ways of working, flexible hours of working, and project-based allocations where members can work independently and decide on the exact pattern and time of fulfilling an assigned project. Empower the employees by giving them more control over their scheduling and workflow, making them satisfied and productive. The opportunities to cross-train allow team members to enter new roles and grow within the organization by adapting to wider professional horizons.

Open communication is the key to creating flexibility. Leaders are supposed to let team members share their thoughts, ideas, and concerns about whatever change in processes or projects happens. Regular check-ins and feedback sessions provide a free flow of communication where employees feel protected when giving their opinions on how things can be done better. This collaborative atmosphere evokes creative problem-solving, reminding everyone that the team shares flexibility as a core value.

Building a culture may also be facilitated by realizing and reinforcing flexible behavior. It's where leadership should highlight when one or other team member positively adapts to changed situations, grasps more responsibility, or collaborates successfully across their role. Celebrating reinforces the value and sets an example for others. In other words, it could go from less formal acknowledgment during the meetings to serious awards celebrating adaptability and innovation.

Conclusion Flexibility within a team is one of the major enablers in negotiating the labyrinthine character of contemporary work. The leaders can facilitate flexible behavior by modeling adaptability, supportive work arrangements, open communication, and recognition of flexible efforts to create an enabling environment for team members to respond with agility and creativity to challenges. By creating a culture of flexibility, organizations position themselves to adapt to the changing landscape. In such a way, flexibility becomes a skill and part of the core identity that will drive success, collaboration, and resilience within a team.

11.3.1 Building a Resilient Mindset

During this period of change and turbulence, nurturing a resilient mindset is paramount for individuals and teams. Resilience can be defined as one's ability to adapt to challenges, bounce back, and prosper through difficult circumstances. It gives team members confidence to manage adversities while focusing on the team's long-term objectives. A resistant state of mind is one in which particular perspectives and methods within a group advertise psychological toughness, versatility, and determination. Typically, the durable frame of mind will certainly entail welcoming obstacles as chances for development. Leaders can embrace this by mounting barriers as not expensive obstacles but beneficial to understanding experiences. By embracing an atmosphere where errors are dealt with as tipping rocks and never fail, employees are extra happy to take threats and introduce them.

This can be sustained by an adjustment in thinking, sharing tales of just how the company has actually encountered misfortune and what was discovered while doing so. Such tales might motivate individuals to consider hardship from a slant of possibility and enhance the concept that strength is constructed via experience.

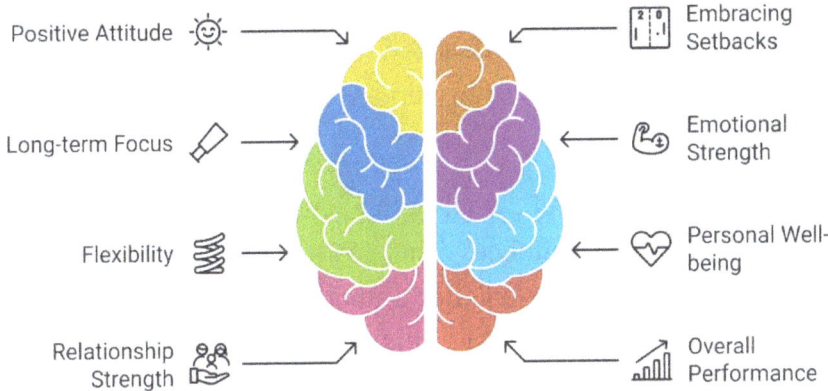

Figure 11.3 Building a Resilient Mindset.

An additional crucial aspect in constructing durability is psychological knowledge. People who can acknowledge feelings, comprehend them as well, and handle their effects are better placed to deal with stress and anxiety plus unpredictability. Leaders can create the capacity for psychological knowledge by preparing training, workshops on self-awareness and compassion, and reliable interaction. The leaders must permit open conversations of sensations and troubles, making the setting non-judgmental. It sustains social partnerships plus supports a feeling of coming from where one can draw upon others in times of difficulty.

A solid support network is additionally essential for strength. Leaders ought to urge partnership and esprit de corps, pointing out the relevance of leaning on each other for assistance. Normal team-building tasks can help reinforce these bonds and construct trust among staff members. When people feel they can contact their associates, they are more likely to seek aid and share their battles, lowering their sensations of seclusion.

Additionally, executing mentorship programs can provide added assistance, permitting less knowledgeable staff members to learn from those who have actually experienced comparable difficulties.

Lastly, self-care and well-being are important in the development of resilience. The leader should indicate the importance of work-life balance and allow his team members to be in practice over self-care. This can involve flexible working policies, wellness initiatives, or an enabling culture where taking time off is allowed. A physically and mentally fine individual will more confidently be able to tackle stress and change. Other mindfulness practices include meditation and relaxation techniques, which enhance emotional regulation and well-being.

11.3.2 Creating a Change Response Plan

Every organization needs to be prepared to respond to the dynamics of change. The Change Response Plan provides a guide that enables leadership and team members to deal effectively with the transition. It enumerates what should be undertaken for changes to progress smoothly with minimal disruptions, resulting in more engagements and a culture of resiliency and adaptability.

The first step in developing a Change Response Plan is the scope and objectives of the change. The leadership should articulate the rationale behind the change, the expected outcomes, and how it aligns with its goals. This will then provide the basic understanding necessary to gain buy-in from stakeholders and ensure that all involved understand the importance of the change. Framing the change within the context of the organization's mission and vision can help give the team members a sense of purpose that may be motivational for them to embrace the transition.

Second, an effect analysis ought to be carried out. This is necessary to establish exactly how the modification will impact the various elements of the company, including the procedures, systems, and employees. Interacting with staff members in this analysis would allow learning more about difficulties or opportunities that might exist. Leaders can obtain a more comprehensive point of view on the circumstance from individuals directly influenced by modification and, therefore, react appropriately.

This will certainly make the strategy more reliable and help staff members feel a part of it. Having assessed the effect, the following action must be to describe concrete actions coupled with timelines for applying adjustment. This consists of establishing functions coupled with obligations, developing essential landmarks, and establishing quantifiable goals. An effectively organized timeline is one certain method to lead the adjustment procedure on the best track and permit clear obligation. Leaders need to additionally consider prospective dangers and barriers throughout the application stage and create contingency plans to attend to these obstacles proactively.

This expectancy allows the company to react rapidly to unanticipated problems, lessening disturbance and preserving energy. A vital element of any Adjustment Response Plan is reliable interaction. Management must establish an interaction method that shows exactly how information will certainly be shared throughout the company. This consists of recognizing vital messages, interaction networks, and also regularity of updates. Openness in interaction assists in minimizing unpredictability and increasing the number of employees, which will keep them educated and involved throughout the modification procedure. Additionally, leaders must urge responses and discussions, allowing staff members to share their concerns and ask inquiries. This two-way interaction produces an encouraging setting where workers feel valued together and listened to.

Ultimately, it assesses the efficiency of the adjustment feedback strategy after application. This includes getting comments from employees on exactly how well the modification purposes were accomplished and what needs to be enhanced. The post-change evaluation enables a company to learn from its experience and embrace much better means of handling adjustment in the future. Sequence plus payment must be commemorated, strengthening society's constant renovation and versatility.

11.4 Learning from Past Change Experiences

In this fast-growing age, companies need to alter every minute. The most effective method for managing adjustment features is gaining from experience. Looking at successful past change endeavors or otherwise provides lessons that guide developing future strategies. Reflective insight into what worked and did not and why allows organizations to build a sound framework for managing change with better adaptability and resilience.

Reflection on past experiences in change allows the view of dynamics that might have influenced the outcomes of such initiatives. This process entails soliciting feedback from employees, stakeholders, and leaders involved in the change. In so doing, an organization can identify common themes and lessons learned by compiling diverse perspectives. For example, if a previously instituted change initiative met resistance, leaders can analyze the reasons behind such pushback as they address similar challenges in future initiatives. This would promote a culture of continuous improvement, whereby the organization would be better positioned to remove obstacles and implement effective solutions.

Lessons learned should be documented throughout the entire change process. Lessons learned may be documented in various forms: post-implementation reviews, case studies, or internal reports. Organizations create a knowledge base for future reference in subsequent change initiatives by capturing quantitative and qualitative data. For example, an organization that has successfully implemented new technology must document the strategies to get employees to buy into the technology, the best training programs, and the metrics defining success. It supports decision-making and prevents important information from being lost over time. It thus allows the establishment of an enabling culture of learning derived from past experiences regarding change. This will call for leaders to model behavior characterized by free dialogue about the events of the change initiatives and how the process has turned out. When employees feel secure sharing their experiences and observations, trust in a collaborative environment will be created. This is furthered within an organizational culture that captures lessons learned and integrates them into training programs so that the new employees start their new jobs with insight from the organization's history. That is how one develops the ability to adapt as an organization within a constantly changing environment.

Learning from experiences does not stop at reflecting upon those experiences; the key idea is to apply insights from these reflections to future change efforts. The best approach would be for organizations to develop ways in which lessons learned systematically could inform their change management strategies. These might take the structures that inform the best methods, danger reduction approaches, and efficient interaction strategies offered from previous experiences. For example, future adjustment initiatives can focus on comparable involvement methods if a previous effort prospered because of strong stakeholder involvement. By proactively using understandings, companies place themselves for even more amazing success in browsing future adjustments. Gaining from the modification experience is an essential part of efficient modification monitoring.

In this respect, a company will certainly be far better able to adjust and become resistant by assessing previous campaigns, recording lessons learned, embracing a discovering society, and using those understandings for future modifications. This aggressive technique readies the company for new difficulties while encouraging workers to accept such modifications confidently. With the modification rate speeding up, leveraging previous experiences will certainly be necessary to flourish in a constantly altering environment.

11.4.1 Celebrating Adaptability and Success

In today's busy globe, both people and companies require versatility. Commemorating convenience and success strengthens that relevance and encourages groups to welcome modification and aim for continual renovation. Identifying success in adaptability develops a resistant cutting-edge society where workers are motivated to encounter obstacles with self-confidence and creative thinking. Adaptability handles unique problems coupled with successfully reacting to every little thing that occurs suddenly.

Simply put, companies can constantly pivot within constant modern technologies, market changes, or modifications in the customer market. Commemorating Adaptability commemorates efforts and successes when it pertains to individuals and groups appearing effective over changes. By highlighting tales of strength, such as exactly how a group adjusted to function from residence throughout a situation or privately accepted brand-new modern technologies, companies can assist in motivating others to do the same. Acknowledging such initiatives supports spirits and enhances that this is valued within society.

Alongside adaptability, the second supportive pillar is celebrating success. Success means anything from reaching milestones within a project to overcoming key challenges. Organizations ensure that successes are recognized publicly and celebrated to create a sense of oneness and shared purpose. Such recognition may be formal, such as award ceremonies or performance bonuses, or informal, such as shoutouts in team meetings or company newsletters. Success celebrations help create a positive work environment; the employees feel valued and appreciated for their contributions, thus motivating them and encouraging teamwork, as employees are inspired to support one another.

Adaptability and success should be celebrated within an organization's recognition culture. This will involve setting clear criteria regarding adaptability and success within the organization. The leaders should encourage open communication and create avenues for employees to share their experiences and achievements. Regular check-ins, team meetings, and social events may allow employees to highlight their efforts and celebrate their colleagues. By promoting a culture of celebration, an organization will ensure that adaptability and success are celebrated and valued at all levels.

Celebrating adaptability and success also creates an opportunity to connect achievements at the individual and team levels to broader organizational goals. When workers see how their initiatives are aiding the company's success, it boosts their feeling of function and involvement. For instance, if a group efficiently adjusts to a brand-new market approach that brings about enhanced income, commemorating this success enhances the significance of versatility in attaining business objectives. This placement encourages staff members and creates a common vision for the future.

11.4.2 Evaluating the Impact of Change

Determining the modification result is considerable in any company's adjustment administration procedure. Organizations that change, either via technical modifications, adjustments in market characteristics, or, sometimes, inner restructuring, are required to recognize the outcomes of these modifications. This will certainly offer the leaders an understanding of exactly how efficient the adjustment has been, plus allow them to make educated choices in the future. This consists of measurable and qualitative dimensions for a complete overview of how the modifications influence various points of view of the company.

Companies should plainly describe the requirements that will certainly be used to review their adjustment initiative's performance. These should remain in performance with the objectives of the adjustment effort plus consist of evaluations of worker efficiency as well as efficiency, client contentment, and also the total results of business. For example, the success signs for a firm executing a brand-new software application to enhance effectiveness might be time conserved on details jobs, mistake prices pre- and post-implementation, plus comments from workers regarding the convenience of usage. Well-defined standards ensure the analysis procedure is concentrated and pertinent, simplifying evaluation.

The next step towards examining modification is organizing information collection. This would consist of measurable information such as sales numbers or performance metrics plus qualitative information such as worker studies or consumer comments. With a study or meeting, it is feasible to discover how employees feel concerning the applied modification and how it affects their work. Efficiency metrics offer more info on where enhancements are required and when issues were encountered throughout the change. A mix of information resources can provide companies with a much more all-natural feeling of the influence of adjustment.

When information is gathered, evaluation starts. This contrasts the results versus the collection examination standards to determine whether the adjustment effort has worked. For example, the goal was to improve consumer satisfaction by enhancing shipment solutions. Consumer comments and complete satisfaction ratings can be assessed before and after the application to see if the desired result was accomplished. This evaluation determines successes and discovers locations that call for additional focus or modification, supplying crucial understandings for future adjustment efforts.

Examining the effect of adjustment is not simply determining success but embracing a society of continual enhancement. Organizations should see analysis as a possibility to pick up from successes and failings. By understanding what functioned plus what didn't, they can improve their procedures of handling adjustment and construct much better methods for future efforts. This step-by-step discovering procedure motivates proactivity relating to modification where companies remain in a placement to adjust plus progress based upon previous experiences.

11.5 Providing Support During Transitions

Adjustments are continuous in today's hectic office, and transitions- whether about brand-new modern technologies, business restructuring, or changes in market method- can be testing for staff members. Throughout these shifts, offering essential assistance is important in supporting a smooth adjustment procedure plus keeping worker spirits. Appropriate assistance aids individuals in handling switches a lot more properly and boosts the durability and efficiency of a company. Shifts are constantly accompanied by sensations such as unpredictability, stress, anxiety, and resistance.

Recognizing the emotional repercussions of adjustment is the primary step towards assistance. For some, it's a worry of the unidentified or a feeling bewildered by brand-new assumptions. Acknowledging sensations enables leaders to react to worries compassionately and supply the assistance they require to smooth shifts. A delicate company minimizes several of the stress factors connected to transformation by supplying a helpful atmosphere where staff members feel recognized. It's among one of the most essential transition-support facets: evident, clear interaction.

For one, it is vital to notify the workers of the applied adjustments and why and also what assumptions. By routinely educating them, one will stay clear of unpredictability and gain count. Such open interaction constantly uses the room and is also a chance for the staff members to review any problems they are experiencing, consequently becoming consistent. It needs to be two-way; energetic paying attention to comments from staff members can offer understanding to aid in notifying the change procedure and indicating various other locations where added assistance may be needed.

An additional location of assistance for staff members throughout the shift includes training and sourcing. Adjustment typically brings brand-new abilities or expertise that might be required, so giving staff members the right device for success is vital. Organizations must offer all-around training programs relating to the adjustments being presented. Whether with workshops, online programs, or individual training, easily accessible training assists workers in becoming confident and proficient in their brand-new duties.

Developing source facilities (such as frequently asked questions, overviews, and tutorials) can be really helpful for the workers throughout the change duration. Recognizing the psychological parts associated with shifts is not to be ignored. Each company ought to have encouraging frameworks like mentorship programs or peer assistance teams where staff members can review their experiences together with dealing techniques. These casual networks offer a sensation of area plus belonging, even more protection against workers from really feeling separated throughout the shift. Supplying accessibility to sources associated with psychological wellness, such as therapy solutions or workshops on handling companies, shows that they genuinely value their employees' health.

Commending the turning points of change significantly enhances spirits and inspiration. Commemorating small successes, such as the effective application of a brand-new system or a turning point in a task, helps to strengthen progression and success. Celebrations can be any kind, from group events to acknowledgment programs that note private payments. By commemorating success, a company inspires its labor force toward a favorable environment, which supports continued participation plus dedication to adjustment.

11.5.1 Instilling a Culture of Continuous Improvement

Constant enhancement entails continuously making procedures the best and eliminating waste to accomplish top-notch outcomes, using the Lean and the 6 Sigma approaches. Continual renovation depends on the reality that no procedure is best; therefore, it constantly supplies space for renovation. This suggestion immediately transforms as soon as a frame of mind change in a company starts: from achieving just short-run results to its growth in constant understanding and technology. This viewpoint places possession right into the hands of the staff members and encourages them to help the company's success.

A continuous improvement culture thrives on the strong commitment of leadership. It requires that leaders model the principle of constant improvement by being proactive in soliciting feedback, encouraging experiments, and embracing failures for the learning that can come from them. Leaders will tell the team that prioritizing these initiatives and committing resources is very important. Furthermore, leaders should provide a safe environment where ideas can be shared and challenged without repercussions. Such a supporting atmosphere is necessary for the development of creativity and collaboration.

A continuous improvement culture can take place only with the involvement of employees. Every organization should encourage all employees to participate in improvement initiatives irrespective of their designation. It might be done by performing routine conceptualizing referral plans with cross-functional groups to deal with certain troubles. Organizations can uncover cutting-edge services and drive purposeful modification by utilizing workers' varied points of view. It additionally identifies and compensates payments to renovation initiatives via official acknowledgment programs or casual validations to strengthen the worth of worker involvement in the continual enhancement procedure.

The other crucial ingredient in creating a continuous improvement culture is investment in training and development. Empower the employees to know when something can be improved, develop solutions, and apply those solutions effectively. Provide workshops, online courses, and mentorship on problem-solving techniques, data analysis, and process optimization. Creating lifelong learning lets an organization empower employees to proactively facilitate business outcomes within teams.

Where continuous improvements are concerned, an organization must establish metrics to measure progress and check results. The constant evaluation of specific performance indicators—efficiency enhancement or any quality improvement—informs how well the improvement process is. Besides, rejoicing in successes—those big or small—reinforces the importance of continuous improvement as a motivator for teams to take on more significant challenges. Recognition can be given in many ways, from team celebrations to sharing success stories in company communications, which builds a sense of accomplishment and unity.

11.6 Case Study: Embracing Change with Confidence

Thriving organizations have footprints in the sand in almost all kinds of continuously evolving business environments. A perfect practical example is Netflix, which has evolved from a DVD rental service to a leader in online streaming channels. The whole transition shows that an ability to change makes all the difference for a winning organization.

Founded in 1997, Netflix began as a DVD rental service, offering customers a far more convenient way to rent movies than traditional video rental stores. However, when digital technology and internet usage started to rise, it became apparent how people consumed entertainment would change. Realizing the potential of streaming technology, Netflix boldly decided to change its business model. In 2007, the business introduced its streaming solution, allowing clients to immediately access a large collection of movies and TV programs. It was a hard job: massive financial investments in innovation, acquiring material, and customer experience needed to be made. However, Netflix was prepared for this change, plus it was transformative.

Netflix's success can mostly be attributed to its creative interpretation of market characteristics and customer choice. With the abrupt need for on-demand material, Netflix changed its offering to fulfill the required progress. It might curate the material involving its target market by examining the pattern of sights and collecting information on individual choices. This data-driven strategy assisted Netflix in maintaining its consumers, drawing in brand-new clients, and enhancing its market share. How the business readjusted its web content technique to adjust to the transforming customer routines is an outstanding example of how companies can flourish by maintaining their finger on the pulse of their consumers.

Besides welcoming modern technology, Netflix revealed it can be dexterous by purchasing initial web content. Understanding that several standard networks and brand-new streaming solutions entered the area of competitors, Netflix altered tracks by developing unique programs and movies. By making this calculated choice, it can range itself from rivals and ultimately accumulate its faithful customer populace. Achieved several collections that earned countless excellent testimonials, "House of Cards "plus "Stranger Things" developed Netflix as an awesome gamer within the show business. Netflix continually showcased development, took threats, and made instance after instance of how adjustment can be a crucial vehicle driver of development.

Netflix's change also drives the demand for a business society of adjustment. The demand for it is likewise based upon the leader's motivation, which makes them appreciate and approve adjustments and brand-new points. Technology and visibility to numerous societies enable Netflix staff members to attempt and gain from blunders.

This way of reasoning influences imagination, which improves durability and can withstand difficulties from the company's method. Thus, Netflix is ensured regarding the capacity of its labor force to handle or adjust to such adjustments; therefore, any adjustment offers a chance instead of danger. Ultimately, this has been Netflix's journey from simply a DVD service to the leviathan of streaming. The trip mirrors how one might adjust and climb with transforming trends.

Netflix showed that organizations can flourish with change by welcoming new modern technologies, remaining in harmony with customer requirements when purchasing initial web content, and advertising a flexible society. This makeover is an influential suggestion that welcoming changes with confidence are needed to accomplish long-lasting success. When unpredictability becomes normal, versatility suggests survival, opening a path for development and development.

11.7 Key Point Donald Trump's potential re-election in 2024

> **Health Care and Social Security:** Promising to protect and improve health care and social security, key issues for older voters.

Along with the 2024 governmental political election, Donald Trump's prospective reelection proposal is extra riveted on two hot-button concerns that might specifically reverberate with older citizens: healthcare and Social Security. As elders make up the bigger blocks in this political election, shielding and enhancing standard solutions will be crucial in understanding citizen beliefs and choosing this political election.

Social Security remains the structure for the monetary protection of countless Americans, specifically those 65 and older. Trump has been attempting to place himself as the guardian of this most hallowed program by promising that the benefits for future and also existing senior citizens would certainly be maintained risk-free. He had struck those seeking to reduce or restructure the Social Security system as attacking senior citizens. By guaranteeing Social Security, Trump attempts to guarantee that older citizens will certainly maintain their advantages.

> **Target Key Demographics**
> Identify and cater to specific voter demographics that align with your vision.
>
> **Stay on Offense**
> Maintain a proactive stance rather than a defensive one in political battles.

Other than social safety and security, health care remains a crucial concern for older Americans, several of whom believe that their clinical costs have increased with the intricacy of their health and wellness requirements. Trump's project is most likely to flaunt that his management has functioned to decrease prescription medicine rates while increasing accessibility to care. His previous initiatives, such as the "Right to Try" regulations permitting incurable clients to gain access to speculative therapies, have some vibration amongst citizens that line up with higher selections relating to medical care. Trump assures to prolong those initiatives, which, with any luck, would interest senior citizens searching for even more budget-friendly coupled with readily available healthcare.

Medicare- the other significant program for the country's seniors- is anticipated to be an additional factor in Trump's project. He can additionally interest older citizens who fidget concerning the boosting price of healthcare by asking for reforms that would certainly boost Medicare solutions and decrease out-of-pocket expenses. It remains the passion of senior citizens who depend on this program for wellness, requiring that Trump vouched to make Medicare lasting with reforms. Highlighting concrete propositions to boost Medicare will certainly stimulate assistance in this market.

On the other hand, Trump's messaging has much to do with paying attention to their problems on healthcare plus Social Security. He will develop a speech for the senior citizens that would connect to them via town hall discussions and social media site systems. It could reinforce his bond with the block of citizens, understanding they have distinct obstacles and looking for their deemed breakthrough. In all, Donald Trump's re-election project for 2024 is most likely to put a high cost on healthcare along with Social Security, two of the most essential concerns for older citizens.

In this manner, Trump guarantees the security and boost of these programs, which would guarantee senior citizens' monetary safety and security along with accessibility to healthcare. As for the political election techniques, his capability to properly articulate his dedication to these problems will undoubtedly be an essential establishment considering his collecting assistance amongst older Americans, which usually affects the results of political elections. In this period, medical care and Social Security have been progressively critical to citizens, and this can be just one of the conclusive aspects of the Trump project approach.

Reference

1. Nyanyo, M. (2021). Embracing change: A journey towards personal growth and success. *Medium*. Retrieved from https://medium.com

2. Deshler, D. (n.d.). Chapter 11 - Evaluating extension programs. In *Title of the Book* (pp. xx-xx). Publisher.

3. Patton, M. Q. (1991). *Utilization-focused evaluation*. Sage Publications.

4. Greene, J. C., Caracelli, V. J., & Graham, W. F. (1989). Toward a conceptual framework for mixed-method evaluation designs. *Educational Evaluation and Policy Analysis*, 11(3), 255-274.

5. Kotter, J. P. (1996). *Leading change*. Harvard Business Review Press.

6. Senge, P. M. (1990). *The fifth discipline: The art and practice of the learning organization*. Doubleday.

7. Dweck, C. S. (2006). *Mindset: The new psychology of success*. Random House.

CHAPTER 12

Legacy of Lions: Building a Sustainable Leadership Culture

Introduction

Within this quickly altering and progressively adjoined globe, the need for a globe with reliable management has never been pushed further. An extremely crucial academic underpinning of such reasoning is a lasting management society. Like lions, which stand for power, endurance, and synchronization within their satisfaction, lasting management needs to produce a society with long-lasting success instead of short-run gains. This method improves business efficiency along with constructs leaders that can influence and also equip future generations.

The Lions' tradition is an effective example of management itself. In the wild, lions are a fantastic instance of esprit de corps and critical partnership to achieve the objectives. A lasting management society motivates synergy, progresses numerous points of view, and creates a comprehensive setting [1]. In this respect, solid partnerships along with count will certainly make the leaders take advantage of their groups' stamina for raised dedication and interaction [2]. This collective spirit is essential for companies looking to adjust and grow within a quickly changing landscape [3]. Lasting management originates from honest habits and also social obligation [4].

Equally, as lions are necessary for eco-friendly equilibriums in their particular ecological communities, leaders need to know their impact on culture and the setting [5]. This consists of decision-making that focuses on the health of the worker, neighborhood, and investor. Considering moral factors in management techniques allows companies to ensure that their society drives efficiency and contributes favorably to the world in which they operate [6].

Another important legacy of Lions in developing leadership is mentorship and succession planning. In the case of the lion pride, the older females always passed on the necessary skills for survival to younger ones for the continuity of the family line [7]. Similarly, a sustainable leadership culture develops its next leaders through mentoring, training, and growth opportunities. Only when an organization focuses on the development of the next generation can a healthy pipeline for leaders be built to continue their missions and values for generations in business [7, 8].

As we dive into how to build a sustainable leadership culture through the legacy of lions, the realization of this approach goes beyond mere fads or flavors of the month to a much-needed evolution in leadership practices. In short, organizations that hold to these values will have the greatest ability to face uncertainty and lead long-term success in a world where both skill and toughness are required [9]. We must teach a leadership culture of collaboration, ethical responsibility, and mentorship that would ensure the legacy of Lions inspires leaders to rise to the occasion for the benefit of all toward a brighter future [10].

12.1 Defining Sustainable Leadership

Sustainable leadership is an evolving concept that embraces a holistic approach to leadership, long-term success, ethical decision-making, and social responsibility. In light of rapid change and growing complexity, the following definition of sustainable leadership could be developed [11, 12]. It requires understanding the core principles of sustainable leadership and their implications for organizations and society.

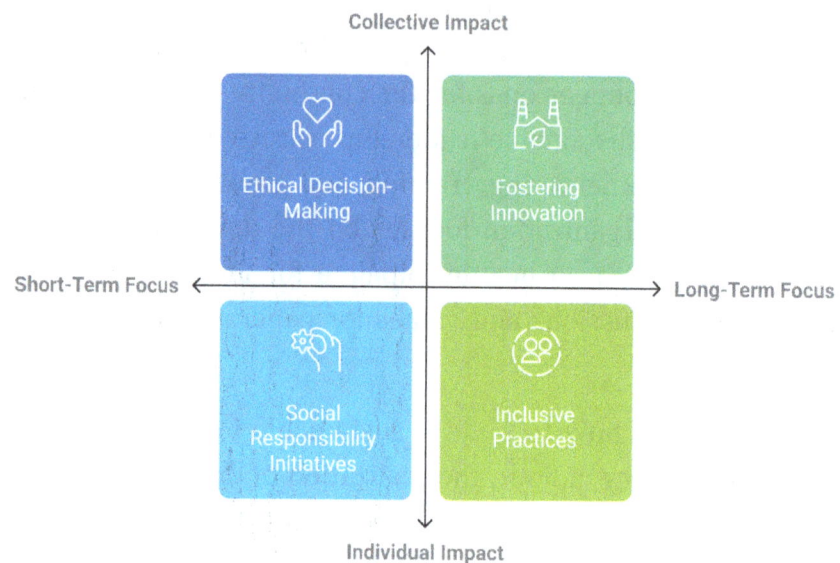

Figure 12.1 Sustainable leadership is an evolving concept.

It brings added value to the organization for employees, customers, society, and the environment. Traditional notions of leadership have been primarily based on profitability and building short-term profits. On the contrary, sustainable leadership is all about vision and long-term resiliency, realizing that a healthy organization is inextricably linked to the health of its stakeholders and the entire ecosystem.

One important aspect of sustainable leadership is ethics in decision-making. Ethics include being upright and clear in deciding and aligning them with individual worths and those of the company. These honest structures count as the basis of any connection within the company. Values established at the management degree dental implant responsibility plus regard right into society, and staff members will certainly carry out to the most effective of their capacities. The other substantial emphasis of lasting management is on partnership and inclusiveness.

Lasting leaders are aware that variety gives areas for advancement and imagination. In such an allowing setting, staff members are motivated to share suggestions and ultimately have the job. That type of esprit de corps in cooperation motivates excellent groups and sounder choices via a large range of understandings and experiences thought about. Lasting management includes a dedication to continual discovery and adjustment.

Leaders have to be certain and open to originalities in this globe where everything experiences consistent adjustment via quick technical improvement, vibrant market change, or changing social assumptions. This can allow companies to react well to arising obstacles and accept possibilities to continue to be appropriate in a significantly transforming globe. Lasting leaders develop a knowing society in their groups, enabling testing and advancement while welcoming failure for understanding.

Besides, much is carefully connected with elements of social together with ecological obligation. The need for larger-scale ramifications of leaders' tasks is progressively pushing environmental adjustment, social inequality, and area well-being. Leaders can make a favorable distinction by integrating sustainability into their business techniques. It will certainly boost their track record and attract clients and staff members with comparable worth. That is to claim, specifying lasting management needs considering it from a multidimensional point of view: moral decision-making, collaboration, versatility, and social obligation.

As businesses struggle to deal with current truths, lasting management has significantly become a design for durability and favorable results. These types of leaders will certainly assist in developing resurgent companies that will certainly overcome obstacles to guarantee the sustenance of the human race and all life. It has to do with efficient, deliberate, and integrity-based management for the good of a far better future.

12.2 Identifying Future Leaders Within Your Team

Identifying future leaders within a group is crucial for any company to accomplish lasting success and sustainability. Establishing a pipeline of qualified leaders ready for new duties is vital for organizations encountering fast modifications and developing obstacles. Such a procedure entails recognizing capacity, supporting ability, and developing an atmosphere where rising leaders can grow.

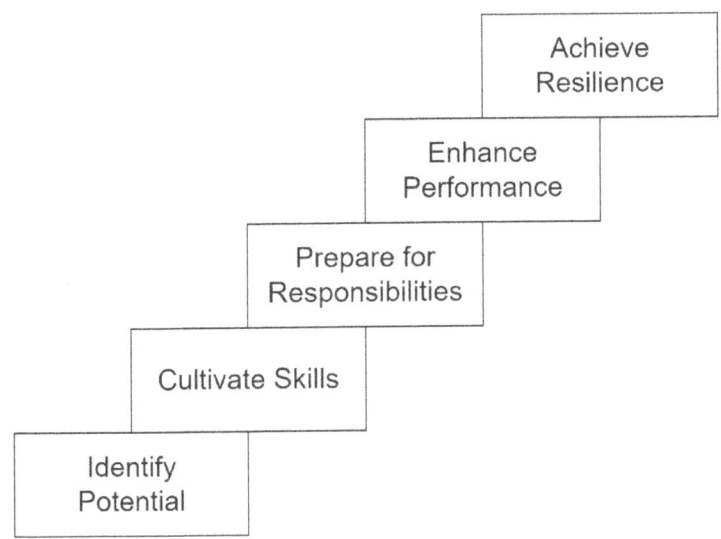

Figure 12.2 Identifying future leaders within your team is essential for any organization.

The initial step in determining future leaders is to observe team participants' actions and features. Secret qualities consist of campaign, adjustability, and solid job principles. Future leaders might reveal that they aspire to overcome obstacles to bring originalities and constantly seek opportunities to enhance points. These individuals can additionally motivate and inspire others while regulating impact and regard amongst their peers.

Normal efficiency evaluations, comment sessions, and less official monitoring commonly reveal that managers can have these management qualities. Employee self-assessments might likewise disclose potential leaders. Developments such as character or management design supplies are devices that people can utilize to assess their toughness and also additional growth needs. They make workers independent in their own job options and also help the supervisor.

Discussions of individual objectives and passions can also clarify this. Growth opportunities must be given where prospective leaders have been recognized. These include mentoring programs, management training, and tough stretch projects. Matching emerging leaders with skilled advisors provides a resource of support, assistance, and useful understanding right into the management trip.

Besides providing opportunities to lead tasks or campaigns, it provides these people with hands-on experience and opportunities to display their capacities. By purchasing their growth, companies can expand the skills of future leaders. An encouraging environment is essential for the development of future leaders. It includes motivating open interaction, cooperation, and a response society.

Leaders must create a safe space for employees to articulate their concepts and problems, making individuals feel like team members and relying on each other. Success must be commemorated, and payments need to be recognized to increase spirits and urge individuals to become leaders. Complete dedication and passion for one's advancement are most likely when workers are valued together and taken care of.

Continuous examination of management expertise amongst staff members is very important in comprehending what awaits a larger function. The company can utilize efficiency testimonials, 360-degree comments, and management analyses to recognize future leaders. These devices might offer substantial insights into a person's expertise, social abilities, and readiness for innovation. When companies embrace a structured analysis technique, recognizing future leaders is reasonable and unbiased.

12.2.1 Creating Leadership Development Programs

Therefore, the advancement of efficient management growth programs plays a quintessential duty in companies' initiatives to construct a solid pipeline of leaders qualified to lead with today's organization intricacies. It will certainly improve private capacities, additional advertise business development and durability. A well-structured management growth program is straightened with the company's objectives, breakthroughs a society of continual discovery, and prepares future leaders to overcome rising obstacles. The primary step in establishing a management growth program requires evaluation.

That implies comprehending the here-and-now state of management, comprehending the spaces, and specifying the proficiencies needed for the leaders of the future. Risk owner engagement—consisting of the existing leaders and employees—gives a useful understanding of what top qualities are required to lead the company successfully. Studies can do this, as meetings and efficiency evaluations suggest where growth is most required. After demands are recognized, clear goals for the management growth program must be defined.

These need to align with the company's critical goals and preferred end results. For example, a management growth program could aim to boost decision-making, psychological knowledge, or shared management among leaders. Quantifiable purposes ensure that a company remains positioned to examine the program's efficiency in meeting individuals' advancement demands. The genuine educational program for management advancement is detailed and varied, ranging from workshops and online training courses to various other kinds of experiential learning, such as work experiences or job projects.

Examples of the subject to be studied might consist of calculated reasoning, problem resolution, interaction, and moral management. Real-world circumstances and study would certainly boost understanding by using one's abilities in functional circumstances.

Mentoring and training are very important facets of any management advancement program. Matching emerging leaders with experienced coaches can supply a wide range of experience, assistance, and understanding into the management trip.

Coaches can share their experiences and offer guidance on browsing difficulties, while trainers can assist people in establishing certain abilities with tailored comments and targeted workouts. This customized technique embraces much deeper knowing and also assists individuals in developing self-confidence in their management capabilities. Comments society is crucial in the success of management growth programs. The program should enable individuals to ask for and offer comments as frequently as feasible, boosting their self-awareness for development. 360-degree comment systems will certainly make it possible for rising leaders to get viewpoints from peers, subordinates, and managers on their toughness and the location for renovation. These continual comments loophole aids individuals in adjusting and refining their management abilities.

Ultimately, the program's efficiency ought to be consistently reviewed. This will certainly be done with individual analysis studies and efficiency metrics. By determining results versus specified purposes, companies can recognize a program's effect and also where it may be enhanced.

Additionally, for the program's sustainability, continued dedication from the management, together with a combination of management growth right into the company's textile, is essential for the company's continued advantage from its financial investment in creating leaders.

12.2.2 Encouraging Knowledge Transfer and Mentorship

Expertise transfer describes sharing information, abilities, and competence among people and groups. It's all about connection, specifically when companies deal with high personnel turnover or are going through change. Efficient expertise transfer ensures lessons learned from experience are not shared but shown to others, possibly boosting decision-making, performance, and analytical abilities at a business level. The expertise transfer procedure also creates a collective job atmosphere where workers are encouraged to share their know-how.

This society of partnerships urges technology, given that various points of view are integrated to fix obstacles and conceptualize originalities. Such companies can adjust to transformed conditions and manipulate possibilities to accomplish lasting success. Mentoring is an essential technique for understanding transfer. In this structure, skilled people are embedded in aiding their less experienced associates in an organized way. The more experienced ones can share their ideas and pointers and assist the less experienced ones in relocating as necessary in their jobs.

These connections will certainly offer wonderful ability growth and a sense of coming from and also linking with the company. The mentoring programs can be formalized with specified objectives and timelines or a casual pairing based on the rate of interest or knowledge. Whatever the style, reliable mentoring calls for dedication from coaches and mentees. Advisors need to be close to being able to spend time with their mentees and open up to sharing experiences.

On the other hand, advisors must be energetic and passionate about their growth, seeking advice, asking inquiries, and responding to responses. This indicates that every company has to inculcate an enabling society for expertise transfer and mentorship to happen. Clear assumptions, ideals, and assistance are needed. Management can play an essential role in modeling the actions preferred in expertise sharing; coupled with mentorship, leaders will establish the company's instance.

The company can execute different programs, such as workshops, networking occasions, and joint jobs that advertise expertise sharing. Arranging online forums for sharing competence amongst staff members, like inner online forums or understanding administration systems, will certainly help with continuous discussion and learning. Acknowledgment and benefits for workers who join energetic mentorship and understanding transfer can help strengthen these worths.

Besides, it is essential to examine and review the efficiency of expertise transfer and mentorship programs for continual renovation. Organizations must develop metrics on how these programs affect worker efficiency, interaction, and retention. Studies, comments, and efficiency evaluations can offer valuable insights into the performance of mentorship partnerships and knowledge-sharing techniques.

12.3 Establishing Core Values for Leadership

Defining core values of leadership becomes a guide toward an organization's behavior, decision-making, and even culture. Core values are the roots on which leaders base their managerial, communicational, and collaborative attitudes. If an organization spells out its core values clearly and promotes them, the work atmosphere will be more harmonious and meaningful, making employees enthusiastic about working while building trust.

Core values are basic guiding philosophies that build an organization's identity and assist in molding the culture. To leaders, these values should signify what they want to live by in performing their roles. Common core values in leadership include integrity, accountability, empathy, collaboration, and innovation. Each value makes a critical difference in contributing to a positive organizational culture and guides leaders through interactions with employees, stakeholders, and the community.

1. Leadership integrity refers to leaders leading by example and earning the trust of their teams. Leaders must be candid and transparent in all their actions and decisions

to set the standard for ethical behavior and give employees the freedom to share their ideas and concerns.

2. There should be accountability for authentic leadership, in which leaders should always show responsibility through their choices and actions. It helps to reinforce accountability within a team or at the workplace by creating ownership in their employees when done between leaders and other teams or among employees.

3. Empathetic leaders understand and appreciate their team members' perspectives and emotions. By adopting an environment of compassion and support, leaders can strengthen relationships, enhance collaboration, and improve employee morale.

4. Collaboration is key to driving innovation and achieving organizational goals. Leaders who prioritize teamwork encourage open communication and the sharing of ideas, allowing diverse perspectives to contribute to problem-solving and decision-making.

5. Innovation is crucial in today's dynamic business environment. Creative and risk-taking leaders inspire their teams to think differently and find new ways of doing things, driving improvement and growth.

Once the core values have been identified, the next step is communicating them well and concisely within the organization. This could be done through induction programs, training, and internal notices. Leaders should also mention them during conversations, strategy formulation, and performance reviews.

Organizations can also insist on core values by embedding them into daily practices and integrating them into their culture.

The leader should articulate the core values and lead by example. It is not easy; it requires much self-awareness and commitment to live a life of values. As the leader models the core values, the employees will follow, which will trickle down into the organization. This is where words meet actions, creating credibility within the organization's culture.

Organizations should provide mechanisms for recognition and reinforcement to maintain an organization's culture of core values. Recognition through awards, shout-outs, or other recognition programs celebrates individuals and teams modeling core values and reinforces the importance of core values to others. Similarly, including core values in employee performance reviews provides a consistent measure to evaluate employees based on their results and how those results reflect the organization's values.

12.3.1 Promoting Diversity in Leadership Roles

In today's interconnected, complex world, there is a moral imperative for any organization to have diverse leadership. This brings diversity in knowledge, experience, and viewpoints, boosting innovation and strengthening decision-making. By paying more attention to diversity in leadership, an organization will better reflect the communities it serves, increase employee engagement, and ensure overall business success.

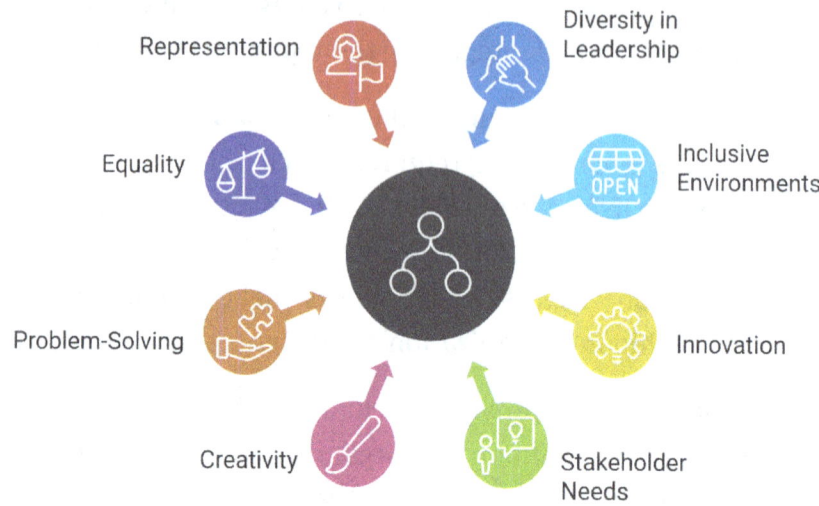

Figure 12.3 Promoting diversity in leadership roles.

Diversity in leadership pertains to differences in race, gender, age, sexual orientation, and cultural background. Studies continue to prove that diverse leading teams outperform less diverse teams. For example, diverse leading teams with women are 21% more likely to achieve above-average profitability. On the other hand, ethnically diverse companies are 33% more likely to outperform their peers regarding financial returns. This correlation indicates the value of diverse perspectives for driving creativity and problem-solving.

The diverse leadership team gives them an edge in connecting even with a wider range of customers. This is because these diverse, representative leaders will make insightful decisions that resonate well with each target audience's customers. This culture strengthens customer satisfaction, brand loyalty, and market reach by boosting cultural competence. Organizations shall now draw on metrics to track change and ensure the effectiveness of diversity initiatives. It would also be enlightening to regularly scan the leadership team for their diversity, analyze the retention rate of employees that constitute diversity, and what effects such diversity training may have. This transparency in reporting such metrics could build employee and stakeholder trust.

12.3.2 Evaluating Leadership Effectiveness

Evaluating management performance is crucial in companies that try to enhance efficiency and accomplish critical purposes. Solid leaders form a company's society, inspire groups, and bring general success to the entity. Management should be straightened with the company's objectives to construct ideal assessment techniques. Determining what efficient management will appear like within the company's context assists leaders in plainly established assumptions plus criteria for examination.

The commonly utilized approach to examining management efficiency is 360-degree comments. It is an all-inclusive technique based upon the payments of all investors, including peers, subordinates, and managers. 360-degree comments create a society of liability and open interaction by stressing a leader's toughness and opportunities for advancement. In addition, some measurable efficiency metrics, such as group performance, worker interaction ratings, and turnover prices, can provide information that can help connect management performance to genuine business results.

This enables leaders to evaluate their influence on total efficiency. Self-assessment is another important measurement in management analysis, which allows leaders to be extra conscious and reflective. In this instance, permitting leaders to evaluate their strengths and weaknesses encourages them to grow. This needs to be stabilized with others' comments to give a view from numerous points of view. Continuous discussions concerning management efficiency can additionally be helped with normal check-ins and one-on-one conferences, where leaders are enabled to analyze workers' complete satisfaction and adjust their designs to best suit the requirements of their groups.

Society must grow for a company to understand the complete worth of management examinations, and comments and constant enhancement must be accepted. This would certainly produce a setting where leaders look for normal comments as chances to expand and establish not to slam them. When accumulated examination outcomes ought to educate the advancement strategies plus techniques at a business degree, as well as the sources plus sustain needed to assist leaders boost their proficiencies need to be geared up. It hence buys the constant advancement and examination of management, making certain that leaders are sufficiently geared up to motivate, involve, and drive success within a frequently transforming organization setting.

12.4 Building a Culture of Accountability

Responsibility is the structure of developing a society that aids companies in enhancing efficiency and constructs depend on making certain outcomes. An answerable society equips staff members to take possession of their obligations, urges clear interaction, plus lines up specific objectives with business goals. Liability brings much better teamwork, increased interaction, and considerable success when instilling right into business principles. Duty in the office suggests individuals oversee their activities, choices, plus results.

Duty consists of establishing assumptions, providing dedication, plus being clear regarding the outcomes. For any company, specifying responsibility at each degree instills a feeling of responsibility within a specific. It specifies functions and duties and also aids staff members in comprehending their payments towards business objectives. Where assumptions have been established, employees feel even more responsible for using up their duties to make up for their efficiencies. Likewise, developing a society of liability requires taking on open interaction throughout the company.

Leaders should motivate staff members to share their ideas, problems, and responses openly. This openness assists in making clear assumptions and dealing with difficulties before they arise. Routine check-ins and comment sessions can promote these conversations, permitting leaders to scale progress and make essential modifications. When workers share their obstacles, companies can determine systemic problems hindering responsibility and work collaboratively to solve them.

Responsibility should be acknowledged, and compensation should be offered to guarantee this social change. Companies ought to identify and compensate teams and people through their activities, and outcomes are shown in liability. Acknowledgment might be found in numerous kinds, from official honors to easy recommendations throughout group conferences. By highlighting instances of responsibility, companies urge others to act in a similar way and also strengthen actions that benefit society. In addition, the actual procedure of connecting responsibility with efficiency evaluations offers to make personnel completely conscious that it is extremely crucial and valued in their job.

Responsibility takes care of specific duties; nonetheless, assistance and resources should additionally be offered to them in search of success. The leaders ought to guarantee groups have access to training devices and also the support required for conference goals. Workers will certainly be dedicated to providing the outcomes when they feel sustained. A development mindset also implies that staff members see obstacles as discovering possibilities instead of failings. This technique instills strength and strengthens a society of responsibility where individuals are encouraged to take dangers and gain from their experiences. Liability is everything about driving business success and producing an encouraging setting within the work environment.

Responsibility is developed by specifying it, motivating open interaction, identifying and fulfilling accountable habits, and giving assistance. It is a business society where staff members really feel encouraged and inspired to take ownership of the job. This society boosts private efficiency and enhances synergy and partnership in initiatives towards much better end results for the company. Responsibility as a core value opens the door to better involvement and performance, hence positioning the company for success.

12.4.1 Creating a Vision for Future Leadership

Establishing a vision for future management will certainly aid companies in navigating a business forest where adjustment is continuously arising. The well-put vision will certainly influence leaders and workers toward usual purposes concerning technical changes, group modification, and market pressures. This will guarantee long-lasting success by infusing an ingenious, comprehensive society into their durability.

Quick advancements in the business atmosphere require a positive strategy for management. Companies encounter quick technical improvements, globalization, and changing labor force demographics, all of which place remarkable needs on leaders who have to assume tactically yet act decisively. A clear vision for future management allows companies to prepare for such difficulties and equips leaders to apply techniques that align with the company's objectives and values. This positioning provides groups with a feeling of function and also encourages them. The vision for future management ought to show the crucial features and expertise required to grow in a vibrant setting.

Because instructions are needed, qualities needed might consist of versatility, psychological knowledge, inclusivity, and a dedication to constant knowing. In the future, leaders should welcome modification, maximize varied viewpoints, and assist the group in working together. The organization can then identify and develop its future leaders by clearly defining such attributes, which will help them be better prepared with the required skills to lead through uncertainty and innovation.

Developing the vision for future leadership should be collaborative among various stakeholders. Consultation regarding the vision with current leadership and employees or customers helps in fruitful insight and brings ownership across all those involved. Workshops, focus groups, and questionnaires provide input and lead discussions around the aspired state for leadership. This inclusive approach ensures that diverse perspectives are considered and helps build consensus around the vision, making it more likely to be embraced and implemented.

Once the vision of future leadership is developed, it must be communicated throughout the organization. The leaders should clearly and convincingly articulate their vision via different channels in a catchy way for all employees. Storytelling can be an effective means for this because it will allow the leaders to illustrate the vision in a way that bestows relevance and attractiveness. It is about creating actionable strategies that implement the vision through programs of leadership development, mentorship, and training focused on those core attributes.

12.4.2 Engaging Employees in the Legacy Process

Worker involvement in the traditional procedure is the only method to assist companies in producing a continual and comprehensive society worth previous payments while producing the course to success for the future. In such instances, the traditional procedure includes recognition, conservation, giving worths, understanding, and methods that specify a company for future generations. By proactively including the team in this procedure, companies can bring possession among them, boost staff member contentment, and raise their commitment to the company's goal and worth. It includes recognizing and recording, plus commemorating a company's background, achievements, and core worths. This is the bridge between the past and the future that might help educate existing techniques while assisting critical instructions. Workers play a substantial duty in this procedure since each has special understandings and experiences to add to the business tale. It concerns the involvement and inclusiveness of various expectations to guarantee the tradition mirrors a cumulative identification. Effective involvement requires companies to construct an atmosphere where individuals can contribute or, at the very least, have their voices listened to.

Ensured workshops, emphasis teams, and expensive suggestion sessions are occasions where individuals might tell tales and share experiences. Other means to advertise addition might include locations for worker payments, such as inner online forums or tip boxes. When workers feel they are being listened to and their suggestions are valued, they are a lot more likely to purchase the traditional procedure and also take satisfaction in their payments. Acknowledgement and commemorating staff member payments are essential to enhance involvement in the traditional procedure.

Specific and group success can be recognized and connected using honors, acknowledgment programs, or narration tasks. Attached are previous payments and future purposes, displaying exactly how staff members have assisted in constructing the company's background and worth. Acknowledgment motivates spirits and also inspires them to proceed in their job of contributing to the heritage.

However, giving employees development opportunities for different organizational values and missions is not the only thing engaging; engaging in the legacy development process also calls for development opportunities. Leadership development training, workshops, mentorship programs, and professional development workshops would let employees play active roles in developing their future by allowing organizational capability for legacy continuity with modifications. This commitment to employee development signifies an organization that values its workforce and is invested in its growth.

Communication of the process is key to engaging employees in the legacy process. The vision for the legacy and how employees can play their part in it should be explained. Updates regarding the progress of initiatives regarding legacy, success stories, and testimonials will reinforce why employee involvement is so important. The organization will continue to keep them informed and inspired to participate in the process through various forms of communication: newsletters, town hall meetings, and social media.

12.5 Celebrating Leadership Achievements

Leadership success should be celebrated in the culture to raise and sustain good organizational behavior; employee morale is enhanced to reinforce those values that drive successful performance. Recognition for the leader's efforts inspires others through leading by example. An organization creates solid grounds for innovation, collaboration, and continuous improvement, where leadership achievements cultivate a culture of celebration.

Recognition is one of the most potent ways to incentivize leaders and their teams. It shows that all the effort and time leaders put into the job is valued. Such recognition can be given at formal ceremonies or quick shout-outs during team meetings. These recognitions of leadership achievement build camaraderie in the team and shared purpose, in addition to raising the morale of those being recognized. When employees witness recognition given to leaders, it creates a culture of appreciation that can make others more productive and engaged.

It is worth noting that every organization should give a formalized program through which leadership achievements are identified and recognized. Such programs include monthly/quarterly awards, leader spotlights within company communications, and recognition events. It is of value to establish the criteria upon which individuals are recognized so their celebration process can easily be facilitated and valid: showing fundamental qualities of leadership, achievement of milestones, and/ or driving meaningful initiatives. A formal system provides avenues whereby leadership achievements can uniformly be ascertained and recognized.

Encouraging peer recognition in addition to formal recognition programs can better amplify the power of celebrating achievements in leadership. Leaders must be motivated to recognize the accomplishments of their colleagues by creating a culture of mutual respect and appreciation. This would be supported through mechanisms that allow employees to share accolades and commendations with peers. Recognition given at many levels reinforces and makes an organization more inclusive and supportive because leadership achievements valued at every level are recognized.

One more robust method to commemorate success is sharing success tales concerning management accomplishments. Success tales can be showcased in internal e-newsletters, social networks, or business conferences. They inspire others to proceed with comparable actions by informing them just how reliable management is, the stimulant for success in group growth, task success, or area interaction. These tales not only commemorate private leaders but also realign and invigorate the workers toward the company's worth and vision.

12.5.1 Ensuring Succession Planning for Longevity

Follow-up preparation guarantees companies' lasting success and durability with the intended business method. It needs to recognize plus create future leaders for an audio pipe of skill that can presume duty with the aid of training when such a requirement occurs. These assist in lessening dangers because abrupt management adjustments together will certainly develop a society of development and connection, resulting in the company's perpetuation. In modern times, companies are tested by several problems, including technical innovation, group changes, and adjustments in market needs.

Sequence preparation assists companies in attending to such intricacies by loading management settings with experienced people who support the organization's values and tactical instructions. Excellent sequence preparation lessens interruption, maintains functional security, and maintains institutional expertise essential for maintaining business efficiency over time. Sequence preparation remains one of the most important factors in determining business leaders. It entails examining the expertise, abilities, and development capacity of workers presently functioning within the company.

The company must determine those with solid technological capacities and those with psychological knowledge, versatility, and critical reasoning. Some methods to determine individuals prepared for improvement include efficiency assessments, 360-degree comments, and professional advancement conversations. Very early recognition by the company allows financial investment in their advancement to outfit them for future management functions. When determined, a company must purchase establishing possible leaders to outfit them for greater duties via tailored growth strategies, management training programs, mentorship chances, and tactical job projects.

This suggests that the management group will certainly be experienced and able to adjust conveniently, given that the staff members will certainly be offered the resources and experience required for development. Additionally, such a culture of continuous learning will encourage employees to seek opportunities for professional development and further enhance their preparedness for leadership roles.

A comprehensive succession plan should reflect specific processes and strategies concerning future leader development. That involves identifying major leading positions, specifying selection criteria for succession candidates, and defining development plans for people selected to fill positions. Naturally, a succession plan has to be regularly reviewed and revised to reflect the dynamic development of the organization's needs and priorities. Engaging current leaders in succession planning will provide great insight into what succession will be effective and ensure the smooth transition of everything when change occurs.

Effective communication is significant for successful succession planning. Every company should connect with all workers regarding the significance of sequence preparation and the fact that it is everybody's duty. Such visibility concerning the procedure would certainly assist in removing the misconception that sequence preparation intimidates work safety and security. Companies can reinforce retention plus spirits by taking on an inclusive environment where workers are encouraged to go after chances to lead while constructing an audio structure for future management.

12.6 Case Study: Building a Sustainable Leadership Culture

"Legacy of Lions" implies that companies are dedicated to a lasting management society proliferating a more recent generation of leaders. Businesses like P&G have long been recognized for their solid, mentorship-based, and succession-oriented management. With this technique, P&G produces private skills that would add to maintaining company worth and critical vision at P&G.

A solid mentorship concentration is assisting pressure in P&G's management society. According to the business, efficient mentorship is essential in structuring qualified leaders who can handle the intricacies of organizations today. P&G leaders participate in mentoring connections, offering assistance to raise ability with experiences and understandings—this mentorship program breakthroughs expertise transfer coupled with workers' feeling of coming from and dedication. Mentorship at P&G is structured yet adaptable.

Mentees can learn from their coaches' experiences while discovering their management styles. The coaches form the abilities and expertise of their mentees through routine face-to-face conferences, comments sessions, and collective jobs. This method develops a helpful atmosphere in which future leaders can establish the self-confidence and capacities required to prosper. Besides mentoring, Procter & Gamble strongly count on sequence preparation.

Totally understanding the characteristics of modification that influence management shifts on business security, Procter & Gamble determines and prepares its prospective leaders ahead of time to hold vital obligations. It places staff members through a demanding ability analysis that checks their proficiencies, efficiency, and ability to provide. Therefore, a skill pipeline arises for various degrees of the company as these jobs open. Sequence preparation at Procter & Gamble does not concern loading openings yet; it concerns maintaining the company in accordance with its long-lasting objectives. By purchasing the advancement of future leaders, Procter & Gamble highlights its dedication to maintaining an audio management structure that personifies the company's core values and goals. Focus on sequence preparation uses connection in a management change, the connection of institutional understanding, and connection in decision-making.

Procter & Gamble has a lasting management company that constantly motivates its employees to discover and establish their abilities. The Firm encourages its leaders to pursue development opportunities and obstacles, allowing them to do so through numerous management training workshops, practical cross-assignments, and international direct exposures. By offering value to expert growth, P & G allows its leaders to fulfill the company's upcoming difficulties together with adjustments. Organizational difficulties drive technology.

Furthermore, PG encourages a response society in which leaders share understandings to gain from each other. Such visibility adds to far better specific efficiency and more powerful team effort in pursuit of typical objectives; thus, partnerships and problem-solving are created. It assists the firm in preparing leaders to navigate unpredictability in the business landscape by producing a discovery and flexible atmosphere. Eventually, the " Legacy of Lions" is a version of how Procter & Gamble protects the foundation of its management society via mentorship and sequence preparation. Cultivating skills with structured mentorship programs, critical sequence preparation, and a dedication to constant understanding, P&G has kept solid management regular with the business's worth. This positive method safeguards the future and constructs a heritage of leaders who can overcome new obstacles tomorrow. As companies attempt to flourish in the ever-changing setting, accepting these concepts will certainly be required to drive and embrace a solid and lasting management society.

12.7 Key Point Donald Trump's potential re-election in 2024

> **Voter Mobilization:** Implementing robust ground game strategies to increase voter turnout, particularly in swing states.

As Donald Trump considers his feasible reelection quote in 2024, citizen mobilization will be vital to the result. Any enhanced citizen turn, specifically in turn states where political elections are won or lost, needs to be appropriately come before by the application of solid ground video game approaches. The Trump project will indeed, for that reason, remain in a far better position to galvanize assistance and ensure an excellent citizen turnover with grass origins arrangements, targeted outreach, and the use of modern technology.

One of the cornerstones in any form of voter mobilization strategy is grassroots organizing. This would include the building up of an army of dedicated volunteers who can reach out to the voters on a personal basis. Grassroots events may involve door-to-door outreach, telephone banking, and other community events that will help representatives connect with constituents directly. By this, a sense of community and urgency for the election can be developed by volunteers who care about the Trump platform, and this could eventually allow more individuals to vote in the process.

> **Use Humor Wisely**
> Incorporate humor to disarm opponents and endear yourself to supporters.
>
> **Highlight Opponent Weaknesses**
> Draw attention to the flaws and failures of opponents.

In swing states, where the voter base is more fluid, grassroots organizing becomes even more important. Thus, areas with a high concentration of undecided or infrequent voters could yield great dividends. The campaign should develop tailored messaging to local concerns and priorities that raise the turnout among groups who might feel slighted in these communities.

Effective voter mobilization also relies on specific targeting of outreach strategies, depending on demographic and behavioral information from various regions, for framing messages. In his case, that would identify the most important issues in each state: economy, health, immigration, and crime.

Beyond this, outreach should not be limited to traditional channels. Social media, local influencers, and community leaders can help a campaign talk back to the voters and create a wider reach for its messages. By building a story of the particular requirements and objectives of the citizens throughout crucial states, the project would certainly even urge individuals to obtain one on Election Day. Innovation creates the foundation of citizen mobilization in contemporary selection procedures. The Trump project must be able to use information analytics to determine and target prospective citizens. By evaluating citizen enrollment information, previous ballot habits, and group details, the project can establish a thorough data source to notify outreach.

In addition, electronic devices can sustain citizen enrollment drives, information regarding ballot places, and electing treatments. Mobile applications and social media networks will certainly advise fans of crucial days and also urge them to share such information within their networks. Hence, the project can use modern technology to ensure much easier and more efficient mobilization for better citizen turnover. This citizen mobilization variable can be important in Donald Trump's feasible 2024 re-election quote. Excellent ground video game approaches, grassroots organizing, efficient outreach, and innovation usage considerably boost the variety of ballots originating from these turn states.

Developing neighborhood visibility and speaking to the citizens on issues dear to them can urge necessity and dedication among advocates. These techniques will certainly be vital in forming the selecting landscape as the political election approaches and will certainly aid in determining the destiny of the 2024 governmental political election.

Reference

1. Kouzes, J. M., & Posner, B. Z. (2017). The Leadership Challenge: How to Make Extraordinary Things Happen in Organizations. Wiley.

2. Schein, E. H. (2010). Organizational Culture and Leadership. Jossey-Bass.

3. Collins, J. (2001). Good to Great: Why Some Companies Make the Leap... and Others Don't. HarperBusiness.

4. Goleman, D. (1998). Working with Emotional Intelligence. Bantam Books.

5. Bennis, W. (2009). On Becoming a Leader. Basic Books.

6. Zenger, J. H., & Folkman, J. (2019). The Extraordinary Leader: Turning Good Managers into Great Leaders. McGraw-Hill Education.

7. Heifetz, R. A., & Laurie, D. L. (1997). The Work of Leadership. Harvard Business Review.

8. Dyer, W. G., & Dyer, J. H. (2013). Team Building: Proven Strategies for Improving Team Performance. Wiley.

9. Kotter, J. P. (1996). Leading Change. Harvard Business Review Press.

10. Senge, P. M. (2006). The Fifth Discipline: The Art & Practice of The Learning Organization. Crown Business.

11. Northouse, P. G. (2018). Leadership: Theory and Practice. Sage Publications.

12. Yukl, G. (2013). Leadership in Organizations. Pearson.

Index

A

Accountability, 17, 99
Achievements, 456
Active Listening, 133
Adaptability, 225
Addressing Conflict, 17
Adjusting Goals, 106
Admitting Mistakes, 184
Adopting Innovation, 388
Aligning Individual, 94
Aligning Strengths, 68
Approachability, 200
Assessments Effectively, 74
Authentic Leadership, 176
Authenticity, 31
Autonomy, 298

B

Barriers, 306
Based Frameworks, 48
Big Wins, 328
Building Diverse, 58
Building Inclusivity, 20
Burnout, 242

C

Celebrating vulnerability, 33
Check-Ins, 28
Coaching, 373
Collaboration, 17
Commitment, 194
Communicating Goals, 96
Communication Norms, 147
Compelling Team Vision, 90
Conducting Skills, 45
Conflict Resolution, 157
Constructive Feedback, 139
Contingency, 232
Cross-Departmental, 266
Cross-Functional, 263
Culture of Recognition, 54

D

Defining, 15
Delegate, 291
Delegated Tasks, 303
Demonstrating Integrity, 179
Development Plans, 64
Dialogue, 12
Diverse Perspectives, 273
Dynamics of Skills, 47

E

Empowerment, 300
Encouraging Peer, 61
Encouraging Risk, 23
Encouraging Transparency, 187

F

Facilitating, 71
Feedback, 103

G

Group Discussions, 160

I

Identifying Key, 51
Impact of Change, 419
Integrity, 17

K

Knowledge Sharing, 365

L

Leadership Roles, 447
Legacy of Leadership, 206
Legacy Process, 454
Leveraging Technology, 163

M

Management Strategies, 403
Managing Emotions, 144
Mentoring, 203
Mentorship, 373
Milestones, 109, 385
Mindset, 228

N

Nature of Change, 398
Navigating Difficult, 136

O

Open-Ended Questions, 141
Opportunities, 360
Outcomes, 331

P

Past Challenges, 238
Perseverance, 245
Posture, 151
Problem-Solving Skills, 224
Promoting Consistency, 192
Promoting Lifelong, 77
Promoting Stress, 234
Psychological, 10

R

Recognition Program, 324
Reflection Sessions, 247
Resilient Mindset, 410
Resources, 371
Retreats, 278
Roadmap, 101

S

Setting Boundaries, 26
Shared Experiences, 269
Sharing Personal, 181
SMART Goals, 91
Stories Publicly, 333
Successful Delegation, 304
Sustainable Leadership, 435

T

Team Engagement, 34
Team Resilience, 218
Team Rituals, 276
Team Roles, 250
Tracking Progress, 99
Transitions, 421
Transparency, 117

U

Utilizing Nonverbal, 150
Utilizing Strengths, 48

V

Vision, 452
Visual Tools, 115

W

Workplace, 401
Workshops, 267